KINSHASA
TALES OF THE INVISIBLE CITY

BY FILIP DE BOECK &
MARIE-FRANÇOISE PLISSART

LEUVEN UNIVERSITY PRESS

Kinshasa ne sera jamais New York. Tant mieux d'ailleurs. Chaque ville a son âme. Chaque ville a son corps, sa peau, son intelligence, sa bêtise, son côté monstre, sa poétique, sa part de mystère...

[Sony Labou Tansi, Kinshasa ne sera jamais]

TABLE OF CONTENTS

7 **PREFACE**
Reflecting on Reflection through Photography and Text

13 **KINSHASA**
Tales of the Invisible City and the Second World. An Introduction

63 **INVISIBLE CITIES I**
The 'Giant of Kinshasa', The Story of a Conversion

75 **BEYOND THE GRAVE**
Memory, Time, Apocalypse and Death in Kinshasa

139 **INVISIBLE CITIES II**
Omba Shako, The Story of a Street Kid

155 **THE SECOND WORLD**
Children, the Street and the Occult in Kinshasa

211 **INVISIBLE CITIES III**
Mado, The Story of a Female Diamond Smuggler

225 **THE POSSIBILITIES OF THE (IM)POSSIBLE**

---

263 Notes

271 References

279 Index of names

284 Index of illustrations

PREFACE: REFLECTING ON REFLECTION THROUGH PHOTOGRAPHY AND TEXT

"Photographe azwui yo photo, abimisi carte ya yo moko. Na yo, na carte, nani akomona moninga? Yo okomona carte; carte ekomonaka yo te. Carte ya photo ekomona yo ata mokolo moko te, ata ba agrandir yango lolenge kani. Ndenge moko biso tozali na Nzambe. Nzambe okomona biso, ye nde akeli biso; biso tokomona ye te."

"A photographer takes your photo and he gives you a paper with your image. Between you and the photo, who looks at whom? You can contemplate the paper with the image; the paper with the image does not see you. It will never be able to contemplate you, no matter how much one aggrandizes the picture. It is exactly the same between us and God. God is able to see us because he created us, but we can't see God."

[Papa Verbalizant, Kinshasa, September 1997]

This reflection on photography by Papa Verbalizant, an inhabitant of Kinshasa, points to the demiurgical qualities inherent in the creation of photographic images. It also points to the power relations at play in the production of the image. Both the camera and the pen are, in a way, ultimately colonial tools, ordering, categorizing, and thereby creating reality in their own image. Each in their own way, photography and writing take possession of the world, freeze it in images and representations, and often kill its vitality in the process.

Surprisingly little has been published about Kinshasa so far. This book is the product of a collaborative effort between myself, an anthropologist, and photographer Marie-Françoise Plissart. Since 1987, I have carried out extensive long term field research in Congo, first in small rural communities along the border between Angola and Congo's Bandundu province, since 1995 also in semi-urban and urban settings such as Kahemba or Kikwit in Southwest Congo, and increasingly also in Kinshasa. The text presented here reflects my long engagement with the urbanscape in Central Africa. In 2000, Marie-Françoise Plissart visited me at home shortly before she was to travel to Kinshasa. She was sent on a short mission by the Flemish Institute of Architecture (VAi) to photograph the vestiges of Belgian colonial architecture for an exhibition and an accompanying book by one of my colleagues at the University of Leuven, Bruno De Meulder. Upon Marie-Françoise's return, we began playing with the idea to return to Kin together to make a book about this intriguing city. During one month in 2001, and again in 2002, we traversed the city together, filming and photographing. The photos in this book are the partial outcome of this joint effort.

Inevitably, my text and the photographic images by Marie-Françoise Plissart are the product of our, the authors' gaze, our lens; they are informed by our own biases, with their specific histories and backgrounds. It is also the strength of their vision: they vindicate the right not merely to reflect or to give proof of having been there, but to select, frame, interpret, stylize and culturalize. And maybe precisely because they do so, they might have the capacity to bring the world back to life transformed. Like the image with which I start this book, namely Italo Calvino's twin cities of Valdrada, cities that are not equal and do not mirror each other symmetrically, our mirror image of Kinshasa does not pretend to reflect the "true" or "objective" reality of the city of Kinshasa, nor does it make an attempt at creating analogons, through art and thought, of the "object" that is Kinshasa. In any event, Kinshasa is a city that not only by its size but by its very shape shifting nature resists objectification, colonization, synthesis and summary. It constantly remains out of focus. It is a city difficult to tame, and impossible to capture in one master narrative. It eludes any order which one imposes upon its realities. Its constant energy and movement refuse to be frozen in static images, in linear text. Its sum is always more than its parts. Rather than offering to encompass it all, the textual accounts and eidetic memories reflect the ways in which we have tried to generate our own personal forms of urban planning, our own subjective, and by definition incomplete, trajectories towards understanding this city. If the city is a writing, as Barthes notes in *The Empire of Signs*, and if the person who walks around in it is a sort of reader, then the text and photos in this book provide our own personal and provisional reading of a city that refuses to be written but that writes itself.

We do hope, though, that the texts and photographs, in spite of, or maybe precisely because of, their necessarily fractal character, add to a better *in-sight* to the city's own internal dynamics. Our reading of the urbanscape's geographical and mental map, the moorings of its imagination, has constantly been shaped in dialogue with, and informed by, the various ways in which Kinshasa's own inhabitants write, read, talk, dance and live their city and its signs. And Kinshasa constantly invents, expresses, indeed verbalizes and reads itself in a voice that is loud and clear though not always in ways that are easy to understand. If the city is a writing, it is often a palimpsestual one, and if the city speaks, it often does so through its own forms of glossolalia. Contrary to Papa Verbalizant's remark about the powerlessness of the represented object, unable to return the gaze through which it is produced, the subjects of Plissart's photographic images do speak: they are constantly making themselves heard in and between the chapters that constitute the body of this book. The different chapters are themselves constructed as a polylogue, in which the voice of the anthropologist and the eye of the photographer are alternated with the voices of some of Kinshasa's inhabitants.

We also hope that the photos, along with these voices, succeed at providing an opening through which to look into other worlds that lie hidden beyond the screen of the city's scene/seen (does not the photographer, like the inhabitants of Kinshasa's "second worlds," have four eyes as well?) Through its very form and nature, photography offers a perfect medium to reflect on some of the themes and theoretical preoccupations upon which this book touches. The photos force us to consider the status of reality and its representation in Kinshasa today. As image, and as a medium that produces an image for a consciousness of absence, of something that is no longer present by the time the spectator beholds it, the phenomenology and aesthetics of photography address the importance of appearance, and the relationship between presence and absence, between the reality of unreality and the unreality of reality, between visible and invisible, between having two eyes and having four eyes, between first and second worlds. Ultimately, photography, like Kinshasa itself, constantly refers to death and the relation with the world of the living, two themes that are central to this book.

The various periods of field research on which this book builds were generously sponsored by the Flemish Fund for Scientific Research (Fonds voor Wetenschappelijk Onderzoek-Vlaanderen). The publication of this book has also been made possible thanks to a grant from the Vlaams Architectuur Instituut (VAi) on whose behalf I co-curated (together with architect and critic Koen Van Synghel) an exhibition on Kinshasa for the Mostra Internazionale di Architettura, Venice 2004. I also thank the Royal Museum for Central Africa of Tervuren and its director, Guido Gryseels, for further financial support and for co-editing this publication. In Kinshasa, I extend my gratitude to Professor Lapika Dimomfu of the University of Kinshasa for inviting me to Kinshasa's campus for a series of lectures as the UNESCO Chair on "Culture et endogénisation" in May 2003. I am equally grateful to Professors Sabakinu Kivilu and Shaje a Tshiluila of the same university for their support. I especially thank Professor Bennetta Jules-Rosette for inviting me to spend a trimester as a visiting associate professor at the University of California, San Diego in the spring of 2002. The months at UCSD provided the much needed time to prepare a large part of the manuscript. Thanks also to Maliq Simone and Vyjayanthi Rao for inviting me to a workshop on *African Cities: Remaking the Urban World* at Yale in December 2003. Without the pressure of having to present a paper there I would never have finalized the last chapter! We also wish to thank the Centre Wallonie-Bruxelles and the Centre Culturel Français in Kinshasa for hosting an exhibition of Marie-Françoise Plissart's photographs in May 2002. This exhibition became possible thanks to the financial support from the Commissariat Général aux Relations Internationales du Ministère de la Communauté Française de Belgique (CGRI). In Kinshasa I especially thank the families Mabaya and Bolya for their hospitality, and Zephyrin Muyika for his invaluable help in the field. Thanks also to Kinshasa based artist Pume Bylex whose utopian constructs helped me to better grasp the Congolese urban context, and to Francis Articlaut, for sharing his passion for photography and the city with us.

Over the years many other friends and colleagues have read and commented on parts of this book, or provided platforms to present some of its ideas. For their encouragement, criticisms, questions and suggestions I wish to thank René Devisch, Ann Cassiman, Steven Van Wolputte, Koen Stroeken, Barbara Drieskens, Knut Graw, Johan Meire, Katrien Pype and the other members of the Africa Research Center of the Department of Social and Cultural Anthropology at the Catholic University of Leuven. My gratitude also goes to Peter Geschiere, Michael Lambek, Bogumil Jewsiewicki, Bruno De Meulder, Birgit Meyer, Achille Mbembe, Alcinda Honwana, Nancy Rose Hunt, Bob White, Léon Tsambu, Koen Van Synghel, Achille Ngoye, Abdoumaliq Simone, Thierry Nlandu, the late T.K. Biaya, Okwui Enwezor, Barbara van der Linden, the late Stefan Bekaert, Gauthier de Villers, Jean-Pierre Jacquemin, Richard Werbner, Pamela Reynolds, John and Jean Comaroff, Nic Argenti, Jean-François Bayart, Jean Omasombo, Brad Weiss, Jan-Lodewijk Grootaers, Danielle de Lame, Yoka Lye Mudaba, Jacques Le Roy, Adelin N'situ, Theodore Trefon, Jean-Luc Vellut, Adeline Masquelier, Mitzi Goheen, David and Catherine Newbury, Danielle de Lame, Boniface Mongo-Mboussa, and Luc de Heusch. In various ways, each of them has contributed to the completion of this book.

Above all, I wish to thank Césarine Sinatu Bolya, who graciously tolerates that I write about Kinshasa, her city, which she has shared so generously with me. Finally, thanks are due to the staff of Ludion, to Sally Bayless at Encinitas, to Philomena Mariani in New York and to Nina Adams in Brussels for their valuable editorial help.

Parts of this book have been published elsewhere in sometimes radically different forms. A shorter version of the first chapter, together with a selection of photographs by Marie-Françoise Plissart, was published in Okwui Enwezor et al. (eds.), 2002, *Under Siege: Four African Cities Freetown, Johannesburg, Kinshasa, Lagos. Documenta11–Platform 4*, Kassel: Hatje Cantz. Chapter 3 is a thoroughly reworked version of a much shorter chapter that appeared in Richard Werbner (ed.) 1998, *Memory and the Postcolony. African Anthropology and the Critique of Power*, London: Zed Books. Chapter 3 also incorporates parts of a text that was published in J.-L. Grootaers (ed.) 2001, *Millenarian Movements in Africa and the Diaspora*, Brussels: Royal Academy of the Overseas Sciences. Chapter 5 is based in part on two texts: one that I published in a special issue on children and politics in Africa which I co-edited with Alcinda Honwana for the journal *Politique Africaine* (2000, n° 80), another which was published in A. Honwana and F. De Boeck (eds.) 2004, *Makers and Breakers, Made and Broken. Children and Youth as Emerging Categories in Postcolonial Africa*, Oxford: James Currey. Mado's story (chapter 6) is lifted out of a longer text which was published in Laurent Monnier, Bogumil Jewsiewicki and Gauthier de Villers (eds.) 2001, *Chasse au diamant au Congo/Zaïre*, Tervuren / Paris: Institut Africain–CEDAF / L'Harmattan. Finally, a selection of the life histories and portraits of "witch-children" on pages 148–153 was published in *Beople. A Magazine About a Certain Belgium* (2003, 6: 46–58) under the title "Geographies of Exclusion: Churches and Childwitches in Kinshasa."

FILIP DE BOECK
Brussels, March 2004

KINSHASA
TALES OF THE "INVISIBLE CITY" AND THE SECOND WORLD

AN INTRODUCTION

The ancients built Valdrada on the shores of a lake, with houses all verandas one above the other, and high streets whose railed parapets look out over the water. Thus the traveler, arriving, sees two cities: one erect above the lake, and the other reflected, upside down. Nothing exists or happens in the one Valdrada that the other Valdrada does not repeat, because the city was so constructed that its every point would be reflected in its mirror, and the Valdrada down in the water contains not only all the flutings and juttings of the facades that rise above the lake, but also the rooms' interiors with ceilings and floors, the perspective of the halls, the mirrors of the wardrobes.
Valdrada's inhabitants know that each of their actions is, at once, that action and its mirror-image, which possesses the special dignity of images, and this awareness prevents them from succumbing for a single moment to chance and forgetfulness. Even when lovers twist their naked bodies, skin against skin, seeking the position that will give one the most pleasure in the other, even when murderers plunge the knife into the black veins of the neck and more clotted blood pours out the more they press the blade that slips between the tendons, it is not so much their copulating or murdering that matters as the copulating or murdering of the images, limpid and cold in the mirror.
At times the mirror increases a thing's value, at times denies it. Not everything that seems valuable above the mirror maintains its force when mirrored. The twin cities are not equal, because nothing that exists or happens in Valdrada is symmetrical: every face and gesture is answered, from the mirror, by a face and gesture inverted, point by point. The two Valdradas live for each other, their eyes interlocked; but there is no love between them.

[Italo Calvino, *Invisible Cities*]

---

¹**im.age** \'im-ij\ n [ME, fr. OF, short for *imagene*, fr. L *imagin-*, *imago*; akin to L *imitare* to imitate] **1**: a reproduction or imitation of the form of a person or thing; esp: an imitation in solid form: **STATUE 2 a**: the optical counterpart of an object produced by an optical device (as a lens or mirror) or an electronic device **b**: a likeness of an object produced on a photographic material **3 a**: exact likeness : **SEMBLANCE** (God created man in his own—

Gen 1:27 **b**: a person strikingly like another person <he is the—of his father>
4 a: a tangible or visible representation: **INCARNATION** <the—of filial devotion>
b *archaic*: an illusory form: **APPARITION 5 a** (1): a mental picture of something not actually present: **IMPRESSION** (2): a mental conception held in common by members of a group and symbolic of a basic attitude and orientation <a disorderly courtroom can seriously tarnish a community's—of justice—Herbert Brownell> **b**: **IDEA, CONCEPT 6**: a vivid or graphic representation or description **7**: **FIGURE OF SPEECH 8**: a popular conception (as of a person, institution, or nation) projected esp. through the mass media <promoting a corporate—of brotherly love and concern—R.C. Buck> **9**: a set of values given by a mathematical function (as a homomorphism) that corresponds to a particular subset of the domain

²**image** *vb* **im.aged; im.ag.ing** *vt* **1**: to call up a mental picture of: **IMAGINE**
2: to describe or portray in language esp. in a vivid manner **3 a**: to create a representation of; also: to form an image of **b**: to represent symbolically
4a: **REFLECT, MIRROR b**: to make appear: **PROJECT**—*vi*: to form an image—**im.ag.er** \er\ n

[*Webster's Ninth New Collegiate Dictionary*]

Standing at Beach Ngobila, along the shores of the Congo river, I try to worm my way through the mass of bodies that engulfs me. Beach Ngobila is one of the only points of straight access to the Congo stream in this city which lives with its back turned toward the river, and in which one is only occasionally reminded of the river's existence by the sight of an orphaned boat, hauled up and stranded deep inside one of the city's sandy back streets. Upon entering Beach Ngobila, the first, violent, impression is that of a cannibalistic space which swallows everyone, and which sucks one down into a swirling maelstrom of soldiers, vendors, custom officials, traders, fishermen, street children and travelers. Beach Ngobila also spits people out. Crossing the river from Brazzaville to Kinshasa, Beach Ngobila is a place of warm welcome and homecoming for some. For others who leave Kinshasa's shores and cross the river in the opposite direction, to Brazzaville and beyond, it is a place of promise, the exit from a city they always dreamt of leaving behind. For others still, the Beach is a place of painful rejection, of expulsion, of the impossibility of returning to a city that once incarnated all their hopes and formed the only imaginable stage of their lives. This is the city to which they are now forced to turn their backs, in bitterness, in tears, with regret or, a distinct possibility, just glad to have caught the ferry and have gotten out alive. And all that remains of this previous life is some insignificant reminder, some shirts, a pair of Nikes, wedding pictures, a cooking pot or a Bible, picked up at random and hastily stowed away in pathetic plastic bags.

And for those who live in tune with the world of the river and the rhythms of its activities, Ngobila offers a livelihood.

Beach Ngobila is Kinshasa's time and space compacted, a place with which it is easy to develop a love–hate relationship, a place in which there is no room for the middle-of-the-road, only for extremes. And like Kinshasa itself, it too constantly assaults one's senses: the smell of the river's warm humidity blowing into one's nostrils, the feel of dampness sticking to one's skin, of heavy air that somehow has become liquid and feels like a fluid, oily blanket of warm water wrapped around one's body; the noise of boisterous laughter, of people shouting, screaming, giving orders, begging, pleading; the touch of complicated hand shakes, of worthless money changing hands; the expressionless gaze of bystanders; the feverish activity of arrivals and farewells, of buying and selling, of nervous movement. And simultaneously of stillness and timelessness.

Imagine yourself set down, surrounded by all your gear, alone on a tropical beach close to a native village. I remember being disappointed when I came here for the first time, many years ago now. The word "beach" had conjured up the promise of an exotic setting of golden sun, pristine sand and palm trees softly swaying in the evening breeze. Instead, Beach Ngobila, once a flourishing industrial port, turned out to be an industrial wasteland, by then a grey concrete strip with rusty hoisting cranes, outlined by a graveyard of moored decaying boat carcasses, the dark brown color of which contrasted sharply, or so I remember it now, with the crisp colors of the neatly folded six and twelve yard *wax hollandais* cloths, all spread out on the ground by the market women along the entrance to the Beach's docks.

When I try to recall this first visit to Beach Ngobila, there is also another color that comes to my mind's eye: the green of old army uniforms. With this memory of tired green comes the hint of lingering, unpredictable danger, the image of muscular men with imitation Ray Ban sunglasses, Mike Tyson haircuts and nonchalant machine guns, asking for cigarettes with broad smiles and with white hand palms turned upward, a gesture that acts out innocence. And then the contrast with the river itself: calm, silent, slow and yet full of swirling movement and underwater currents. It must have been during the period of rain for, in my memory, the water does not have the muddy brown color it takes on during the dry season, but it is dark and black, with tufts of green upon its gliding surface, little miniature forest islands indifferently drifting past the city on their long downstream journey from the equatorial forest. Hard not to think of *Heart of Darkness*, although I distinctly remember being angry with myself for allowing this cliché to take over.

Looking out over the river, with the crowded docks behind me, and behind them the vast anthill of this city named Kinshasa, Léopoldville, Lipopo, Kin-Malebo, I remember, also, being overwhelmed by a sense of perspective, of distance, of horizon. To the right, the upstream side, where the river widens into the Malebo Pool and rather successfully tries to imitate the vastness of an ocean, the distant line which divides water and sky is blurred by the heat. The horizon is lined with the shimmering silhouettes of trees, drawn with black Chinese ink by an unsteady hand against the sky, hinting at the existence of islands in the stream, or merely suggesting the idea of islands, shapeshifting sand banks, with names nonetheless: Mbamu, Mimosa, Kandolo, Lumbu, Mabanga.

Straight ahead, across the river, west of Kinshasa, one makes out the modest skyline of Brazzaville, with its landmark Elf skyscraper. To me it was the silhouette of just another city, back then. Now it has become a skyline which has lost its innocence, for it is still pockmarked and scarred by the months of war and violence which reduced the capital of the other Congo to a shadow of itself in 1997. *Poto-poto mboka monene, solo Kinshasa poto moyindo*, "Brazzaville is a big city, but only Kinshasa is an African Europe," the proud inhabitants of Kinshasa used to sing. But then they also sang *ata ndele mokili ekobaluka*, "sooner or later, the world will change."

Along the river, close to Kinshasa's shores, a fisherman glides by in a small dug out canoe, oblivious of change, his image reflecting in the water, a double broken and fragmented by the waves.

In 1997, while Brazzaville was busy bombing itself out of existence, and while rockets fired from the city's presidential palace in the direction of Kinshasa fell on Kintambo and other riverine neighborhoods, leaving tens of Kinois dead, historian Ch. Didier Gondola published his *Villes miroirs. Migrations et identités urbaines à Kinshasa et Brazzaville 1930–1970*. Gondola's book is a history of the twin cities of Kinshasa and Brazzaville, mirroring each other across the Congo river, like an imperfect materialization of the city of Valdrada which Italo Calvino describes in *Le città invisibili*. This other book, *Invisible Cities*, tells the story of a Venetian traveler, Marco Polo, who diverts the aged Tartar emperor Kublai Khan with tales of the cities he has seen in his travels around the empire. Soon it becomes clear that each of the fantastic places that Marco Polo describes is really one and the same place, the city of Venice.

Our book about Kinshasa, a joint project between an anthropologist and a photographer, is not a historian's history of Kinshasa. Nor is it a demographer's or an architect's. All of them would have written radically different portraits of Kinshasa. The Kinshasa described here resembles Calvino's invisible

Venice, for it contains many cities in one as well. It is at once a city of memory, a city of desire, a hidden city, a trading city, a city of the dead, a city of signs, a city of words, an oneiric city, a city of utopia. And like Calvino's Venice and Gondola's twin cities, this Kinshasa too cannot be understood without reflecting upon reflection, upon reflecting realities, mirrors, images, imitation, imagination, and (self) representation. This book presents Kinshasa as a vast mirror hall. Starting from but drastically expanding Gondola's notion of mirroring cities, we seek to analyze the various levels of mirroring which fracture Kinshasa's urban world into a series of kaleidoscopic, multiple,

but simultaneously existing, worlds. Each of these micro cities constantly reflects the others, though this reflection is not always symmetrical. Some of these cities, and some levels of mirroring between them, are more visible than others.

Above all, this book tries to capture Kinshasa's constant urge to move beyond the tarnish left upon the surface of its mirroring realities; the ways in which this city, sometimes playfully, sometimes desperately, but always with tremendous vitality, tries to break through the layers of dust and dirt, the palimpsests of colonization, de-, re- and neocolonization that have settled upon its surface and have dulled, sometimes even destroyed, its luster. Living in an urban reality stained by a film of increasing poverty, by the tears and blood drops of physical and symbolical violence, as well as by a pervasive sense of societal crisis and loss, Kinshasa's inhabitants struggle to reach beyond the fractures inflicted by the postcolonial world and the disjunctions at play in the myths of modernity *and* tradition. This is also where the metaphor of the mirror is pushed to its limits. Kinshasa does not merely reflect. It is not merely represented in the mirrors held up by precolonial pasts, colonialist modernities or nationalist myths. Certainly, to an important extent it is animated by the reflecting images of these imposed representations. Simultaneously, however, it resists, shatters, transforms and moves beyond all of these in often unexpected and surprising ways.

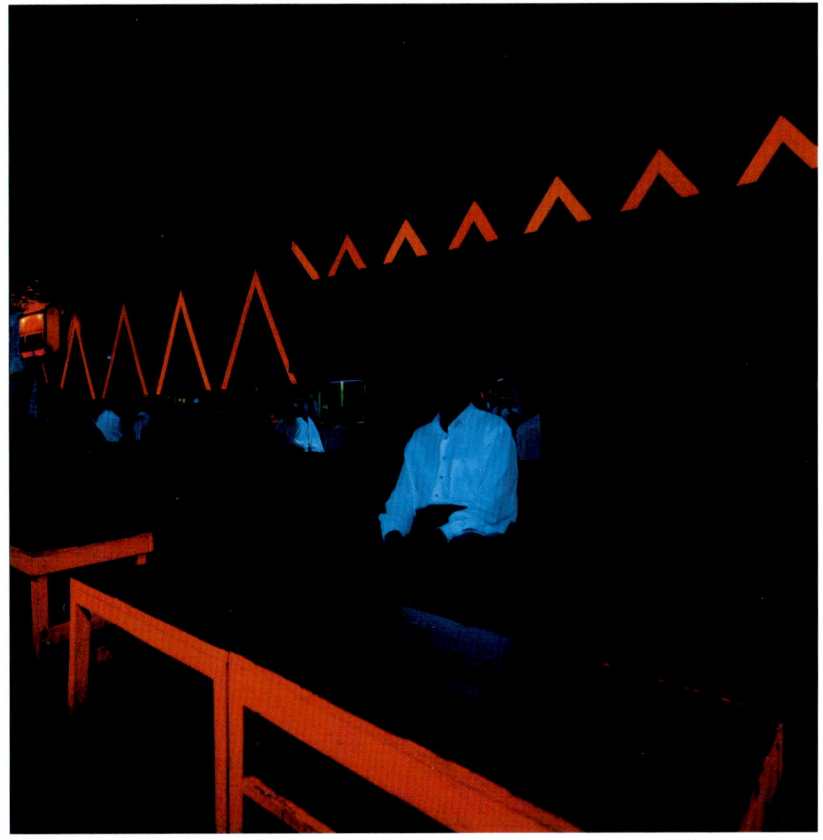

Paradigms of resistance against the hegemonies of state, money and market fail to fully capture the complexities of the realities lived by many in Congo today. Nor do they manage to seize the dynamics of subversion by means of which the metaphor of the mirror becomes alive in the urban world of Kinshasa. Both literally and figuratively, Congo's capital constantly smashes its own mirrors. At the same time, it never stops piecing itself back together. In ways that often leave the observer perplexed, the city constantly activates and undergoes the effervescent push and pull of destruction and regeneration. The incessant and chaotic crossing of the borders between these two forces somehow seems to generate the energetic source from which Kinshasa taps the power to embody, animate and sustain its own *eidos*, its own ongoing attempts at societal creation. In its most essential form, this power is operated by a frontier logic of mutation. It is, in a way, the power of the fetish. Like the fetish, the city of Kinshasa is a constant border-crossing phenomenon, resisting fixture, refusing capture. And like the fetish itself, like the magic activated through the mirror in the bellies of Congo's power objects, the city's moving force of mutation is generated in "the slippage between the dominance and the subordination of the surface."[1] Mentally and materially, the city emerges in unstable space. It is a product of a profound mixture between different cultural itineraries and sites. Its content is composite and is generated through crossing various borders and mediating between different opposites. As such, it is also extremely well adapted to carrying this mutant message, for it presents in and of itself a space of confrontation, mutation and movement. Out of the breccia of broken glass, the debris of its own pasts, the city thus feverishly transforms and goes on. In a sustained effort to recreate and institutionalize itself, the city tirelessly energizes an ever-growing web of plural meanings and social imaginary significations.

The following sections offer an introduction to the major themes that run through the chapters of this book. In part, they provide a summary of the different mirrors in which Kinshasa is captured and authored by external gazes and representations. More importantly, however, they also set the stage to move beyond such identity play which reduces Kinshasa to the mere role of "significant other," in an attempt to start understanding Kinshasa's originality, its internal struggle to contemplate and create its own identity.

MIRRORS AND MODELS: THE COLONIAL SPECULUM

One level of reflection through which Kinshasa is made to exist is quite obvious: it takes place in the European mirror of colonialism which invented and created the primitivist idea of the Congo and its counter-image, the urban landscape. The history of the creation and evolution of the city that is called Kinshasa today, from its origins as a small trade station, established by King Leopold's envoy Stanley upon his arrival in Ngaliema Bay on the first of December, 1881, its subsequent rebirth as Léopoldville, capital of Belgian Congo, between 1908 and 1960, to the large city of at least 6 million people it has become now, is a trajectory that cannot be appreciated without taking into account the military, monetary, medical and moral dynamics of the colonizing context in which it emerged.

1961. Lumumba murdered, Congo in crisis. I was born in 1961, a postcolonial subject. I was born not in Congo, but in Antwerp, in a street named *Beschavingstraat*, Civilization Street. Standing in the shadow of the Church of Christ the King, our house was one of many similar houses in a new suburban housing estate, erected after the Second World War. A couple of streets away, on a little square and opposite my grandparents' house, stood one of the only two houses that Le Corbusier built in Belgium. In 1961, this house, a 1926 realization, was still inhabited by its original resident, Mister Guiette, an Antwerp painter who, so my father tells me, also had two beautiful daughters. The house still exists, the daughters have gone. The postwar modernism of my childhood neighborhood, a modest reprise of Le Corbusier's architectural ideals, reflected the optimism of that period.

Our own street ended on the *Tentoonstellingslaan,* Exhibition Avenue, close to what then was still the *Kolonielaan,* the Colony Avenue, which has undergone a name change since. The port of Antwerp was the umbilical cord which connected tiny Belgium to its giant baby of a colony. Yet, this was not the reason for all the colonial references in the street names of my early childhood neighborhood. Only recently did I realize why the streets were so full of colonial memories. Going through some personal papers and documents of my grandmother's after her death, I found some photos of the World Exhibition that was held in Antwerp in 1930. No doubt the photos had been made by my grandfather, who worked in a small photo-shop in Antwerp in that period. An important section of the 1930 World Exhibition was dedicated to Flemish Art, appropriately housed in the Church of Christ the King. On a plot next to this church, in the area where my childhood neighborhood would be erected two decades later, stood an imposing, resolutely modernist, Congo pavilion in which Belgium's colonial oeuvre was proudly put on display. In line with a tradition that started with Universal Exhibitions at the end of the nineteenth century, including Tervuren's famous example of 1898, the 1930 Congo display also included a *village africain,* a "negro-village." This "African Village" was built in a way that imitated the *style soudanais,* a vague pseudo Arabic architectural style which never really existed as such in precolonial Congo, but which referred to a crucial element of the Leopoldian colonial mythology. In this mythological construction, the colonizing drive that was set in motion by King Leopold II and that swept through the Congo in the last decades of the nineteenth century, was invariably legitimated as a humanitarian struggle against "Arab" slave traders such as the legendary Tippo Tip. The adobe style of the 1930 African Village provided an invented architectural commemoration of this era, which culminated in the *campagne arabe* of 1892–1895 and similar events of the time, including that other, equally famous but slightly surreal, colonial founding myth, Stanley's rescue of Emin Pasha. Throughout the colonial period, the pseudo Arabic style remained popular in the Belgian Congo as well. The architecture of the colonial prisons that the Belgians erected throughout the country and which continue to be used today still bears witness to this colonial orientalism.

The 1930 African Village conveys the complexities and ambiguities that are inherent in the notion of "place" as it existed in the colonial discourse and imagination. The image of Congo which was created in this Antwerp display, next to a Le Corbusier house of the same period, calls into being a completely imaginary reconstruction of an equally imaginary traditional Africa. Within the Exhibition display, this colonial reflection is mirrored in and juxtaposed by the "modern" imperialist Congo pavilion and the Flemish Art in the equally imperialist Church of Christ the King. The Congo has, of course, always

fascinated the western imagination, from Conrad's *Heart of Darkness* to Naipaul's *A Bend in the River* and de Villiers' SAS pulp fiction airport literature, with titles such as *Panique au Zaire* and *Adieu Zaire*, spectacularly racist cocktails of exoticism, sex, violence, intrigue and betrayal, with an African pin up girl on the cover. In varying degrees, "Congo" appears in these works of fiction as a powerful negative image of the Western Self, in which the West constantly projects all of its fears and fantasies. For example, in the wake of the 1995 Ebola outbreak in Kikwit, 500 kilometers south east of Kinshasa, a leading Belgian newspaper characterized the virus as symptomatic of a wild and undomesticated country. In the same way, Hollywood has associated the outbreaks of AIDS with the Central African forest and phantasmagoric constructions of the ways in which the virus jumped from monkeys to Africans. The great discrepancy which is generated in the mirroring process between this topos, the Congo of the imagination, and the topicality of the physical Congo, seems to go unnoticed by most. The strength of the imagined place renders *invisible* the reality of the African site. What the African Village of the 1930 World Exhibition revealed is precisely this rupture, this fault line between representation and reality which is so characteristic of the problematic place of "place" in the colonial and postcolonial contexts. As Edouard Glissant explains: "On voit

beaucoup l'Afrique à la télévision – le sida, les massacres, les guerres tribales, les misères... Mais en fait, on ne voit pas l'Afrique. Elle est invisible." [We see a lot of Africa on television – AIDS, massacres, tribal wars, misery... But in fact we don't see Africa. She is invisible.][2] In the recent ninth edition of the Lonely Planet travel guide, *Africa on a Shoestring: Discover the Rhythms of Africa*, "Kinshasa," and the lives of its millions of inhabitants, is thus totally obliterated and rendered invisible in half a page: "The rest of Congo (Zaïre) may be pretty wild and untamed but Kinshasa, the capital, sprang from the jungle into the fast lane a long time ago. It's huge, muggy and very dangerous but, despite the widespread destruction, there are still a few decent shops, restaurants and hotels. [...] Kinshasa is a dangerous city at any time of the day. Thieves and muggers abound, violent crime is common and police and army personnel constantly target travellers for bribes. When you arrive in Kinshasa by air, you'll be surrounded by gangs of military personnel in civilian clothes who will hold you, your luggage and your passport hostage until you give them money. If at all possible, have someone who knows the ropes meet you at the airport."[3] Similarly, the limits of the city are defined by its geographic invisibility. No map that I have ever seen of Kinshasa reproduces the city in its integrality. Hundreds of thousands of lives that are lived in those areas which expanded after independence are quite literally not "on the map." Every city has its elsewheres, geographically (for example through its diasporic networks) and through its local imaginaries, but Kinshasa often strikes one as a city that is, in and of itself elsewhere, invisible.

It was not a coincidence that the World Exhibition of 1930 was organized in the same year that Belgium celebrated its hundredth anniversary as an independent nation state. The works of colonial imperialism are intimately linked to the rise and consecration of the western nation state, for which the colony served as its external expansion. Within eighteenth and nineteenth century Europe, the changing nature of internal mechanisms of state control was based on processes of what Foucault has called "sequestration."[4] This term refers to the creation of new technologies of (state) supervision within new types of institutions: the prison, the asylum, the labor camp, the colony, the hospital, the *cité*... The genealogy of such spaces of social control illustrates changing conceptualizations of normality and deviance within western society and within the expanding model of the modern nation state as unifying moral project. These new institutions, as spaces of organized repression, thus became the depositories of new social categories of the irrational, the marginal and the deviant.

People who, in these emerging definitions, no longer occupied an unproblematic niche within society, who found themselves on the wrong side of the new lines of fracture of social acceptability, were readily subjected to the state technologies of power and control. In addition, the nation state, as a panoptical, rationalizing project, developed new "geographies of perversion."[5] These "othered" the criminal, the madman, the beggar, the vagrant, the laborer, the prostitute and the homosexual. They redefined these categories of people into readily identifiable targets for the nation state's programs of social engineering, education, civilization and reeducation. Paradoxically, then, the state, as homogenizing project and as upholder of (the illusion of) unity, continuously produced difference as well, a difference which it simultaneously and systematically excluded, stigmatized and pathologized. It is indeed interesting to see how, together with the rise of the European nation state, new images and theories of atavism, degeneration (*dégénérescence*) and sociobiological decline emerged in European culture and politics.[6]

Within the hegemonic discourse of the state, the notion of degeneration was often linked to the sociocultural sites of those whom the state defined as deviant. Culture, in other words, became centrally implicated in forms of both physical and social disease. This also implies that medical intervention, at that point, became a form of *moral* sanitation. As a result, many of the techniques

Work: The base for progress. Agriculture: Efficient remedy against hunger.

of state control did not hesitate to penetrate deeply into the lives and daily sociocultural locales of citizens. Very often, these techniques centered on the body, and aimed at imposing new norms of hygiene, at controlling sexual behavior, at changing the ways in which people were dressed and housed, and even at redefining kinship relations. As such, the structures of the working class family, this basic building block of the nation state, are thus reoriented towards a more acceptable nuclear form, which can then function as the nation state's image on the local level.[7] The nineteenth century proletarian was thus perceived to be a kind of western "nigger" *avant la lettre*, the state's internal precursor of the later colonial subject.

The relations to the working and peasant classes which the colonial forces exported to their colonies differed greatly from one colonial context to the other. Consider the contrast between the British, who exported few workers, and the Italians, who used colonies as plantations to absorb excess peasants from home. In the Belgian colonial context, where an attempt was made to create an indigenous working class, the formula used seemed to replicate many of the strategies and trajectories that the Belgian state applied at home vis-à-vis its own working classes and other problematic groups. Once that internal other was domesticated, his alterity defined, labeled and then eradicated, the state embarked upon the same homogenizing sanitizing and environmental project in its colony.

In colonial Africa, writes Jean Comaroff, "as an object of European speculation, Africans personified suffering and degeneracy, their environment a hothouse of fever and affliction."[8] Although this statement, in its sweeping generalization, disregards the multiplicity of ideals that motivated missionaries and other agents of colonialism, certainly when viewed in the Belgian colonial context, it undoubtedly also captures something of the Belgian sentiment with regard to its colony in the early decades of its colonial endeavor. Therefore, after a first period in which medicine aimed primarily at the protection of the expatriate colonial agents and military, the major imperialist interventions were often both medical and moral, in a joint venture between the cure and the cross.[9] They focused on issues such as disease control and, especially in the early mission medicine but also afterwards, on the regulation of the colonial subjects' unruly minds and bodies.[10] These bodies had to be clothed, educated, housed and fed in drastically new ways. During the heyday of colonialism, nutritional studies in Africa, for example, were often prompted by colonial efforts to deal with the "problems of African native diet." As such, they were designed to provide ways of altering local attitudes to food production and consumption, in an attempt to reduce malnutrition, disease and poor health, and heighten the "effective performance of individuals and communities."[11] More generally, and again for a variety of combined reasons ranging

from moral and medical to economical, one of the major aims of colonial medicine was to control and diminish indigenous morbidity and mortality. This occurred while, on another level, the colony clearly functioned as an exploitative "space of death." On that level, the colonial negrophile often turned out to be Africa's necrophile and necrophore. For the same reasons, the Belgian colonial administration interfered drastically in local modes of residence, sanitizing the spatial layout of villages, creating new types of settlement, and controlling and restricting the movement of its colonial subjects.

Colonial medicine was also seen as "the greatest force for conceptual change, compelling Africans to abandon their unscientific worldview."[12] Thus, colonialist modernity—of which medicine was an outspoken icon—intervened in the most intimate aspects of the colonized's culture, through its attempts at domesticating and controlling indigenous sexuality. It worked at imposing new concepts of space, time, causality, production and accumulation upon the colonial subject in an attempt to reconfigure the colonial mind, and even at genetically engineering a new race of ideal workers.[13]

Many studies of colonial medicine have taken the medicine as social control approach which I briefly outlined above. In such approaches, the politics of the state, both at home and abroad, is perceived, in a very real sense, as biosocial eugenics, a body politics, an "anatomy of power" which, as an implicit or explicit system of power, knowledge and coercion, defined the relations between ruler and ruled: "Medicine and imperialism in nineteenth century Africa are seen to be inseparably joined in practice and in concept. The evolving field of biomedicine, introduced by missionary healers, provided images of an ailing human body that would justify the intervention of a colonial state as it imposed its own order of domination [...]."[14] As hegemonic discourse and practice closely related to the ideology of the state, or more generally as a tool of empire, biomedicine was —and still is— centrally concerned with *difference*. As a metaphor for a more general colonial ideology and praxis, it is thus illustrative of many of the mechanisms that contributed in the creation and development of the urban colonial landscape, and of Léopoldville in particular.

Throughout its emergence and gradual development, Léopoldville, as colonial speculum and as a large scale project in social engineering, grafted upon its urban geography and ecology many of the evolutionist oppositions that also underpinned the cultural construction of difference in the medical colonial intervention. The difference between metropolitan Prospero and colonial Caliban, between Self and Other, Culture and Nature, Rationality and Irrationality, Man and Woman, writing and speech, knowledge and ignorance, modernity and tradition, or peace and war, is constantly generated in this European speculation. It is also the same mirror that gives birth to Léopoldville's two reflecting halves, the western Ville and the indigenous Cité. In these complementary but opposing spaces qualities such as "public" and "private" acquire radically different meanings.

The colonial triumvirate of sword, cross and money, that is, of the colonial administration and its military arm, the church and its proselytizing activities, and the colony's powerful trade and industry circles, often had different and sometimes even contradictory agendas. They did not necessarily hold the same views on the development of the urban landscape and its inhabitants, and their actions were not always concerted. Nevertheless these three pillars of Belgian colonialism in Congo shared the same underlying, although often vaguely defined, ideal of colonialist modernity as outlined above. It is this shared ideological configuration that underpinned to a large extent the ways in which the city was shaped and designed.

During the postwar period in which the modernist suburban housing estate of my childhood years was built, Belgian modernism was also given a second life in Congo. In 1940, Léopoldville was home to some 50,000 inhabitants. At the end of World War II the number of inhabitants had doubled, reaching 200,000 in 1950, 400,000 at independence and well over a million in 1970. In the early decades of the twentieth century, Léopoldville developed itself along the axis Kintambo–Kalina. Kintambo developed out of Stanley's early trading

post and consisted of the city's oldest industrial and residential sites. Kalina, currently Gombe, developed into the capital's administrative area, housing the colonial administration's offices and residential villas. Gombe has very much kept that function today. Kintambo and Kalina were soon connected by a railroad. Around this axis gradually developed commercial centers and several *cités indigènes,* native quarters and settlements inhabited by Congolese workers. On the Kintambo side, the labor camps arose along the river, in proximity to the industrial activities of that part of the city, its shipyards, metallurgy and other activities such as the confection industry of Utex Léo. On the Kalina side, a considerably larger space was set aside for the development of several indigenous neighborhoods, most notably Kinshasa, Barumbu and Lingwala. Consisting of a large number of small *parcelles*, plots and compounds, these neighborhoods were laid out according to a well ordered grid which continued the original ground plan of an army camp that had been located there previously. These indigenous neighborhoods, camps and, after the Second World War, *cités jardins*, garden cities, consisted of houses that were either individually constructed and owned (and there existed a *Fonds d'Avance,* a lending agency to encourage such individual ownership) or were built by colonial employers and companies. Here too, these neighborhoods existed in close proximity with the administrative and residential centers of Léopoldville. Yet, they were consistently separated from these central areas by stretches of no man's land, by the main railroad (which also connected the city to the port of Matadi in the Lower Congo), as well as by a number of other buffer zones, such as the city's botanical gardens, commercial zones, an ethnographic museum displaying indigenous lifestyles, a zoological garden, mission posts and army camps.

In terms of its spatial layout, the extended booming urban conglomeration that Léopoldville was rapidly becoming thus emerged from the very beginning as a racially segregated city, with a strict demarcation line between a central white Ville, with its administrative and residential areas (Kintambo, Ngaliema and the current Gombe, later expanded into the residential neighborhoods of Limete), and a "peripheral" African city, the *cité indigène*.

On top of the racial lines of segregation that structured the city of Léopoldville, or Lipopo as the city was called by its Congolese inhabitants, the colonial economic demands and necessities also occasioned a demographic, strongly gendered, segregation. In the early decades of the Belgian Congo's existence, the colonial population mainly consisted of men. It was only very slowly that families, wives and children became an established fact of Léopoldville's urban social make-up. Hesitantly, they started to emerge in Léopoldville during the interbellum period, but it was only after World War II that wives and family became a standard part of the colonial city's social make-up. This demographic imbalance, however, was not a reality that characterized the lives of the white colonials alone. Before 1930, the male–female ratio in Léopoldville's indigenous neighborhoods was three to one. At the end of World War II men still outnumbered women two to one, and special taxes were imposed on single women who were living in the *cités indigènes*. This reflected not only the colonial endeavor to control the city's growth rate, but also the simple fact that these indigenous quarters mainly functioned as depots of cheap African labor, in which there was room for neither women nor the unemployed. Especially after the war, in a vain attempt to diminish and contain the mounting social and political tensions in the city, the colonial administration developed a strict policy of cleaning up the streets. Those without jobs were rounded up by the colonial armed forces, the *Force Publique*, and sent back to the interior. Paralleling the city's segregated spatial and demographic development, the *Force Publique*, strategically located in army garrisons throughout Léopoldville, was built along equally strict segregated lines, with a superstructure of Belgian officers on the one hand, and a body of Congolese recruits, mostly Bangala from the Congo's Equateur province, on the other. It was mainly these soldiers who became the driving force behind the development of Lingala, their native language, as the city's major *lingua franca*.

Despite a vast array of far reaching colonial measures which aimed at restricting and controlling the rural migration to the city, Léopoldville kept expanding. In 1949, faced with a demographic explosion and the increasing social unrest it engendered, the Belgian colonial administration started to implement a large urbanization program through the newly created *Office de Cités Indigènes de Léopoldville* (OCIL). One of the office's projects was the Renkin neighborhood (named after Belgium's first Minister of Colonial Affairs), which formed the heart of what would later on become Matonge, the vibrant core of Kinshasa's night life.

In 1952, the OCIL was succeeded by the *Office de Cités Africaines* (OCA). This office was created to coordinate better the government's response to the increasingly pressing needs of a rapidly growing city.[15] The goal OCA set for itself was ambitious: the construction of 40,000 new "quality homes" throughout the colony over the next ten years. Twenty thousand of these homes would be built in Léopoldville alone. Between 1952 and 1960, the city thus expanded drastically, giving birth to an impressive number of new satellite *cités* such as Bandalungwa, Yolo Nord and Yolo Sud, Matete, Lemba, Ndjili and, finally, Kinkole.[16] Still, OCA's housing program and urban planning efforts, impressive as they may appear today, fell short of providing a satisfactory solution to the city's enormous demographic expansion and increasingly chaotic character. The colonial government concentrated all of its efforts at urban expansion in OCA while barring all nongovernmental housing programs and initiatives. The government refused, for example, to sell land to private companies to construct new homes for their employees. And yet, the rate at which the much needed new houses were constructed within the OCA program was far too slow to match the population growth. Even worse, many of the new houses remained empty because they were too expensive for Kinshasa's commoners. As a result, shantytowns started to spring up everywhere across the city. The situation worsened during the first years after independence. At first, the unfulfilled OCA plans continued to be realized, though at a much slower pace. This effort at continued urban planning was coordinated by the *Office*

National de Logement (ONL) and financed by the *Caisse National d'Epargne et de Crédit Immobilier*. Gradually, however, the government abandoned all efforts at urban planning. No longer restrained by government supervision, the shantytowns started to expand into the endless and still growing sprawl of popular neighborhoods, the vast peripheral city, the *zones annexes* of which Kinshasa consists today. In the process, the capital grew far beyond its colonial borders: towards the Lower Congo in the western direction, and in the eastern and southern directions, over the hill range that once contained the city, towards the Bateke plateau and the Kwango. As a result of this unbridled growth, the city has grown away from its old colonial heart. This evolution was recently consolidated by Laurent Kabila's decision to order the building of a new major market square in Masina, in an attempt to alleviate the pressure on the old central market area near the Rue du Commerce. Its construction confirms the fact that the colonial city center, which was also the geographic center of the city during colonial times, long since ceased to be either, and had become peripheral to the daily experience of the majority of Kinshasa's population.

It is in Camp Luka, Masina, Kimbanseke, Kingasani, Kisenso, Ngaba, Makala, Selembao, large parts of Mont Ngafula, Malweka and the many other similar annexed areas and *communes urbano-rurales* of postcolonial Kinshasa that the failure of modernist urban planning, as conceived by the colonial government and the early postcolonial state, is most clearly illustrated. It is here, also, that Kinshasa began to reinvent itself into the city that it has become today. The growth of this new Kinshasa (and it is growing fast: Kinshasa has currently a yearly deficit of 200,000 houses)[17] has also marked a mental move away from the "place" of colonialism (and this place is both a spatial reality and a language, French). It has, in other words, moved away from the mimetic reproduction of an alienating model of colonialist modernity, imposed by the colonial and the Mobutist state upon the city's population through a wide ranging arsenal of physical and symbolic forms of violence. For the past four decades, the city has also moved away from the secular time of the (post)colonial nation and the official religious time of the Catholic Church which accompanied these efforts at nation building. It is in these increasingly numerous informal urban areas, with its complex patchwork of multiple local ethnic identities, that the city's inhabitants have started to reterritorialize and reclaim the urban space, develop their own specific forms of what De Meulder has called "proto-urbanism," and infuse the city with their own praxis, values, moralities and temporal dynamics. This process, which is perhaps better referred to as a form of "post urbanism," began at Kinshasa's margins and has now engulfed the city as a whole. Unhindered by any kind of formal industrialization or economic development, the city has bypassed, redefined or smashed the (neo)colonial logics that were stamped onto its surface. It has done so spatially, in terms of its architectural and urban development, as well as in terms of its sociocultural and economic imprint. Reaching across the formation period of high colonialism and its modernist ideals, Kinshasa is, to some extent, rejoining its earlier rural roots. Today, aided by an unending political and economic crisis, the city is undergoing a large scale process of informal *villagization*, in which a new type of agrarian urbanity and even a new type of ethnicity is generated.[18]

For an external observer it is not always easy to read this new urban landscape. Related to the western failure to reach beyond its blurred vision of a largely fictitious Congo is the development of a second form of cataract, which is becoming increasingly apparent in the incapacity of much academic discourse to grasp fully and make visible the changing realities in contemporary Congo and Kinshasa. Faced with worlds and interactions that no longer correspond to the social interweave as we tend to conceptualize and experience it, one becomes acutely aware that it is futile to explain some of the processes currently taking place in Congolese society by means of the standard vocabularies used by social and political scientists, economists, demographers and urban planners. Terms and concepts such as state, administration, government, governability, democracy, army, citizenship, law, justice, or even education and healthcare no longer seem to apply unequivocally to the realities usually covered by those terms.

Why is a building called a national bank, university, state department, hospital, or school when the activities which take place in it cannot be given the standard meanings and realities usually covered by those words? In January 1995, for example, Belgian newspapers reported that the national bank's total stock of foreign currency amounted to US$ 2,000 and a handful of Swiss francs. Similarly, university professors today earn US$ 200 a month—that is, if they are paid at all—and most departments of Kinshasa's national university have not bought books, or produced a single doctoral dissertation since the Zaireanization in the early 1970s. What does it mean to be a city with an estimated six million inhabitants in which there is hardly any car traffic or public transportation, for the simple reason that, at frequent intervals, there is not a drop of fuel available for weeks or even months? Why continue the social convention of referring to a banknote as "money" when one is confronted daily with the fact that it is just a worthless slip of paper? The withdrawal, in November 1993, of the IMF and the World Bank from the country attested to the fact that Congo was no longer partaking of the formal world economy. But what is the use of distinguishing between formal and informal or parallel economies when the informal has become the common and the formal has almost disappeared?

For years now, Congo's second or shadow economy has become the first and virtually only one. For Kinois it has long since become a cliché to say that no economic model can explain how a city like Kinshasa survives. For the *pousse-pousseurs* (the pushcart persons), the *quados* (informal car-mechanics), the *khaddafis* (illegal vendors of fuel), the *cambistes* (money changers), taxi drivers, shoe shiners, night watchmen and *ligablos* (street vendors) who daily experience in the flesh the continuing deterioration of their standards of living, and whose lives unfold in Poverty Street, the common discourses of political, economic and other analysts and "experts" are therefore totally devoid of sense. To them, *Kinshasa-la-belle* has long since become *Kinshasa-la-poubelle*, referred to as *Koweit City rive gauche*, *Sarajevo* or, more recently, *Kosovo*, *Chechnya*, *Afghanistan* or *Baghdad*.

Mirroring the constant attempts of Kinshasa's inhabitants to rename and thereby reclaim their city, the colonial and postcolonial authorities invested a lot of energy in the construction of their vision of the urban space. The colonizing dynamics of naming and renaming the city and its composite parts are typical of the colonial, the Mobutist and the Kabilist period. During colonial times, not only the city's name, Léopoldville, referred to the colonial master but so did the names of many a neighborhood: Belge I, Belge II, Bruxelles. Similarly, Mobutu stamped himself onto the city's map by renaming streets, buildings (Mama Yemo hospital, Stade Kamanyola), military camps and neighborhoods (Cité Mama Mobutu, Camp Mobutu). These acts of name giving illustrate the constant attempts at mastering the city, at producing domination, at defining place and encapsulating it in language. And yet, the names themselves immediately become sites of opposition against the official order.

The breakdown of the colonial city model and its local appropriation, transformation and cultural reterritorialization had already started during the colonial period itself. In 1959, more than half of Léopoldville's population was under the age of eighteen, and of this large group, only half was schooled. In 1960, the capital, already overpopulated, was flooded by another wave of youngsters who were fleeing from the rebellion and warfare in the interior (a process that is currently repeating itself). It is against this background of a decade of rising insecurity and socioeconomic and political unrest that street gangs of youngsters without schooling or salaried job started to make an appearance in the streets of Léopoldville.[19]

Between 1957 and 1959, in the same period in which the administrative reform took place, six movie theaters in all opened their doors: SIBIKA in the Kintambo neighborhood, and ASTRA, MBONGO–MPASI, MACAULEY, MOUSTAPHA and SILUVANGI in the popular neighborhoods of Lingwala, Kinshasa and Barumbu. These movie theaters, which flourished all over the city except in the "European" neighborhoods of Ngaliema, Léopoldville and Limete, soon became favorite meeting places of Léopoldville's youth, especially those youngsters at the margins of the colonial urban order, at risk of being expelled by the authorities. Hollywood westerns, in particular, had a tremendous impact on the way in which the urban youth subcultures of that time chose to express themselves, and were a decisive factor in the creation of Billism. In particular the image of the buffalo hunter and culture hero Buffalo Bill, alongside other cowboys such as Pecos Bill, left a deep impression.[20] These cowboys provided ideal role models for the young Kinois, who imitated the appearance (blue jeans, checkered shirt, neckerchief, lasso) and the tics of the Hollywood actors. After each movie, these young urban cowboys circulated on their "bicycle-horses" to announce the message of the western (*mofewana*, Lingala deformation of Far West), crying loudly *Bill oyee!*, upon which the bystanders would reply with *serumba!*

Billism appropriated and transformed the image of the cowboy-hunter to make it its own. Most of the members of these ludic groups of young urban "terrorists," more generally known as "The Spongers of the Far West" (*Les écumeurs du Far West*), lived on the margins of colonial society. The movement produced various competing youth gangs. Around 1957, most of these gangs, such as the "Yankees of Ngiri-Ngiri," shaped up around a few leaders. Amongst these early "ancestors," "priests" (*prêtres*), "sheriffs," or *grand maîtres* of the street gangs figured predominantly two persons known as William Booth and Gazin. Others followed soon: Grand Billy, Ross Samson, Néron (Monerona, author of a popular song, *Wele Kingo*), Tex Bill, Mive John, Mobarona, Khroutchev, Long Li Su, Azevedo, Eboma, Vieux Porain Zanga-Zanga, Libre, De Goum, Moruma, Demayo. Most of these were well known local

delinquents. Initially, the youngsters circling around these leaders lived together in houses (called "ranches" or "temples"). Later groups hung out in what became known as *nganda*, a meeting place around a bar-restaurant. Well known *ngandas* included Dynamic and Mofewana in Ngiri-Ngiri, or L'Enfer and Okinawa in Ndjili. These groups organized themselves in little territorial fiefdoms throughout the city (in Ngiri-Ngiri, Saint-Jean, Camp Luka, Bandal, Kintambo, Bandalungwa, Barumbu, Kinshasa and later Lemba, Ndjili, Matete, Yolo) and like sheriffs, they "made the law" (*kodondwa*) and "created order" (*tobongisa*, one of the Bills' slogans) in their neighborhood, while stealing for a living and fighting over territory with neighboring gangs.[21] Each territory, with its ranches and *ngandas*, thus had its chiefs and subchiefs, its ritual specialists known as *professeurs*, its own laws and rules, declared by the master of each particular gang, its own systems of taxation (making other citizens pay for a safe passage through gang territory), and its own passtime rit

uals, such as weight-lifting, gangbanging neighborhood girls, or smoking marijuana. Billism also strongly focused on music and guitars. The movement itself was at the origin of the birth of multiple local orchestras, some of which evolved later on into well known bands, such as Zaiko. Billism mobilized and channeled the social forces from the margin, and greatly contributed to the establishment of one of the most powerful forms of expression in Kinshasa's flamboyant popular culture.

Furthermore, each of these street groups had its own rituals of initiation. They usually consisted of a period of seclusion in the bush (thereby imitating the older rural model of the *mukanda* circumcision camp). There, one was trained into a specific style of ritualized combat, called *bilayi*, in which one had to learn how to butt one's head into a person during a fight. Overall, the Billies placed great value on violence, endurance, physical strength and courage (qualities which are stressed in the nicknames the Bills bestowed upon each other such as "hard wood" (*bois dur* or *bois fort*); the same stress on violence recurs in popular slogans of Billism: *azongaka sima te*, "a Bill never retreats," *tokende liboso*, "we go forward").[22]

What distinguished the Bills above all was the use of a particular argot, known as Hindubill, a mixture of French, Lingala, English and local vernacular languages. In a counterhegemonic inversion, "Hindu" refers to "Indian," the cowboys' natural enemies (that is, the state agents). It also makes reference to the "Indian" marijuana the Bills smoked. "Hindu" possibly also betrays the influence of Hindi movies shown in the theaters of Léopoldville during that period. This Indian cinematographic influence is partly responsible for the way in which the emerging figure of the *mami wata*—half woman and half fish, who promises access to wealth in return for human lives—began to dominate the city's imagination in the 1960s. In Kinshasa's popular paintings, *mami wata* invariably appears as a white skinned "Indian" lady (and this in spite of the West African origin of the *mami wata* figure).[23]

As the language of youth, Hindubill formed the hidden transcript of the youthful underdogs of Kinshasa who were excluded from education and salaried jobs and thus from the world of "adults." With Hindubill, the urban cowboys created their own modes of inclusion and exclusion. At the same time the persona of the Cowboy emerges as emancipatory figure, representing the spirit of the coming independence. The Bills played an important role in the lootings and the uprising that spread through Kinshasa in January 1959. They also reterritorialized the city in yet another way, by renaming various areas, markets, schools, bars and other public spaces of the city. On these they bestowed names such as Texas, Dallas, Casamar, and Godzilla. This reterritorialization was an explicit criticism of the Belgians' insufficient and segregationist urbanization of a too rapidly expanding Léopoldville. Undoubtedly, the Billies' practice of reclaiming and renaming parodied the colonizer's imperialist obsession with mapping and labeling, while at the same time playfully commenting upon the claims of the emergent nationalist movement.

From November 1960 onwards, with the mounting "Congo crisis" and the increasing unrest throughout the country, many new youth gangs appeared. These still made use of the vocabulary of the Bills but at the same time they increasingly shifted from the figure of the Cowboy to that of the Soldier, with references, for example, to the United Nations Blue Helmets, thereby reflecting in their vocabulary and organization the changing context of the period in which they emerged.

Billism laid the foundation for much of the contemporary urban youth culture. Kinshasa's movie theaters have long since disappeared. Instead, movies have become available through television, or they are watched in small neighborhood video theaters, where one usually pays for a full evening program including clips of the latest Congolese hits and concerts, a movie à la Ninja or Rambo, some soccer and, to top it off, a porn movie. Yet, the way in which western action movie hunters/warriors are captured and localized by Kinshasa's youth, but even more by the military, is reminiscent of the Billies in the 1950s. Zorro, Rambo, Superman, Terminator, Godzilla and the Power Rangers have become common role models for Kabila's *kadogos* (child soldiers) and for urban youth in general. Kinshasa's youth, a major focus throughout this book, share with their forebears the same capacity for fracturing and reinventing urban public space. Street children in Kinshasa sing: "It is said that water that sleeps does not move. The sleeping water only moves when one throws a stone into it." Often, Kin's youngsters are like such a stone, shattering the water's reflecting surface and sending ripples and waves through the pool in which Kinshasa beholds itself. They inscribe themselves in new temporalities. They also recycle and generate surprising, oftentimes embodied, cultural vocabularies and aesthetics. Now, as in the past, these feverishly reflect Kinshasa's social history while providing a subversive comment upon the banalization of violence, the militarization of society, the apocalyptic gale-force sound and fury of the city's constant religious transfiguration, and the material hardships in today's urbanscape.

THE VILLAGE AND THE FOREST CITY

The growing ruralization of Kinshasa is a strong reminder of the fact that the capital has not only looked into the mirror of modernity to design itself, but that it has always contained a second mirror as well. This mirror is provided by the village, the rural hinterland that constitutes Kinshasa's demographic and ethnic make-up. The countryside feeds Kinshasa, forms its natural backdrop, and exists in the city by way of contrast. It is this contrast that allowed the city to fashion itself as city, to define itself as *centre extra-coutumier*, outside of tradition, and, as marker of difference in opposition to the village, to place itself outside of the normative order of a rural and more traditional world that was, and often is, considered to be backward and primitive. And yet, at the same time, the construction of Kinshasa's urban space and identity has always remained a contested and dislocatory presence, a reminder of an artificial breach. In reality, this urban identity has constantly been invaded and formed by, blending with and depending on the village's traditions, moralities and pasts.

Three decades ago, someone like Henri Lefebvre, in his acclaimed work *The Production of Space*, could still, somewhat naively, write: "Much as they might like to, anthropologists cannot hide the fact that the space and tendencies of modernity (i.e. of modern capitalism) will never be discovered either in Kenya or among French or any other peasants."[24] Lefebvre thereby continued the same long modernist tradition which underpinned the creation of *difference* in the colonial period, and which is characterized by its conceptualization of the world within a polarized framework opposing, for example, modernity and tradition, city and countryside, center and periphery, "warm" and "cold" societies, culture and nature, male and female, the "hard rationality" of liberal capitalism generated in the urban space and the "soft irrationality" of a rural "economy of affection," and so forth. However, the distinctions between urban and rural realities, between modern and traditional worlds, or between what is situated locally and what is considered to be global, can no longer be taken for granted. It is no doubt a perceptual error to concentrate exclusively on the center, or the city, in order to understand the production of modernity (or the construction of, for example, "modern" male African identity.)[25] Rather than scrutinize the processes of modernity's construction from the metropole's perspective, this book also looks at the fringes, at the periphery, at those sites, whether located in the rural countryside or in the city itself, where "modernity" has not solidified but is a fluid and negotiable reality, an unfinished hegemony.

In the postcolony, moreover, categories such as center and periphery, or city and village, and the string of qualities attached to them, have often themselves become states of mind rather than objective qualities of space. The way in which the urban and the rural are constantly deconstructed in the postcolony necessitates an imaginative theorizing of that reality. For example, whereas the space of the city has not only undergone a marked ruralization, it has also, and increasingly, become, in the collective social instituting imaginary, the space of the forest. The hunter's landscape, which is one of the potentially dangerous, frontier like margin, is thus constantly mapped onto the urban, and thus "central" landscape. Hence, Werrason, the current uncrowned king of Kinshasa's popular music scene, refers to himself as "the king of the forest" (*le roi de la forêt*) and the "chief of the animals" (*mokonzi ya banyama*). It is no coincidence that the bar, a most crucial site in the urban landscape, is often redefined as village, such as Village Syllo, with its pastoral setting, along the Avenue Lumumba, or Limete's Village Bercy. In the latter, the light bulbs are put inside Aladdin lamps, which function as *pars pro toto* for the local, conjuring up the rural and the village. At the same time the notion of the village blends into an interesting palimpsest through a reference to an Icon of the global western world, the Stade de Bercy in Paris, where a number of Kinshasa's orchestras have given concerts in recent years. Often also, the bar is conceptualized as a forest. Werrason's headquarters is an open-air bar called *zamba playa* (*zamba* meaning "forest" in Lingala). In the social imaginary, the nocturnal environment of the bar is no doubt one of the most important locales

in which the city most fully displays its urbanity and modernity, and in which "diamond-hunters" and others who have access to dollars track down and capture, through ostensive consumption of beer, women and consumer goods, their interpretation of the good life as promised by and defined in their notion of modernity.

Similarly, the city/forest has become the site of the hunter's female counterpart, the gatherer. Once a week, huge bus-trucks called CITY-TATA ("City father") leave Kinshasa to transport passengers to Kikwit, 500 kilometers southeast of the capital, along a ravaged and dangerous road that once used to be a smoothly asphalted highway. Analogous to these trucks, the name CITY-MAMA has been bestowed upon small baskets that are used by an increasing number of urban women, the *mamas miteke*, who are without an income or a garden or field to till. These women take to the bush and swamps around the city to collect what little roots and grubs they can find there. Like the passengers in the CITY-TATA

bus, the roots are then transported back to the city in the "basket-bus" on the women's heads. (Ironically, Kinshasa is being redefined in terms of the sylvan margin at a time when woods and forests around the city are rapidly disappearing, a fact that has even changed its microclimate.)

It thus seems that, in Kinshasa today, modernity as exemplified by the city is contested or unfinished not only at its fringes, that is, the rural hinterland, but also in its very heart, the polis. There the local logic of hunting and gathering has infused the urban world, both metaphorically and practically, with its own moralities, its own ethics of accumulation, expenditure and redistribution, and its own specific pathways of self realization. Especially for the urban young, the hunter provides a model for identification and a figure of success and eminence. It is no coincidence that it was Buffalo Bill precisely, a buffalo hunter, who became a culture hero for Kinshasa's youngsters. Even today, the image of the hunter continues to have a strongly epistemic power. It offers the possibility of remaking both identity and place, and generating, to some extent at least, a social environment in the midst of chaos and change. For the *bana Lunda* ("children of Lunda") or *basali ya mbongo* ("those who work money"), the numerous youngsters who leave Kinshasa and other urban centers to travel hundreds of kilometers to the Angolan diamond fields of Lunda Norte, hunting diamonds and dollars constitutes a crucial part of the active capturing of the urban space. It allows them to refashion the city (and thereby modernity, the West, the *mundele* or white man) in their own terms, which are those of longstanding moralities, rooted in local rural pasts. Congolese youngsters' engagement in more global economies of diamond export and dollarization is thus often shaped from an utterly local perspective and out of a memory that is rooted in the *longue durée*. It is this enduring long term reality that forms the tain, the tinfoil, the lusterless back of the mirror in which Kinshasa beholds itself today. Without this gritty surface, without the past lingering

on into the present, the mirror wouldn't reflect anything.[26] Although memory and history in the urban context are of a specific kind and have undergone some radical transformations over the past decades, the expanding peripheral city is thus not without history, unlike Koolhaas's notion of the "generic city."[27] To conquer the city and shape their own moral and social economies in this urban space, the urban young tap into sources and routes of rural identity formation, thereby negotiating and reinventing the content and architecture of the intermediate world in which they find themselves. The passage into Angola is thus a contemporary version of a much older strategy of self realization, as hunters and warriors. It constitutes a veritable rite of passage, modelled upon the old *mukanda* circumcision ritual which is still practised in the countryside, and to which youngsters explicitly refer when they share and discuss their experiences in the Angolan diamond fields. It is important, however, to stress that the past (represented in the form of hunting logics, the village morality of capture and redistribution, the ultimately rural modes of self making as hunter and/or warrior) which is thus carried into the urban present is *not* a static model. On the contrary, for the urban youth the past becomes, if not reflexively at least in practice, a source for active engagement with the present, in ways that give shape both to very creative and outgoing forms of collective imagination and to a constant invention of a future for tradition, as imagined, for example, by Kinshasa's musicians in their video clips. There the persona of the "traditional chief" is frequently reenacted and recreated as a potent icon of power. More generally rural "folkloristic" music has been continuously recycled by urban bands such as Swede-Swede and its lead singer Boketshu Premier since the 1980s.

At the same time, the rural periphery has (once again) gained in importance. As elsewhere in the world, where processes of globalization are played out in a context of frontier expansion,[28] the Congolese hinterland has become most central to the capitalist dynamics. Whereas the city has become peripheral and in some respects village-like, the bush is the place where dollars are generated, where the good life is shaped and where villages are transformed into booming diamond settlements, where life focuses on money and the consumption of women and beer.[29] The little diamond boomtowns of Kahemba and Tembo, along the border between Congo's Bandundu province and the

Angolan province of Lunda Norte, have become most central to capitalist dynamics and the dollarization of local economies. Thus, the diamond traffic, and the phenomenon of dollarization which has followed in its wake, are also emblematic of a return to the Léopoldian trading post economy that has marked the origin of Kinshasa and so many other cities throughout Africa. The political economy of the *comptoir* has always been colonial in its very essence. In the past it contributed a lot to the urbanization of the African material and mental landscape. The contemporary *comptoir* economy in Congo and Angola has continued to contribute a great deal to the frontier urbanization of places such Mbuji-Mayi or Tshikapa (in the Kasai), Kahemba and Tembo (in southern Bandundu), as well as the Kwango river diamond settlements in Angola, or the diamond "ranches" around Kisangani. These local sites have become, in certain ways, globalized spaces, the economic and cultural dynamics of which are linked to many other different places on the globe that play a role in a semi-formal world economy, from Luanda, Kinshasa, Brazzaville, Bangui and Bujumbura, to Antwerp, Mumbai, Beirut, Tel Aviv and Johannesburg. At the same time, these locally generated bush dollars have also engendered the further development, revival, sometimes even (relative) gentrification, of certain areas in Kinshasa: Masina's *quartier Sans Fil*, Ndjili's *quartier sept*, and some parts of Lemba, such as the more residential areas of Salongo and Righini.

DIASPORIC MOVEMENT AND THE MIRRORING OF MODERNITY

The local creation of modernities leads us to a third mirror in which Kinshasa generates an image of itself, contemplates and reflects upon itself, and projects itself outward. This mirror is situated in the context of the diaspora. Effectively barred from traveling abroad during the colonial period, the Congolese were quick to insert themselves into waves of increasingly intensive migration after independence. This mobility intensified and was accentuated by the gradual economic decline that started to manifest itself in the latter half of the 1970s and that reached mind-boggling dimensions towards the end of Mobutu's long and disastrous reign. The breakdown of the Zairean state and the increasingly harsh living conditions in Kinshasa and the country at large prompted a huge exodus. From this period onwards, the city also materializes as a huge machine of evacuation. It starts to develop complex (semi)informal economies, involving the production, selling and buying of these rare goods called visa, passport, *prises en charge* and all the other documents and stamps needed to move out and beyond the increasingly confining horizon of sheer survival that Kinshasa has become. In recent years, these informal economies of evacuation have rotated around Kinshasa's musicians. Every time orchestras go and play concerts outside of Congo they travel with an increasing number of "musicians" who, once abroad, "shed their body" (*kobwaka nzoto*) and start an existence as illegal aliens (*ngulu*).³⁰

Almost invariably, the first stop along the often difficult path of diasporic existence was Belgium, and even today the focal point of Kinshasa's diasporic mirror remains the neighborhood of Matonge, in Brussels. In many respects this Belgian Matonge continues to be the social and cultural nexus of Europe's Congolese migration. It is named after one of Kinshasa's most vibrant neighborhoods, the fast-beating heart of the city's night life and popular music scene, with its effervescent central square, *Rond Point Victoire*, with its night clubs and open air bars and *ngandas*, with its West African *commerçants* in their suave *boubous*, the proud descendants of the Coastmen who arrived in Kinshasa in the 1930s, with its freshly roasted *kamundele* goat meat, and its crowded *Djakarta* market, lit up by hundreds of little kerosene lamps at night.

Both the colonial mirror, the mirror offered by the village and the mirror activated by the diasporic movement constantly echo a deeper level of speculation. This underlying mirror is often a broken and deforming one, a mirror that reflects Kinshasa's complex relationship with the outside and the beyond of a more global, transnational world, with the real and imagined qualities of modernity and of the wider, whiter, world of the West. Driving along Kinshasa's Bypass, as the road which leads from the *Rond Point Ngaba* to the *Echangeur* of Limete is named, the observant eye might notice a dry cleaner or laundry *(blanchisserie* or whitener in French), named Modernisation. On the façade of the house, stuck into the whitewashed cement, little shards of broken mirror form the letters of the word *Modernisation*. Filled with irony, mirroring modernity, assimilating to the West, and inscribing oneself in the project of what is, in the end, still a very colonialist modernity, is here shown for the whitewash operation that it has always been at heart. The colonial *évolué*, this prototype of Naipaul's *mimic man*, or Kinshasa's *mundele ndombe* (the "Black White"), or Fanon's *Black Skin, White Masks*, or today's pale youngsters, whitened (*kotela*) by disastrous "beauty" skin products—all of these figures illustrate the processes of imitation and the creation of image embedded in this mirroring. To some extent, the young diamond hunters of Kinshasa have moved beyond the mimetic. But it requires still a complex process to break the spell of this image in the mirror, the image of this "African Europe" that colonial administrators, missionaries, expatriates and the elites of the postcolonial state held up for so long to Kinshasa as a model to which it should aspire.

In Congo, as elsewhere in Africa, the mirror of the West conjures up the property of the marvelous. The collective social imaginary concerning the West (referred to as Putu, Miguel, Mikili or Zwenebele) is rich in fairy tale images that conjure up the wonderland of modernity, and the luxurious, almost

paradisiacal lifestyle of the West. In Lingala, for example, Belgium is referred to as *lola*, "heaven," and one would do almost anything "to die" (*fwa ku Mputu*) in this Mputuville.³¹ "The West," as a topos of the Congolese imaginary, where one enjoys the benefits of endless sources of wealth for free, sums up all the qualities of the good life. The lifestyle of a local rich urban elite and of the expatriate confirms the reality of this Idea of the West. This image of the West is also reinforced by weekly local television broadcasts of *Mputuville*, a program that further mythologizes Congolese life in the European diaspora. Also, rather than deconstructing this myth for the home front, people who live and undergo themselves the often harsh realities of life in the diaspora usually go to great lengths to deny this grim picture and to confirm the exactitude of the collective imaginary. Admitting that life in the West often is a life of poverty does not invalidate the topos of the Western Paradise for those who remained behind on the home front. Instead, it is interpreted as a sign of personal failure and weakness of the *mikiliste* who followed the trail of the diaspora. Rather than revealing that life in the diaspora is not that easy, Congolese living abroad therefore often prefer to send home pictures of themselves in front of a Mercedes, neglecting to mention that the Mercedes actually belongs to the neighbor. Europe (and increasingly the United States, as the ultimate Land of Cocaigne, "the Putu of the *banoko*" [the Uncles, that is, the Belgians]) continues to be framed in these positive terms. Europe is *malili*, cool, whereas Africa is *moto*, hot, full of suffering. For most, the ideal of Putu conjures up a world without responsibilities: "Something is broke? Not to worry. Bring it to the white man and he will fix it" sang *feu* Pepe Kalle in one of his songs.

Nevertheless this myth of the West is developing holes in it. Another phrase of Pepe Kalle's goes as follows: *bakende Putu, bakweyi na désert*, "they went to Europe, but landed in the desert." The phrase conveys the demythologization of the Idea of Europe. Those who are now living in the diaspora have discovered that life in Putu is in reality a desert, a life of poverty filled with problems concerning money, housing, visas, and so forth. Simultaneously, the phrase also conveys a second meaning: "We Congolese started *en route* towards an insertion into a global ecumene of modernity, but we never attained our goal. Somewhere along the way we ran out of fuel and had to land in the

desert." The world of modernity, with its tempting promises of boundless consumerism embedded in a vision of an expansive capitalism in the service of the nation state, has become the fool's paradise in which the Congolese nation is no longer capable of living. It is out of reach for all except those who partake in the lottery of politics, have salaried jobs, know how to access international organizations and businesses, or have access to diamond dollars.

Blame for the impossibility of accessing this western version of the good life is not only placed on the excesses of the Mobutu era, but increasingly is also laid on the doorstep of the West itself. "When the Belgians left, they gave us Independence, but at the same time they threw the key to open the door to development into the ocean" is a frequently heard remark in Congo. One shopkeeper of a store which recently opened its doors painted the following motto above the entrance: *A qui la faute? Chez le blanc!*, "Who is to blame? The White Man!" As such, the motto translates a growing breakaway from the world of modernity as defined by the metropole, a definition which reduces an increasing number of people in Congo to a subaltern status as part of a swelling Third World proletariat. In *Ma Personnalité*, a song from his 2002 hit album *A la queue leu-leu*, Werrason sings:

Mundele alobi ye moto asala *dindon*, eeh!	The White Man says that he invented the turkey!
Po ye alia mokongo,	For he eats the turkey's breast,
Na Ethiopiens balei mopende,	The Ethiopians eat the drumsticks,
Bachinois balei mapapu.	The Chinese eat the wings.
Ah biso tolei libabe!	Ah! We eat the fat of the turkey's behind [misfortune]!

Werrason toys with the word *libabe*, which means "misfortune" but in this context also refers to the *tiges*, the small (imported) sticks of roasted turkey fat that have become part of the Kinois' diet in recent years, mostly because they are so cheap. These lines, which were immediately picked up by Kinshasa's youth, are indicative of the complex and multi-faceted relation that Congo continues to maintain with the outside and the beyond of a more global, transnational world (from the White Man and the West to Ethiopia and China).

For an ever growing number of "malcontents," then, the world of modernity as defined and propagated by the West and its agents—the state agent, the missionary, the development worker, the dwindling local urban elites—has indeed become an inaccessible chimera. Some observers have therefore interpreted *la grande fête de Kinshasa*, the wave of lethal and yet ludic lootings which swept through the city and demolished the country's economy in 1991 and 1993, as a radical break with the West. What was being demolished in the plundering were the icons of western modernity: fancy restaurants, supermarkets and industrial plants such as General Motors. Similarly, in 1997, Congo's new leaders, who to a large extent were recruited from the diaspora, were contemptuously nicknamed "Europe's leavings" (*occasions d'Europe*) upon their arrival in Congo. In other words: the members of this new ruling elite were perceived to be like second hand cars. No longer wanted in Europe and the States where they could not obtain a steady position, they returned to Congo like *Bounties* (the brand name of a bar of chocolate with a coconut filling): black on the surface and white at heart. This second rate, hybridized version of the West is the best one can get, but it never quite is the genuine article...

Although the tendency to turn away from the modernist position, in a true spirit of resistance against western domination, is certainly there, this does not mean that people resist or reject modernity's promise of the good life itself. A painting by Chéri Samba, one of Kinshasa's most acclaimed artists, entitled "Woman and Her First Desires" (*La femme et ses premiers désirs*)[32] shows the painter's wife, Fifi, sitting in a bourgeois living room in Kinshasa, surrounded by the signs of her and her husband's status: refrigerator, television set, rotating fan, a cooking furnace. These are the fruits, the bourgeois contents of modernity that everybody, in the end, wishes for. What people increasingly object to, however, is the ideological hegemony of modernity, the fact that the West imposes upon them, from above and from outside, its own definition of "the good life." Much of the cultural and political struggle in Congo today focuses on control over a politics of identity as self representation, which implies that it is self generated and self constructed. To a large extent the arguments of identity today center round the question of who represents whom, and to/for whom. Who is author, who is subject of representation? Recourse to colonial and postcolonial stereotypes is inevitable in situations where identities are at play.

A SECRET CITY OF PUBLIC WORDS

Behind the garden city, the forest city and the village city lurks yet another city, an invisible but very audible city of whispers, what Kinois call *les on dit*, consisting of fleeting words, questions, harmful suspicions and treacherous accusations. Powerful and relentless gossip and rumor constantly run through the city. Shamelessly, leaving no subject untouched, it spreads like a bush fire through all of Kinshasa's communities. Kinshasa's urban space is very much structured through rumor. It is a city in which the spoken form regularly seems to dominate the built form. Often a weapon of the weak, it enters the scene from the margin and takes over the whole entity, pumping its words like blood through the veins and arteries of this giant urban body. The motor of Kinshasa's public life, of the city as body politic,[33] the capillary biopower of this *Radio Trottoir*, Radio Sidewalk, punctuates the city's heart beat and constitutes its public eye. Uniting and dividing the city through the force of words, it generates the capital's urban mythologies, its aesthetics of laughter, its cultural repertoires and collective imaginaries; it creates its heroes and damages the reputation of its most powerful and prominent citizens. It amplifies itself in the columns of the numerous newspapers that have started to proliferate since the end of Mobutu's one party system. These are read and commented upon collectively at several points throughout the city by the "politicians" of the street, the *parlementaires debout*. Urban rumor solidifies in the paintings of Kinshasa's artists. It translates into the scripts of its popular street theater and locally produced TV soaps. It is echoed in the lyrics of Kinshasa's urban trou-

badours. It is spelled out in actions such as Radio Blackboard, *radio tableau*, where international radio news (RFI, BBC, Canal Afrique, Afrique N° Un) is written out on a blackboard in the street and commented upon by the owners of small portable radios. Meanwhile the whole neighborhood contributes batteries to keep the radio working. It is a way of escaping and redirecting interpretations and representations imposed upon them from elsewhere.

In spite of its formidable creative force, Kinois have rarely something good to say about their gossip mechanisms. Franco, the most prominent musician that the city ever produced, bitterly addresses *Radio Trottoir* in one of his songs: "You sabotaged me, *Radio Trottoir*, You broke my marriage. With an information that you spread around but did not even bother to verify. You broke my marriage with your gossip!" In a similar vein his contemporary, Tabu Ley, complains in a song: "Gossip kills this city. Friends, you might hear something today, but try to see it with your own eyes before you start spreading illness for nothing." The invisible space of rumor and gossip constantly fractures and reshapes the composite anatomy of the city's public and private spaces.[34] It produces the awkward intimacy of a public secrecy, a crowded and promiscuous common living space, shared by all of the city's inhabitants. In colonial times, the qualities and characteristics of "private" and "public" had distinctly different connotations in the "white" city and the indigenous peripheries. At sunset a curfew banned the Congolese from the European areas of town. Both sides retreated into the privacy of their own living areas, ignorant of and often uninterested in each other's lives. The neighborhoods and houses where both worlds touched each other geographically were often the literally intermediate and blended worlds of *métissage*, of those who did not belong firmly to either space or who crossed the social or racial lines that pervaded colonial society and thus had no fixed place in it. Mixed African-Euro-

pean households, mostly set up by Portuguese or Greek traders and shopkeepers, formed a buffer zone between African and European neighborhoods. The colonials retreated to their residences, offices, clubs and restaurants, and restricted their contact with indigenous worlds to a functional minimum, living in ways not much different from the lifestyles chosen by many expatriates in Kinshasa today.

Life in the African parts of town, on the other hand, was played out in the compound, *parcelle*, and in the street. The *parcelle* is a space that is typical of Kinshasa. Often surrounded by a wall and with an iron gate that marks its entrance, the *parcelle*, with its house or houses, and usually with its mango or palm tree and little garden of vegetables and crops, creates a small island of more or less private domesticity, in the shared intimacy of one's (extended) family and ethnic affiliations. In many areas of the city, though, the *parcelle* has been invaded by and lives in close proximity and symbiosis with the street. As such, many *parcelles* are rather "public" private spaces. Simultaneously, Kinshasa also generates "private" public spaces, such as the recreational places of the bar, the night-club, the hotel and the *nganda* (originally the retreat where fishermen rest after their work, but now the name given to "formally informal" restaurants, often in the backyards of private homes). Here men and women meet their friends, lovers, mistresses and concubines in an atmosphere of privacy and secrecy. And yet invariably this is also in view of all, within reach of *Radio Trottoir*'s tentacles and subject to the gaze of the public eye. The *phonie* is another place where private and public become interchangeable. Every neighborhood has its small *phonie* enterprises, where one can enter into contact with otherwise unreachable friends and relatives in the interior of the country through radio wave communication. Often the *phonie* is also a meeting point for people from the same regional or ethnic background. Money matters, love affairs, marriages, births, divorces, illnesses, deaths and other private family matters are shouted into the microphone as well as into the ears of the neighborhood's and indeed onto the country's sidewalks. In Kinshasa, the private life of the individual and the moralities generated by the collective gaze are constantly living in a sometimes uneasy, often contradictory cohabitation.

Like many capitals around the world, Kinshasa has always been a narcissistic city, very much fascinated and preoccupied by the events within its own microcosmos. To an outsider who is unfamiliar with the city's inner argot, its signs and secrets, Kinshasa's urban codes therefore often appear difficult to crack. At the same time, Kinshasa constantly displays and puts itself on stage. Just like the city they live in, Kinois are extremely skillful at managing not just one but several identities at the same time. The constant negotiation between these individual and collective identities almost always takes place or is commented upon in the public sphere. Kinshasa exists in the public eye and through its public appearance. Nourished by the force of pretense, the make believe and "as if," the *faire croire* and *faire semblant* that pervades the urban praxis, Kinshasa is essentially an exhibitionist city or, as Yoka says, *une ville-spectacle*, a spectacle city.[35] The urban aesthetics of display and public appearance are most clearly illustrated in the city's most private space, which is simultaneously also its most public theater: the body. Outdoing Proust's Paris, Kinshasa is a city of *flâneurs* and idle strollers, a proudly sensuous city where both male and female bodies are constantly dressing up and taking themselves out into the dusty streets and alleys of each neighborhood to be seen, to display themselves in feigned indifference to the public gaze (which is often a predominantly masculine gaze). It is a city, also, where there are always eyes to see and behold. Spectators constantly comment upon the outfit, the kind of *pagne* or wax cloth a woman is wearing, the bearing of the body that passes by, its *kinoiseries*: the slow rotating movement of the buttocks (*evunda*, "the bodywork filled with goods"), the shape of the legs, ideally in the form of a beer bottle turned upside down (*mipende ya milangi*), the placement of the hands on the hips, a sign of assurance, the number of creases in a woman's neck (*kingo muambe*), the style of the hairdress, in short the whole bearing, appearance and stature of passers-by, their whole social skin and social skill. In fact, the eyes of the beholders offer a mirror which constantly reflects one's own social strength. In spite of, or maybe precisely because of its extreme poverty, Kinshasa's aesthetic regime of the body has turned into a veritable cult of elegance, culminating in the movement of the *Sape*, an acronym for the Society of Fun Lovers and Elegant Persons, *Société des ambianceurs et des personnes élégantes*. Begun in the early 1980s around "King of Sape" Papa Wemba, a popular musician, this movement escalated into real fashion contests and potlatches in which youngsters would display their European fashion designer clothes, in an attempt to outdo each other. Today, youngsters ironically refer to their designer gear as "bad clothes" (*bilamba mabe*). Recently, also, this spirit of elegance has found a second breath in the flourishing context of Pentecostalist and other Christian fundamentalist churches, in which the city's new figures of success, its most famed preachers such as Fernando Kutino or Soni "Rockman" Kafuta, show off their Armani and Versace suits to their admiring and ecstatic followers, under the motto that "one has to appear clean before God" (*Il faut être propre devant Dieu*).

Pushing the mirror metaphor to the limit of reflection and beyond, the religious transformation which Congolese society is currently undergoing has contributed to a reconfiguration, if not an obliteration, of the dividing lines between public and private space, as well as an increasing theatralization of the city. This process goes hand in hand with an increasing celebrity making (*starisation*) of those who occupy the front stage, the preachers and musicians.

The new *vedettariat* in the popular music scene has given rise to new forms of violence. Not only do the music and its accompanying dance styles reflect, and reflect upon, the violence that pervades the city and Congolese society at large, but the frequent clashes between avid followers of rival bands have themselves become increasingly responsible for the mounting insecurity in Kinshasa's public spaces. Home to street children and military, Kinshasa's main arteries, crossroads, markets, sport stadia, and administrative sites have often become a social no man's land, governed by the predatory violence of the street. At the same time, the enchanting space of the church, with its new moral economies and its own forms of physical and symbolic violence, has swallowed and encompassed the space of popular culture. It has also claimed and drastically reconfigured the public space as such. In all corners of the city, and at all times of the day and the night, thousands upon thousands of Kinois gather to pray. In the process, the space of the church has become the city's main stage, a space of *témoignage* also where people publicly bear witness of their sins and their conversion, where they display and act out their poverty or wealth, their misery or blessings, leaving no stone of their personal lives unturned, no intimate detail unmentioned. In the process, the religious dynamics in these churches have also impacted thoroughly on private space and contribute to a radical restructuring of the social networks and moral and ethic matrices of the family, of kin relations, and ethnic affiliations. Within the church context, the changed relations between the public and private spaces are indicative of deeper changes in the relationship between subjectivity and intersubjectivity in Kinshasa today. While representing a vast effort to recreate a new, all-inclusive intersubjectivity on a moral basis, the religious praxis pushes aside the intersubjective moral model which has always been provided by the village, with its ethics of kin solidarity, reciprocity, and gift logic. Paradoxically, this effort thus contributes to an increasing demonization of social life as it has been lived until now.

THE FIRST AND SECOND WORLDS OF KINSHASA

While taking into account these various levels which constitute Kinshasa's ecology today, there is yet another, and more fundamental, mirroring process that impacts on all the previous ones: that between the visible city of the "first world" and of the day, and an invisible Kinshasa that exists in what Kinois themselves refer to as the nocturnal "second world" or "second city," an occult city of the shadow, as it exists in the local mind and imagination. "If there can be a better way for the real world to include the one of images, it will require an ecology not only of real things but of images as well" wrote Susan Sontag.[36] Throughout this book, the urbanscape of Kinshasa, its activities, its praxis, and its specific meaningful sites (the compound, the bar, the church, the street) will be read not only as geographical, visible and palpable urban realities but also, and primarily so, as a *mundus imaginalis*, a local mental landscape, a topography and historiography of the local Congolese imagination that is no less real than its physical counterpart, a second world, an "underneath of things"[37] that is collectively shared by all social layers in Kinshasa, uniting its *beau monde* and its demimonde. In this second world, the dimension of the marvelous combines with the dimension of terror to form the tain, the back of the mirror that reflects these qualities back into the daily life experience of the Kinois.

In the autochthonous experience, daily life constantly uses the processes of mirroring and reflecting to make sense of itself. The activities of the day constantly include the world of the night, of the dream and of the shadow. To interpret the world of the living, a diviner opens up another space time, another world, the world of ancestors, through a mirror, or by means of the unmoving surface of water in a gourd. Dreams are beacons in the night but they impact in very tangible ways on decisions one has to make during the day: whether or not to travel today, whether to meet so-and-so, whether to set out on a hunt or postpone it. The material realness of the mask, as image, as double, and as dancing representation of the dead, doesn't make the existence of the dead any less real. Rather, the mask *becomes, is, posits* the ancestor while simultaneously being a mask made of raffia and wood. "To consider the obverse and the reverse of the world," writes Mbembe, "as opposed, with the former partaking of a 'being there' (*real presence*) and the latter of a 'being elsewhere' or a 'non-being' (*irremediable absence*) — or, worse, of the order of unreality — would be to misunderstand. The reverse of the world and its obverse did not communicate with each other only through a tight interplay of correspondences and complex intertwined relations. They were also governed by relations of similarity, relations far from making the one a mere copy or model of the other. These links of similarity were thought to unite them, but also to distinguish them, according to the wholly autochthonous principle of *simultaneous multiplicities*."38

One of the main questions that this book will address, though, relates to the changes that seem to have appeared in the mechanisms operating this simultaneous multiplicity of the two different worlds that exist on each side of the mirror, and thus also in and through each other. In urban Congo, something seems to have changed in the slippage between visible and invisible, between reality and what we can call, for lack of better words, its double, its shadow, specter, reflection, image, or *elili*, as it is referred to in Lingala.

What is it, then, that has affected the praxis and rhetoric of the image in Kinshasa today? Within the local experiential frame, rendered in Kinois' accounts of their lives and of their city, the double, this other, nocturnal ghost of a city which lurks underneath the surface of the visible world, somehow seems to have taken the upper hand. Today, mirroring the way in which the second or shadow economy has taken over the first or formal economy, this other, "second world" (*deuxième monde*), "second city" (*deuxième cité*), "pandemonium world" (*monde pandemonium*), or "fourth dimension" (*quatrième dimension*, that is, one of the multiple "invisible" worlds of what is referred to as *kindo-*

*kinisme*³⁹) increasingly seems to push aside and take over the first world of daily reality. "The second world is the world of the invisible," says one inhabitant of Kinshasa, "and those who live in it and *know* are those who have four eyes, those who see clearly both during the day and during the night. Their eyes are a mirror. A man with two eyes only cannot know this world. The second world is a world that is superior to ours. The second world rules the first world." This, and many other, similar accounts, seems indicative of the widespread feeling that what you see is not what you see (unless you have four eyes), and what is there is not what is "really" there or, more important, is not what matters most. The seen and the unseen, it thus seems, no longer reflect, balance and produce each other in equal, and equally *real* ways. Somehow, the reverse has become more *ontological* than the obverse. It is no longer experienced as a similar but parallel reality, but, on the contrary, as the reality that has come to inhabit and overgrow its opposite. Symptomatic of this more general change is the invasion of the space of the living by the dead. A term which is currently used in Lingala to describe this new quality of mounting *Unheimlichkeit* and elusiveness of the world, is *mystique*. In the postcolonial *Afrique fantôme* that Congo seems to have become, it is increasingly frequent to designate people and situations as *mystique*, difficult to place, interpret and attribute meaning to.

This changed nature of the point of inflection between different but simultaneously real worlds, the change in the mirroring mechanisms of reflection and retroflection that constitute the passage between the obverse and the reverse of the world, has a heavy impact on daily life in Kinshasa. For example, it continuously transforms the qualities and realities of what constitutes life and death, as well as the ways in which they relate to each other. Similarly, as will be illustrated at length throughout this book, the changed relationship between obverse and reverse constantly promotes a religious transfiguration of daily reality.

All of these changes are characteristic of some deeper alterations that Congolese society as a whole is undergoing. Without dealing with the historical roots of these changes here, this evolution may be summarized as a generalized crisis, situated in the Congolese capital's capacity for semiosis and semiotics, at observing and interpreting the syntax, semantics and pragmatics of the sign *as sign*. Not that Kinshasa's inhabitants do not know how to work with signs, or have stopped doing so. Quite to the contrary, one could even argue that Kinshasa is marked not by a lack but by a constant overproduction of leading signs and meanings, and that it is precisely this "overheating," this excess of the signifier, that leads to the crisis of meaningfulness. But it is also in the nature itself of the transcription of one reality into the other, and therefore in the nature of the representational, that the changes have ensconced themselves. In the process, something has happened to the relationship between image and reality. A change has occurred in the ways in which the representation and the represented reality relate to each other.

Applying a linguistic and sociological perspective to the daily scene in Kinshasa, one could say that the rupture between discourse, representation, action and structure is total. The urban reality has gradually turned into a world in which fact and fiction are interchangeable. In Kinshasa today, it is no longer possible to forget or deny the Saussurian arbitrariness of the sign, or the facticity of the social fact. What Taussig has termed the "mimetic faculty,"[40] the capacity to pretend that one lives facts, not fictions, has often ceased to operate in an adequate way. To put it differently, there is a strong sense of what Baudrillard has termed the "precession of simulacra," thereby pointing out the changing relations between the signifying "real" and the representational "imaginary," or the liquidation of all referentials.[41] The common links and paths of transfers between signifier and signified, or between predicate and subject, have imploded or are subverted. What I have previously called the *faire croire* and *faire semblant* have often taken over from reality. In Kinshasa, as a consequence, more than anywhere else, there is no reality that is strong enough to resist language. Often, the discrepancies between signifier and signified allow for the generation of a specific kind of Kinois humor, enabling, for example, the tenant of an old and decrepit shack to refer to his dwelling as the *palais du peuple*, "the people's palace," after the imposing parliamentary building of the same name which was constructed in the heart of Kinshasa by the Chinese. But in that specific Kinois language, the shifts are often less benign. Very often what poses as true is actually false, the lie becomes truth. As a result, to give but one example, the boundaries between legal and illegal are continuously shifting. Such shifts are operated by the widespread mechanism of reversibility that is constantly at work in the daily lives of most Kinois. Hence, also, as I noted earlier, the important place which this city attributes to appearance. Undoubtedly, this crisis of meaning that can be observed at all levels of Congolese society has profoundly alienating effects on both macro and micro levels of societal life.

But this sociological level only captures the more obvious effects of the crisis of meaningfulness that may be observed in Kinshasa. On another, deeper, level, one could stand the argumentation on its head and say that Kinshasa's "image repertoire" does not so much suffer from a lack but rather from an excess of overlap between the signifying and the signified, or between the structures of the symbolic, the "real" that resists language, and the level of the imaginary. On this level, the problem with notions such as "fact" and "fiction" is that they do not take into account the autochthonous experience of the realness of the double, but risk reducing it to something unreal, a mere "fantasy." But if, on the contrary, one takes the reality of the thing and its double

seriously, one starts to see that the deeper crisis situates itself primarily in the changing functions and qualities of junction and disjunction (such as the disjunction between life and death), and hence of the role of the imaginary, which operates that disjunction or *dédoublement*. Much of the current Congolese societal crisis, the subjectivity of which is lived and experienced most strongly in precisely the urban locale, situates itself in this slippage. Put in a different way, the societal crisis in Congo essentially evolves around the containment, the struggle to reestablish control over an increasingly overflowing imaginary. And at the heart of this struggle lies the ever more problematic possibility of positing or "siting" of the double (for example, death as the double of the living, or the double as the living and familiar figure of death). What may be

observed here is, in a way, the *liquidation* of the double, the unwholesome coalescence of the reflecting sides into one, or the gradual take-over of one by the other. In its more extreme forms, this process of liquidation operates a killing, a destroying of reality, an annihilation or *néantisation* of the world in its most essential structure. And through this liquidation, which produces Kinshasa as idol and as cidolon, the imaginary ceaselessly creates its own level of autonomy, with all of its excesses, its witchcraft, its diabolization of social life. This new "siting" of the city's imaginary forms the undercurrent that runs throughout this book.

Please take this seriously.
You are in the workshop of Master Cheri Samba.
This is not a family house.
Silence.

INVISIBLE CITIES I
THE STORY OF ELVIS, "THE GIANT OF KINSHASA"

During a public moment of confession and "witnessing" (*témoignage*) in a Pentecostal church, Elvis tells the assembly about his conversion. He recalls how he was swallowed by the forces of evil for a long time. His narrative draws from several themes and story lines, such as the "Giant of Kinshasa," the siren (*mami wata*), or the snake that vomits money (*nguma*), which are part of Kinshasa's collective mythology. These urban myths constantly feed into the cultural repertoire of *Radio Trottoir*'s rumor mill:

My name is Elvis Mutombo. Mutombo was also the name of my grandfather. He was a village headman and a big sorcerer. When you give a name to a child, the child also takes on the character of the person whose name he inherits. Well, I inherited the name of Mutombo. My grandfather was the first to carry me after my birth. Because of that he was able to put magic onto my body, and to transfer his characteristics into me, so that I would also inherit his habits and the authority he had in the world of the obscure.

Shortly after my birth my father died and then my mother died. Both their families met to find out about the causes of their death, especially my father's. And they discovered that these deaths had originated on my father's side. My paternal aunts were held responsible for these deaths. My father was someone who liked to use magical power objects, and he observed many ritual prescriptions and taboos. But he didn't always respect these rules and so they were able to kill him.

After his death I grew up with one of my maternal aunts. According to our custom I should have grown up with my father's younger brothers. They are the ones who are usually responsible. And after a while, therefore, I left my aunt's and moved in with one of my father's brothers. He lived in the Equateur Province. I led an unhappy life there. I was badly treated. Our families are large, and orphans are not looked after very well. I suffered a lot from the injustices and lies in my family. A man who has to raise his brother's children will always accuse them of everything that goes wrong in the household. He will say: "You stole things from the house, you did this, you did that." Ah, orphans are constantly maltreated. Many people say that orphans are witches, but God will take vengeance in their name. One day I was badly beaten by my uncle because some money had disappeared at home. I had not stolen it. All of this made me very sad.

THE THREE LADIES

I had a friend, Adelard, to whom I told everything. He took me to the house of Kibai Samba Sabu. This man introduced me to witchcraft. Sabu summoned The Three Ladies. I was going to school by then. The exam period was approaching and I had to study. Every evening, because of that, I had a terrible headache. So he called The Three Ladies. He put three glasses of water upon the table, along with some bread and three white napkins. He called The Three Ladies so that I could talk to them. But I was afraid to behold them. I was still a child. Sabu took some dust and put it in my eyes. It blocked my eyesight. Then The Three Ladies arrived. I could not see them. But I saw how the three glasses were lifted from the table by invisible hands. The water in the glasses disappeared. They were drinking. And I saw how the bread disappeared, but I could not see them eating. And then I felt that they were coming closer to me. I heard them decide amongst themselves who would address me.

I was frightened and tried to escape from the room. A female voice cried out in anger: "Sabu! Why is this child afraid? Did he not call us?" But Sabu did not reply, because he too was frightened. I gathered all my courage and I said: "No! I did not want to meet you with my eyes. All I want is to get rid of my headache. It is not necessary for me to be able to see you, just heal me and discuss things with Sabu, not with me." This upset The Three Ladies. They spoke: "Why do you pretend not to know us?" You see, they had known me all my life. They knew me because of the marks that my grandfather had left on my body. Many people have signed pacts in their life without even knowing it. Many people went to the homes of witch doctors who left tattoos on their bodies. Many people have been ritually treated with powerful animal substances, so that they take on the characteristics of this animal. If you graft a tattoo onto someone's body with a fish bone, the person in question will become like this fish. It is the demon that is introduced into their bodies. The demon that reflects the character of the animal that enters your body with the tattoos. Sometimes it is a leopard which is being cut into your body, sometimes it is a fish. In the first case you will become ferocious as a leopard, in the latter case your body will start to tremble like a fish's. These demons enter someone's body to corrupt it. Through the tattoos [*bilayi*, a Hindubill term] the demon installs itself into your body. In this way, many mothers have knowingly introduced witchcraft in their children's bodies.

THE PENTACLE OF DOMINATION AND PROTECTION

Finally, The Three Ladies left the room. Thereupon, Sabu fabricated a pentacle of domination and protection which he gave to me. I slipped it into the left pocket of my trousers. I carried it with me everywhere I went. And always I kept my left hand in my pocket. When I touched the pentacle I had power over other people and I could dominate and control them. I used it a lot at school. It was a success. I made everybody love me: the teachers, the girls. I was still a child but already then I loved girls a lot. At the age of thirteen I had already known a lot of girls and women. At school the girls were fighting to go out with me. I was very undisciplined. Every day I was punished. But the girls who were fighting over me were those who were the teachers' girlfriends. And the teachers hated me because I had so much success. All the girls loved me. But to me it was painful because I knew they only loved me because of the magic I possessed. And every time it caused problems for me. The girls became pregnant. And the more the girls loved me, the more the teachers became angry with me. I lived in pain and sadness. In the beginning I liked the pentacle because I could dominate people with it, but in the end it only created problems. Rather than curing my headache, it only increased it. So I decided to return to Sabu. I told him: "What you gave me is insufficient. My headache is still there! I didn't come for you to give me powers of domination over other people. I just wanted to be cured from my headache."

This headache of mine, I inherited it from my father. He died from it. At times I was afraid that I would die in the same way. Brothers, the Bible tells us that we should not be afraid. Those who can kill our body cannot kill our soul. Fear the one who can kill both body and soul. But instead we fear the Uncles, the fetishists, the magicians and wizards. We are afraid of evil spirits. Why? Because we do not possess authority and power. Authority only comes from God. It is God who gives us the power to defeat evil spirits.

THE PRIEST'S INITIATION

Sabu asked me to find some ingredients so that he could proceed with the fabrication of the magical protective devices that I needed. He told me he needed red candles and incense. I went to the Catholic Church. Sabu had told me to enter there. Upon entering, he had told me, I should touch the pentacle in my left pocket. Then I had to shake hands with a priest. He had also told me to go along with everything that the priest would ask of me.

And so I went and greeted the priest. He was Belgian, a Flemish missionary. He asked me: "Was it you who came to see me yesterday? Was it you who came to see me yesterday?" His Lingala was not very good, and he spoke with a strong accent. Since Sabu had told me to say "yes" to everything the priest would ask me, I said it was indeed me who had come to see him the day before. He replied: "Was it you who came yesterday and asked to become an altar-boy?" I told him, Yes. And so I became an altar-boy. I took the red candles from the altar and gave them to Sabu.

One day, the priest told me: "Come to see me after mass, there is something that I have to tell you." So I went to see him at his house. When I was seated he said: "Child, I like you a lot. I want you to know all the things in this world. I want you to succeed in life. You are an orphan, but I want you to become successful." I was very happy. Finally someone liked me. He told me: "I will show you all the things that are hidden in this world. You will have everything. You will have money. You will be known by all." His words touched me.

And one evening, the priest said: "Come, I have to show you something." We left the house and went to a tree where the mothers usually sell oranges and many other things: bananas, groundnuts, sweets, biscuits, lots of little things. He bought everything. I thought that we were going to go to the old people's home because that is what priests usually do: they help the ill and the old. But he took me back home and we started to talk. When the evening came we left the house again. He ordered me to sit next to him in his Land Rover, and then we drove off towards a school complex at the edge of the city. Next to the school was a cemetery. I didn't dare ask him where we were going. We stopped at the entrance of the cemetery. Night had already fallen. When he got out of his car, he drew some lines in the sand. The sand drawing was in the form of a pentacle! Then he murmured some words. He ordered me to stand erect in the middle of the pentacle. He said: "Do not move, even when you notice that someone is approaching! Stay in the pentacle, it will protect you." Then he left. From a distance he called out to me: "Look behind you!" And I turned round, and just as I was going to tell him that I didn't see anything, I noticed a light. It became stronger and stronger, and then a path opened up. All of a sudden I was on this path. The world around looked beautiful. A file of young girls passed, followed by a file of young men, and then a file of fathers and file of mothers, a file of old people, and a file of babies. They all walked past me, happily talking amongst themselves. I saw the priest distributing all the goods that we had bought. Although the quantity of things that we had bought was much smaller than the number of people which passed, he did not run out of gifts. The goods seemed to multiply themselves.

One of the people in the crowd was a well-dressed soldier. He stopped to talk to the priest. He pointed his finger at me. I was afraid that he was going to arrest me. I wanted to protest, but the priest made a sign that I should keep silent. Afterwards, the priest approached me and wiped out the pentacle in the sand. All the people disappeared. The priest said: "Since you are my friend I told the soldier that all these gifts came from you. And he said that the people would remember this and come to your rescue when necessary." "But who are these people?" "These people are the dead. They aren't evil spirits, they are just dead people. You can greet them and talk to them. The Bible says that one cannot talk to the dead. In Leviticus and Isaiah it is stated that one cannot talk with the dead. But I have received the power to talk with the dead and to ask things from them. I want to teach you this as well." I asked him: "But you say that the Bible interdicts this!" The priest laughed and just said: "In your tradition, it is believed that one can control the spirit of a deceased person just by collecting a bone from the skeleton, or some earth from the tomb, or a piece of cloth that belonged to the deceased." And only then did I realize that this priest was in reality working not for God, but for other forces, the forces of evil.

THE GIANT DEMON NAMED KINSHASA

And I followed him on that same path. I started to wander around at night to hang out with the dead. We would enter people's homes. One day, I heard someone tell a story about a Giant Man Called Kinshasa who wandered around in the city at night. And I decided to shapeshift and to become this Man Called Kinshasa. And so I did. Every night, around 11 pm I became Kinshasa. I would go to the Rond Point Ngaba, to the *quartier* of Rhigini, to Salongo. I posted myself along the road, near to the house of Mungul Diaka, the former Governor of the city of Kinshasa, next to the little lake in front of his house. And there I would sing an occult song, and my body would start to grow. I grew and I grew and I grew. Every time a car would pass the driver would be so frightened upon seeing me that he would drive his car head on into the lake. I had a hell of a good time. From that day onwards, my friends started to call me Kinshasa. This Kinshasa has never really existed. He is an invention of witches and wizards. They use him to frighten people. I did too. I would become the Giant Kinshasa and post myself along the Lumumba Boulevard, between the twelfth and the eighteenth street. I would provoke a lot of accidents. Many car drivers died along the Lumumba Boulevard. And the next morning, I would send out messenger spirits who would start spreading the news about the Giant Kinshasa and what he had done throughout the city. All of this happened in 1992 and 1993. I stopped doing these things after my conversion. You can check for yourself: the car accidents between the twelfth and the eighteenth street became less numerous after that period.

THE MARRIAGE WITH AICHA OF THE INVISIBLE WORLD

By the time I became the Giant Kinshasa, I felt totally at ease in the invisible worlds and in the company of the evil spirits. One day, I called the Three Ladies. They came. I asked one of them, Aicha, the Queen of the Coast, to become my mistress. She lived in the water. We took to meeting each other daily. I carried a ring on the second finger of my left hand. Every time I wanted to see her, I kissed this ring and she would appear. She used to give me a lot of money. But it did not bring me peace, for Aicha was terribly jealous. Every time I turned my head to admire a pretty girl passing in the street, Aicha would throw a fit and say: "You! Elvis! Watch out!" I constantly had to control myself. It was not a life. So, I made up my mind and told her: "Aicha, *en tout cas*, Aicha! Since you don't seem to trust me and you constantly make a scene even though I only touch the girls with my eyes, I only see one solution, and that is to leave you." I started to take the ring from my finger. Suddenly she started to cry. She said: "Don't do this to me. If it has to be like this, then I give you the permission to love all the women of this world, but on one condition: give me a child and marry me!" I said: "*Bon, ça va.*" And that was the beginning of the pact that I signed with her. She said: "If you agree to marry me we will go to my world. You will meet my parents there." And so we went to the World of the Invisible. We arrived in the fourth dimension. The fourth dimension is like the sky. It is full of spirits. She presented me to her parents: "I have loved this man for a long time. And since I love him so much I want him to give me a child. Therefore, we want to get married officially. We want to inform you of this. Give us your blessing so that we can live forever." Her parents were overjoyed. They said: "Here in the Invisible World we don't ask for bridewealth. So, since you love each other, organize your own wedding party!" And so I set about organizing a grandiose party here in this world of ours. I engaged a bar. And people came, and everybody looked at her, she was so beautiful, I have no words to convey her beauty. All of this took place in the bar that is called Trois Mille, in the neighborhood of Lemba. It was the most luxurious wedding party. We started in that bar and ended in another bar, the one that people call Ixelles [the name of a commune in Brussels, Belgium]. Everybody celebrated this marriage, but nobody saw the family of the bridegroom, nobody knew the family of the bride. All they saw was a magnificent party. It was even videotaped. Afterwards, Aicha gave birth to a child. The marriage ended when I became a member of the church.

REAL AND FALSE NECROMANCY

My involvement with the world of magic did not end there. I used to hunt for souls at night. One has to understand about the principle of undoubling. Suppose you go to a cemetery. There you take the mud of someone who is dead, the mud of his body, his "traces." You also take his nails and hair. Let me tell you how this is done. When someone dies his body turns into mud after three days. His belly explodes, like a cannon. And then you take the mud from this body and smear your own body with it. When you recite a certain formula, you will start to shift into the shape of the deceased person. I often did this, just for fun. It is called necromancy. There are two forms of necromancy: real and false. In real necromancy someone is really dead and comes to haunt and frighten people. It happens all the time. But I want to talk about false necromancy, which is based on a principle of undoubling. Let me give you an example. There was once a young girl who died. I used to change into her form all the time, because she was so beautiful. She was from Rhigini, like me. She was buried in the cemetery of Kintambo. Three days after the burial I went to the cemetery and took the mud from her body. When she was still alive she drove around town in her father's car. So, every evening, shortly after sunset I would change into her form and go to her father's house.
The first time, I entered the house and said: "All right, I come to take the car. I have to go somewhere." Stupefied, the whole family looked at me and started screaming: "Oooh! Look! Our deceased sister!" Everybody ran away, terrified. I walked to the father's room and called out: "Papa!" He too was frightened. I just told him: "Just tell me where you keep the keys to the car. I have to go somewhere. Why are you frightened of me? You used to love me when I was alive in this world, but now that I am dead you are afraid of me. Why?" With shaking hands, the father pointed out the keys. I drove around all night and returned the car the next morning. When they saw me arrive they said: "Ah, *vraiment*, this child of ours! She is dead but she can't leave the car behind. She loves it too much!" In the end they sold the car because they were too frightened of me.

THE PYTHON THAT VOMITS MONEY

I also learned how to dominate a python that vomits money. I made this python work for me. Upon my uttering some words the python would come and out of his mouth would come dollars. And in this city today, the people love nothing but dollars, dollars, dollars. But if you give these dollars to someone, someone will always die elsewhere in the city.

Brothers, I will tell you the secret of this city of Kinshasa. The city
of Kinshasa that you see all around you is full of hidden things!

Do you know this house in Binza, just before the market of Binza IPN,
when you come from Cité Verte? It is a house in a *parcelle* with a high
wall around it. The house is white. Nobody has ever seen any movement
in this house. Nobody has ever heard children play in the garden. People
say that it is inhabited by *mami wata* spirits. This is the house where
my python lived, together with his wife. She is a business woman.
Every Saturday she goes to Europe and she returns on Sunday.

One night a young man was sitting in a bar, drinking a lemonade all by
himself. All of a sudden, a big, shiny Mercedes parked in front of the bar.
A woman walked into the bar. It was the python's wife. She started drinking
a beer when she noticed the young man. She walked over and sat down at
his table. She asked him to buy her another beer. The man replied: "Please,
Tantine, pardon me, but I do not have any money left. I did not even have
enough to buy myself a beer. That is why you see me drinking a lemonade."
The woman asked him what taste he preferred, and bought him a big bottle
of PRIMUS beer. They started talking. After a while the woman told the young
man: "I like you. I want you to become my *petit poussin*, my lover. I will
buy you clothes and everything else you need, even money. Will you accept
my offer?" It didn't take long for the young man to accept. Thereupon
the woman gave him the address of her white house in Binza. She told him:
"You can visit me but only during the day, and only on Mondays, Tuesdays,
Wednesdays and Saturdays. Don't try to come and see me on any other day."

And so they started seeing each other regularly. This young man, however,
was married. He lived with his wife and two children somewhere in a small
house. Soon, the wife noticed some changes in their life. He came home with
money and all kinds of goods. She asked her husband: "Where does all this
come from?" The man told her that he had found a job, somewhere in the
city: "I work for a business woman who frequently travels to Europe." They
lived a happy life for many months. And then the young man became seriously
ill. As soon as he felt better again he went over to the house of his lover.

It was a Thursday. He remembered that the woman had told him to visit
her only on Mondays, Tuesdays, Wednesdays and Saturdays. But it had been
so long since he had seen her, and he wanted to be with her so badly, that
he didn't care. And so he went to the white house. The gate was locked. He
climbed over the wall and looked through a window. And what did he see?

The woman, totally naked, was playing with a large python on the floor. The snake saw the young man. The latter was very frightened and jumped over the wall into the street. He ran home as fast as he could. In the meantime, the python was very angry with his wife. He hissed: "You have been betraying me with this man." He started biting the woman and she died. Four days later, on a Monday, the young man went to the house of his lover again. Again the gate was closed, but he could see a huge swarm of flies around the house. He climbed over the wall and went inside the house. There he found the rotting corpse of the woman. Her swollen dead body, full of python bites, was lying on the floor, covered by flies. He left the house and informed the police. Together they returned to the house and after some questions the police took the body and buried it in the cemetery. The house remained empty.

At home the man told his wife about his lover and everything that had happened. The wife fainted on the spot. The next day, the young man was walking along a street when a car drove up to him. He bent over to have a look at the driver and with a shock he recognized the deceased lady. She addressed him: "I was looking for you. I want to take you with me. I had warned you not to visit the house on a Thursday. Because of you, my husband punished me. Now that I am dead, he makes me work day and night for him, to produce money. I come to fetch you so that you can help me to produce money for my husband." The man ran away as fast as he could. At home he broke down and started crying. Later on, in the middle of the night, he woke his wife and the neighbors with his screaming. When they came rushing to his bedside he told them that the dead woman was in the house. But no matter how hard they searched, they couldn't see her. The man was very agitated, as if possessed by a demon. The neighbors started praying till, suddenly, the man died.

When you see people blessed with wealth, Brothers, we always have to ask ourselves what is hiding behind this blessing. Is it the blessing of God or is it a diabolical blessing that produces nothing but pain and suffering in the end?

BEYOND THE GRAVE
MEMORY, TIME, APOCALYPSE AND DEATH

Mokolo mosusu ngai nakanisi,	The other day, I was picturing,
Naloti lokola ngai nakolala,	in my dreams, while I was asleep,
Aa mama aa, mokolo nakokufa.	Oh mother, the day I will die.
Mokolo nakokufa, nani akolela ngai?	Who will mourn me on the day of my death?
Nakoyeba te.	I do not know.
Tika namilela.	Let me mourn for myself.
Liwa ya zamba soki mpe liwa ya mboka?	Will death come in the forest or in the village?
Liwa ya pasi soki mpe liwa ya mai?	Will death come with illness or will I drown?
Aa mama aa mokolo nakokufa aa	Oh mother, the day I die.

[Excerpt from *Mokolo nakokufa*, Tabu Ley Rochereau and African Fiesta]

"[...] the dead theater of Death, the foreclosure of the Tragic, excludes all purification, all *catharsis*."

[Roland Barthes, *Camera Lucida*, 90.]

"Quand l'un mourait, il ressuscitait en double. Il ne servait à rien de les tuer. Morts, ils se relevaient et se multipliaient" [Whenever one died, he would resuscitate, doubled. It was no use killing them. Dead, they would get up again and multiply.]

[Amadou Koné, *Les coupeurs de têtes*]

TAXI CONVERSATIONS I [Kinshasa, May 1998]: A bright morning. I am trying to board a taxi at a parking lot annex local market near the Rond Point Ngaba. The sun burns in my neck, I can feel the sweat starting to run down my chest. Mud, music blaring out of two loudspeakers from a nearby bar, gesticulating arms, the penetrating smell of dried fish and burning rubber, yelling policemen, honking horns. At this time, the sea of morning rush hour people has already somewhat ebbed. Yet, every time a *Tetanos*, one of the old 1970s Toyota Corolla taxis, drives past, painted in what once was a bright yellow but now looks like a cadaveric patchwork of rusty brown, people rush forward and try to squeeze themselves in. Hanging from the open doors of Volkswagen *fula fula* taxi buses, the *reçeveurs*, the boys who collect the fare from clients, shout the destination to the bystanders: *Rond Point Victoire! Lemba Terminus! Campus!*

It is only after numerous taxis have passed that I manage to get into a front seat, next to the driver. Driving away from the crowd, the noise recedes while we pick up speed. In the back of the car sits a boy. After some minutes he exclaims: *"Aah mawa, petite wana a cassé!"* [Sorrow, the girl has died!] and then he breaks down in tears. The driver asks: *"Ndenge nini?"* [What happened?] "Well, for three months my girlfriend didn't have her period. It turned out she was pregnant. She asked me to arrange an abortion. I said that was out of the question." "Why did you refuse?" asked the driver. "Because I don't have the money. The cost of the abortion itself is already excessive, but on top of that one needs to pay for rich food to make her better again afterwards. I am just a poor schoolboy. I am sixteen, she was fourteen. Where would I find the money to cover all these expenses?" *"Bongo, akufi ndenge nini?"* [How did she die, then?]. "She told me she felt a lot of heat in her heart and that she needed milk to cool it down. I didn't know how to refuse and so I gave her some money to buy a box of milk powder. After that she went home. She didn't use the money to buy milk, however, but she paid some woman to provoke an abortion. And now she is dead!" "And do her parents know that you made her pregnant?" "She lived with her brother and his wife. Her sister-in-law knew that I was her boyfriend. After she died, a whole group of her family came to my father's house and threatened to kill me. My father told them that I was not in Kinshasa. He told them that I had gone to the village to buy some pigs. But they didn't believe my father. My friends came to warn me that I shouldn't return home. *Aah, moto, 'bapic' bazo luka ngai!* [Aah, friend, the soldiers are looking for me!]. Please, drop me on avenue Kianza, at the place where the trucks from Bandundu province come to sell their merchandise. I hope to find a truck there that will get me out of Kinshasa tonight. I have to leave the city, I don't know what to do!"

Rereading Malinowski's *Argonauts of the Western Pacific* and one of its famous opening lines: *Imagine yourself suddenly set down surrounded by all your gear, alone on a tropical beach close to a native village...* There was a time when ethnographies started like fairy tales (mirror, mirror on the wall), even when, at the very heart of the tale, there lay already, dormant but present, the kernel of a doubt, the awareness of falsehood, the smell of death. "Ethnology is in the sadly ludicrous, not to say tragic, position," writes Malinowski, "that at the very moment when it begins to put its workshop together, to forge its proper tools, to start ready for work on its appointed task, the material of its study melts away with hopeless rapidity. Just now, [...] when men fully trained for the work have begun to travel into savage countries and study their inhabitants—these die away under our very eyes."[42] Walking in the churchyard of the town of Tervuren, where Belgium's King Leopold's Royal Museum of Central Africa is located, I was reminded of Malinowski's phrase when my eye caught sight of seven identical weather beaten and derelict tombstones, which were lined up, in veritable fairy tale fashion, against one of the church's walls. A recent tourist office sign provided the visitor with the following information:

> "Brussels Universal Exhibition 1897. On the occasion of the International Exhibition of Brussels in 1897 three African villages were erected along the lake of Tervuren. During daytime these villages were inhabited by 267 Congolese. Seven amongst them – EKIA, GEMBA, KITUKWA, MPEIA, ZAO, SAMBO and MIBANGE – did not survive the chilly summer and lie buried here."

Within the framework of the modernist celebration of universality, the exploitative nature of the capitalist nation state as motor of a global imperial enterprise (even if, strictly speaking, the then Congo Free State was not yet a Belgian colony, but King Leopold's private property) is here disclosed as a despotic machine of subjection, a machine geared towards the production of displacement and/in (physical and cultural) death. Hochschild's recent book about King Leopold's Congo, "revealing the terror which lay hidden in Congo," strengthens this image which lives in the western collective imaginary about the Congo as "heart of darkness." In doing so, Hochschild makes use of a black and white, highly moralizing Hollywood script about Good and Evil. On the book's dust cover, *King Leopold's Ghost* is marketed as "the haunting account of a megalomaniac of monstrous proportions, a man as cunning, charming and cruel as any of the great Shakespearian villains. It is also the deeply moving portrait of those who fought Leopold: a brave handful of missionaries, travelers, and young idealists who went to Africa for work or adventure and unexpectedly found themselves witnesses to a holocaust." Undoubtedly, the history of Belgian colonialism is much more complex and ambivalent than Hochschild's interpretation allows for, and certainly, the Belgian Congo was not a proto Nazi enterprise. Nevertheless, the painfully brutal side of the space of colonialism and its political economy of violence, in which the colonial subject is detribalized and retribalized, pressured into paying taxes, exploited by traders, reduced to forced labor, displayed, humiliated, violated and disciplined by the whip (*chicotte*), is undeniable. The displaced graves of seven colonized subjects make the colonial space excruciatingly tangible as site of death, as *terra morta*.[43]

However, once the space of colonialism has been defined as a "space of death," to use Michael Taussig's phrase, the question then becomes how to speak about the postcolonial afterlife, that which lies beyond the grave. What remains to be told in the *post*, in the postcolonial as *post mortem*, but the unspeakable, with words that have themselves run cold from *rigor mortis*?

A century after Malinowski. Imagine yourself set down, surrounded by all your gear, close to a native city, Kinshasa, for example. In the evening, in the quickly receding sunlight filtered by the smoke of thousands of small wood fires rising from between the corrugated iron roofs of Kinshasa's cement brick houses, from between the thousands of mango and palm trees in the compounds in which these houses stand, upwards, towards a darkening sky, it is as if this forest of a city, this warm, dusty, grey green body full of sounds and smells, takes a deep breath and comes back to life, glad to have survived the heat of the past day. Sauntering in the soft evening light through the sandy alleys of Kinshasa's more peripheral *cités*, the underbelly of this urban body, people greet neighbors and acquaintances sitting in front of their houses playing checkers, while making way for the determined pace of women returning from their faraway markets, fields and rivers; young and old women gleaming with tired sweat, smelling of the cassava roots and wood they carry on their head, wet with the water spilling from the buckets and plastic gourds they balance on their heads. Everywhere around them is the sound of voices, and laughter, and rumba music from blaring cassette players, and church hymns, and drums announcing a funeral wake, and the frenzied rhythmical sounds of wood against glass, as the *bana petrol*, the "kerosene children," like fireflies, start appearing in the streets to advertise their merchandise by drumming with small sticks against tiny bottles filled with kerosene, crying out: "*kolo-kolo, kolo-kolooo!*" If, on such an evening, there is a little money left, parents, grandparents, aunts or uncles will send other children out into the street to buy some kerosene in order to fill the Aladdin lamp made in China and make a little light into the darkness that is setting in, because SNEL, the national electricity company, switched off the light months ago, and the moon has not appeared yet.

Imagine yourself set down in such a shantytown, on such an evening. Hand in hand, a group of three or four young men, strolling along one of Kinshasa's many potholed asphalt roads (*princes*), starts singing. Hesitantly at first, searching for words and melody, then more confidently, each of them in turn invents a new song line in a high-pitched lead voice, while the others join in, providing an improvised *a capella* version of *Milonga ya Kwango*, an old song by the orchestra Victoria and "King" Kester Emeneya, one of Kinshasa's beloved music performers:

> My uncle from the village wrote a letter, asking me to buy a dog. I bought him a dog,
> and he was very happy. He returned to the bush. Hunt, my dog, catch
> the game, *nganga* dog. His name is Seti.
> Illness, where did you come from? My brothers, my uncle became ill.
> He wrote to me, Ndeti Marko, urging me to come to the village,
> so that I would know our village's secrets.
> Forest, and rivers and then the bush.
> I was in Kinshasa and thought: 'When will I arrive in Mayumbu?'
> Uncle Musize, tell me the truth, the river Kwango I do not know,
> my brother, I find myself in despair, too much sorrow.
> I arrived too late, my uncle had died. I am in Kinshasa. I found the people
> seated on the floor, crying. I went to Mayumbu, crying, with my arms
> on my head. I keep asking myself "why?" and I weep. I went to the village
> and arrived too late, my uncle had already been buried. I wept.
> "Where have you been? Why do you arrive too late? Your uncle died
> with your name on his lips, Ndeti Marko, ayeee. You, little one, what were
> you doing in Kinshasa? Our uncle has gone, he was waiting for you."
> Our slaves have become chiefs, they have become the major chiefs.
> And now they are selling the forests for money, but the money has already
> gone, and now they are going to chase us from this land. Too much suffering.
> Our forests and our rivers are for us, and the bush is for us as well, and
> today one can buy this with money, following the example of Papa Mobutu,
> the bad example he gave.
> Our slaves have become our chiefs, they have become the most important,
> and now they start selling our forests, and the money is almost gone,
> and they will make us leave from here. Too much sorrow.
> Brothers, you cannot deceive wisdom. The courageous one fell down
> on the ground.

On this evening the voices sing about loss and despair, about displacement and dislocation, about poverty and estrangement, about fragmented memories and a deeply felt sense of personal and communal crisis that has pervaded all levels of society in Kinshasa and Congo as a whole. Imagine yourself living this crisis, and you will notice that it takes the shape of a Russian doll: *wana nde tobengaka makambo nakati ya makambo*, "it is what we call problems inside of other problems." Now imagine yourself to be thinking about these problems, seated at the desk of your university office, or in your cosy living room, removed from these subjectivities of the crisis, what name would you give the crisis then? Is all that remains in the postcolony, the *post mortem*, an autopsy of crisis?

In popular discourse, an often recurring theme is the loss of ancestral land, inalienable for its inhabitants, and yet seized by outsiders who are perceived to be rich, powerful and associated with *Leta*, the State. Beyond the complex legal problems surrounding land tenure in Congo,[44] this theme also reveals a more general sense of insecurity, displacement, deterritorialization and loss of place in the Congolese postcolony. Like King Kester's song, many popular songs bemoan the "lack of a place to which one fully belongs" (*kozanga esika*), thereby indicating a deeply felt rupture with one's lived world.[45] There is a generalized *malaise*, a widespread sense of crisis. This crisis originated in the violent and alienating discrepancies and dislocations generated in and by the colonial project, and was further aggravated in the past decades. It is a crisis which has profoundly disturbing effects on both macro and micro levels of societal life. Indeed, life has itself become, in the words of the actors, deadly, ominous, downgraded, wrecked and rotten (*cadavéré, sinistré, déclassé, épavé, pourri*). *Mboka ekufi*, "the country has died" was a frequently heard expression in Mobutu's Zaire, and it still is said of the Kabila dynasty in the new Congo.

The concept of praxis or habitus, now so central to social theory and to the bodies of discourse that surround it, necessarily depends on a particular historico-cultural starting point from which it is more or less unproblematically reproduced and transmitted.[46] However, against that is the growing sense of loss of a viable basis of social relations and of the shared epistemological truths on which it rests. Such loss increasingly seems to imperil people's ability to continue to construct and transmit a meaningful reality out of the social, political and economical paradoxes in which they are caught. The violent breaking up of what Bourdieu (and before him Marcel Mauss) calls the "doxic experience," attacks the quality of a world that goes without saying for those who experience, live in and belong to it. The consequences of this breakdown reach far beyond the general atmosphere of *fin-de-régime* which characterized Mobutu's Zaire, and beyond, also, the experience of crisis brought on by the war under Laurent Kabila. These consequences jeopardize the continuity and the very existence of local historico-cultural systems (which had already lost a great deal of their cohesiveness during the colonial period); they undermine the notion of historicity itself, the "natural" economy of habitus and the cultural identities that result from it. Yet many people in Kinshasa and elsewhere in Congo and Central Africa have no choice but to continue to live in a world that seems to be falling apart before their very eyes. If and how they achieve this, endure, and cope with the fundamental ruptures in their lives and identities is a major question. By and large, social scientists, usually not so "fully trained for the work" of crisis analysis, have failed to answer satisfactorily or have only just begun to explore it.[47]

In this chapter, and indeed throughout this book, I respond to that challenge—to explore if and how people seek to overcome the manifold, daily experienced ruptures and breaches in their lives. How do they continue to make sense of a world that seems to have lost much of its "taken-for-grantedness" and that has arrived at "the end of history?" It is, for example, no coincidence that the book of the Apocalypse, which projects one's own time frame against the screen of the completion of history and humanity, is one of the most popular and frequently read books of the Bible in recent years. I look at available pathways and strategies by means of which people in contemporary Kinshasa have tried to overcome this deeply felt sense of loss, occasioned by the continuing fragmentation of their world.

Central to this query are the ways in which postcolonial subjects in Kinshasa and its hinterland address issues of history, temporality and memory and, through them, the issue of the crisis of their own Selves as postcolonial subjects. In my analysis, the subjectivity of crisis—which, I argue below, is itself intimately tied to a generalized *memory crisis* and the breakdown of the production of history—is linked to an impossibility to place or *posit* death.

Barthes, reflecting upon the relationship between history and death, cites a passage written by Michelet:

> Each soul, among vulgar things, possesses certain special, individual aspects which do not come down to the same thing, and which must be noted when this soul passes and proceeds into the unknown world.
> Suppose we were to constitute a guardian of graves, a kind of tutor and protector of the dead?
> I have spoken elsewhere of the duty which concerned Camoens on the deadly shores of India: *administrator of the property of the deceased*. Yes, each dead man leaves a small property, his memory, and asks that it be cared for. For the one who has no friends, the magistrate must supply one. For the law, for justice is more reliable than all our forgetful affections, our tears so quickly dried.
> This magistracy is History. And the dead are, to speak in the fashion of Roman Law, those *miserabilis personae* with whom the magistrate must be concerned. Never in my career have I lost sight of that duty of the Historian. I have given many of the too-forgotten dead the assistance which I shall myself require.
> I have exhumed them for a second life. [...] Now they live with us, and we feel we are their relatives, their friends. Thus is constituted a family, a city shared by the living and the dead.

Mirroring Michelet's thoughts, Michel de Certeau notes that the quest for historical meaning "aims at calming the dead who still haunt the present, and at offering them scriptural tombs."⁴⁸ History "deals with death as an object of knowledge," he writes, "and, in doing so, causes the production of an exchange among living souls." In his view, then, the role of the historian does not consist in the exhumation of the dead for a second life, but rather in the establishing of a contract between the living and the dead. In the postcolonial "beyond the grave," however, this contract has been broken. Increasingly, the dead exhume themselves, while the living seem condemned to live in the disturbing company of these severed restless souls wandering around, these dead who are unable to "liberate the apartment for the living.⁴⁹" Kinshasa has indeed become a city shared by the living and the dead, but the terms of that coevality form constant grounds for dispute.

TRADITION AND/OR MODERNITY: A CATCH-22

In the King Kester song quoted above, the individual experience of crisis and loss (the death of the uncle, the personal sense of rupture occasioned by the economic migration to the city of Kinshasa, the sale of homeland) is lifted to a more collective level of awareness of alienation brought about by a general political and economic crisis (slaves who become chiefs, the power of money and the growing abyss between haves and have nots). In the song, individual and collective experiences of the crisis are expressed by means of reference to death, ancestral land and thus to roots. As such it echoes other commentaries that are generated in the streets of Kinshasa and other towns throughout Congo.

In 1995 the Ebola virus surfaced 500 kilometers southeast of Kinshasa in the city of Kikwit, leaving more than 200 people dead in the span of a few weeks. One among many different explanations *Radio Trottoir*, the rumor machine that punctuates Kinshasa's pulsating heartbeat and opens a window onto the city's popular imagination, provided to account for the appearance of the deadly virus centered on the burial site of Kungu Pemba. Kungu Pemba was a *chef de terre*, land chief of the village of Kipuka, which later would become Kikwit. He was the first traditional authority of the area to encounter the white man and resist the intrusion of the colonial state, at a time, according to one of my informants, "when Kikwit itself was still densely forested and called *makaku* by the whites because of the many monkeys which could be found in its forests." Two palm trees are planted on Kungu Pemba's grave, which can still be visited today. These palm trees are the soldiers guarding his body. At night they exclaim to all those who want to approach the grave: "Everyone who tries to sell the soil of Kikwit will die." Many are those who did. Popular lore has it that one of the most prominent people having died from Kungu

Pemba's curse while attempting to get hold of some of the soil of his grave, is Zairean President Mobutu's own mother, Mama Yemo.

> One day Mama Yemo arrived from Kinshasa at Kikwit's small airport in her private DC30. A Mercedes car was waiting for her to drive her to the hotel. During the night she ordered her chauffeur to take her to Kungu Pemba's grave. Upon her arrival Kungu Pemba's 'guards' exclaimed: "Never will the soil of Kikwit belong to anyone else. It is the soil of power [*la terre qui rafferme le pouvoir*]." Despite this warning, Mama Yemo, on behalf of her son, collected some of the earth from the grave and returned to her hotel. The following day, after her return to Kinshasa, the hotel and the neighboring market burned down. Mama Yemo herself died shortly after these events.
> Many are the politicians who have tried to get hold of some earth of Kungu Pemba's grave in order to inherit from his power. All those who did so for opportunistic reasons, or tried to tame and incorporate Kungu Pemba's power in the postcolonial state, have died from his curse. In this way, Ebola was seen by some as the result of Kungu Pemba's curse, triggered by trespassers who tried to get hold of his power.
>
> [Interview, Kikwit, September 1995]

Kungu Pemba's grave holds another secret. Popular lore in Kinshasa and Kikwit has it that the "golden book," the *livre d'or* signed by Congo's first Prime Minister, Patrice Lumumba, by the Belgian ministers and King Baudouin on June 30, 1960, during Independence Day (or, according to other voices in the street, during the Brussels Round Table conference of January–February 1960), ended up in the hands of Antoine Gizenga, Vice-Prime Minister in the Lumumba and Adoula governments, and currently leader of the PALU opposition party.[50] Gizenga was rumored to be involved with the Brazzaville based *Front National de Libération* and with the mid-1960s Mulelist Kwilu revolts, which caused Kikwit to lose favor in the eyes of the central government in Kinshasa. According to *Radio Trottoir* Gizenga buried the "golden book" in the grave of Kungu Pemba, where it has remained to this day.

Taken together, the youngsters' song, the stories of Kungu Pemba and the burial of the *livre d'or* are emblematic of much of the current crisis that Kinshasa, and indeed Congo as a whole, is undergoing. Beyond the obvious political debacle of the Mobutu years, beyond the disastrous effects of the war that started in 1998 in an attempt to topple L.D. Kabila's regime, this crisis is rooted in a catch-22 situation. It is perceived, somewhat like Scylla and Charybdis, in extreme spaces between which people find their way only at their peril. The space of tradition, on the one hand, is often only a poor image and faint reminder of a past long gone. On the other hand is the space of modernity, projected by colonialism and by the often exuberant lifestyles of expatriates and indigenous urban elites in such wealthy Kinshasa neighborhoods as Gombe, Binza Ma Campagne or Limete. This modernity, however, is a mirage. It only presents an illusion of development while remaining beyond the reach of most citizens. In between these extremes of "tradition" and "modernity," between a transformed and distant past and a turbid vision of what seems to be an equally distant future, what conscripts most people in Kinshasa's *cités* and shantytowns and forms the daily context of their lives is an architecture of chaos and decay, a geography of shortage, of lack and of loss. Most people's lives thus unfold in a space which one could describe, as Mudimbe does, as a space of marginality, in which, to name but one element, the traditional socioeconomic realms are disrupted and transformed by a new division of labor.[51]

The stories surrounding Kungu Pemba's grave exemplify the ambivalence and paradoxes inherent in this intermediary location from which escape seems so difficult. Seen from one point of view, Kungu Pemba stands for resistance, defending local identity, autonomy and independence in the clash with colonial hegemonic rule. Tradition, personified by Kungu Pemba as custodian of the ancestral land (his name is both a reference to Kongo, the precolonial nation, and to the whiteness, *pembe*, of the ancestors), is also made the preserver of the dreams of the Congolese nationalists, exemplified by Gizenga, defending those dreams and visions against their postcolonial usurpers (represented in the story by Mobutu and his mother). At the same time, Kungu Pemba's curse is not only about resistance and counterhegemony. A complaint often heard in Congo is that "the Belgian Uncles" (*banoko*) "taught us about progress and development, but at independence they threw the key to open the door to development into the ocean," thereby denying the former colonial subjects access to the benefits of modernity. In the Kungu Pemba story, however, it is not so much the former colonizers who deny the (postcolonial) subjects access to the spaces of modernity but, rather, tradition which stands in the way of development. As a power object in its own right, the "golden book," empowered by the signatures of those representing Bula Matadi, the "Breaker of Stone," as the colonial state machinery was referred to, is a *pars pro toto* for the legacy of colonialism formed by the tools of Prospero, the total colonial library, its "signs taken for wonders," to use Bhabha's expression, its technologies of remembering, knowing, ordering, controlling and acting upon the world.[52] Kungu Pemba has rendered this legacy of colonialist modernity inaccessible. Worse still, Kungu Pemba, who evokes a time of plenty, when villages were surrounded by forests full of game, has become the enigmatic shorthand for a nostalgic notion of precolonial self-sufficiency, identity and ancestral wisdom. Yet, this same local culture hero has become a curse; he has turned against his heirs, spreading Ebola amongst those who turn to him.

The road to modernity has become an equally hazardous one. I want to stress the point that in modernity the technology for constituting a viable social memory in the postcolony (that is, the technology of writing, the colonial mnemonics, as exemplified in the *livre d'or*) has been buried and has, therefore, become inaccessible. This has to be taken quite literally, for in Congo books are simply not available. At the same time, modernity itself, somewhat like Elvis changing into The Giant Named Kinshasa, has turned out to be an unreliable and deadly shapeshifting trickster. This interpretation is again illustrated by an alternative explanation which circulated in Kikwit and Kinshasa concerning the possible cause of the Ebola outbreak:

> During the first weeks of the Ebola epidemics, popular discourse focused on Dr. Fontaine, an American medical doctor and missionary working in nearby Vanga hospital, as the most likely agent of the viral spread. Everything started on the day when Dr. Fontaine transformed himself into a hippopotamus and hid in the Kwilu river, where he started to attack and frighten the riverine population. Due to this conduct, the other missionaries of Vanga decided to chase Dr. Fontaine from their hospital when he shifted back into his human form. Outraged, Dr. Fontaine traveled to Gbadolite, the presidential palace in the north of the country, to seek help from his friend, the *maréchal* Mobutu. Since the latter had disliked Kikwit ever since the Kwilu revolts of the sixties, he advised the American missionary to bewitch the city of Kikwit by way of revenge. Making use of an invitation to attend a conference on AIDS and a Bible seminar, Dr. Fontaine returned to Kikwit, spread poison in Kikwit's main hospital and put a spell on the city which occasioned the outbreak of the deadly virus.[53]

In this account, the legacy of colonialist modernity (the mission, with its own "golden book," the Bible, biomedical healthcare, the postcolonial state) literally turns out to be a poisoned one. In this instance, the collective imagination comments not so much on the modernity of witchcraft, but on the witchcraft of modernity, or modernity as witchcraft. Ironically, the collective discourse on the witchcraft of (post)colonialist modernity often uses the missionaries' biblical arguments against "traditional" witchcraft, turning their discourse back against itself, by playing on the ambivalence of the biblical references. This is, for example, how one should understand the frequent reference to Matthew 10:28, quoted by "Giant Kinshasa" Elvis in the previous chapter, and illustrated by the Congolese painter Midgi (known as Paepm, *Peintre Artiste Effort Personnel Midgi*): "Do not fear those who kill the body but cannot kill the soul [that is, the African witches]; rather fear him who can destroy both soul and body in hell." Not only is this verse used as an argument against indigenous witchcraft, but it simultaneously underpins the local vision of the colonizer's Christian God as super witch outdoing the others.

Cut off both from a unproblematic return to precolonial "communitarian" cultural sources as a possibility for replenishing the present, and from the pathways of modernity that may open up a future in the global ecumene (a modernity that in itself leads to enchantment rather than to the *Entzauberung* of the world that Max Weber predicted), Congo's postcolonial subjects are faced with a dilemma that, as Mamdani has pointed out, may be characteristic of a more global African impasse: how to arrive at a creative synthesis between two positions, modernist on the one hand, and communitarianist or traditionalist on the other, that are both perceived, to varying degrees, as somehow paralyzing and marginalizing? In the next sections I will investigate this question by focusing on issues of memory and memory crisis in the Congolese postcolony.[54]

HISTORY, MEMORY, AND THE "FAILED" STATE

In his book *Present Past. Modernity and the Memory Crisis*, through an analysis of a number of key literary works, Richard Terdiman historicizes the rise of a memory crisis within the time frame of the emerging modernity of the nineteenth century. Given the intrinsic link between memory and identity, the construction of new, more global and encompassing national identities followed the speeding up of processes of space/time compression and globalization (in terms of rapidly expanding means of communication and travel) so characteristic of the nineteenth century, and celebrated in the invention of the Universal Exhibition.[55] This inevitably also led to the construction of new, more global and encompassing national identities. The nineteenth century witnessed not only the consecration of the identity of the nation state, but also, as I noted in the introduction, the external expansion of the nation state in the works of colonial imperialism. This globalizing process brings rapid social change and the dissolving of familiar social environments and "chronotopic frames."[56] The inevitable flip side of this process is a growing sense of nostalgia for these disappearing worlds, for small-scale parochial identities unambiguously linked to a clearly defined sense of place.[57] The crisis of local identities in the West, and of western identity as such, went hand in hand with a growing fascination for the Other. Hence, also, the birth of the ethnographic museum in the nineteenth century. The seven graves in the Tervuren churchyard indeed remind one of the intimate interconnection behind the projects of the Universal Exhibition and the ethnographic museum. A substantial part of the museum site's meaning, itself grounded in the evolutionist canon of natural history, derived from the fact that it erected a shrine for the premodern; that it represented and spatialized a nostalgia for lost worlds and identities, a "rage to preserve" as a "reaction to anxieties generated by modernist amnesia."[58] Nineteenth century memory is thus predominantly about a sense of loss, a Proustian search for *le temps perdu*. The memory crisis is characterized by the fact that memory itself becomes a museum, a burial place where lost identities are mourned, in a desperate attempt to keep their atrophied representations alive. In this context at least, memory evolves into a site of death, of something past, a distant monumentalism that is no longer evocative of a living, taken-for-granted context. Here, memory is no longer produced out of experience, nor does it have the force actively to reshape or influence habitus and experience. Memory has become alienated memorial.

For Bourdieu the habitus, as product of history, produces individual and collective practices (that is, history) conforming to the schemes engendered by history.[59] The habitus is embodied, internalized history, and therefore *forgotten* as history. The strained relationship with history is perhaps what colonialist modernity and the postcolonial condition have most (although not exclusively) in common. Although for different reasons, in both the colonial and postcolonial periods it was/is no longer possible unproblematically to (re)produce habitus, and therefore history; and for the same reason, it is not possible in either context to forget about habitus as history. It is not by accident that the "Golden Book," containing the history of the colonization and decolonization of the Congo (metonymically represented by the signatures of the major political players on both sides), is buried in the grave of Kungu Pemba, "Mr. Antecolonial-and-First-Contact-History" personified. If colonialism is a site of death, erected upon but also contained by the buried body of Kungu Pemba, then the Congolese postcolony is everything that takes place beyond Kungu Pemba's grave. Rather than being a postmodern "non-place" of hyper-modernity, as Augé calls it, it is a postcolonial "out of the world," to use Mbembe's phrase, in which history, "the forever-remnant trace of a beginning," can neither be recovered, produced or forgotten.[60]

Inevitably, this has repercussions for the construction of the historical narrative. On the one hand, Congo's "factual" history of the past century is not readily available, and one is indeed continuously confronted with this impossibility to gain access to "objective" historical realities in Congo today. On the other hand, history books that attempt to provide a historical master text, such as Ndaywel's voluminous *Histoire du Zaire. De l'héritage ancien à l'âge contemporain* (1997), are not accessible to most and therefore not very influential in the Congo itself. The state, always one of the major producers of homogeneous, closed, unified official history, had, in the Congolese case and especially towards the end of the Mobutu years, become a nonentity, a virtual reality.

Today, although Zaire has become Congo again, the country is still struggling with that heritage. In "The Colonial Debt" [*La dette coloniale*], a Congolese novel set against the backdrop of the Mobutu epoch, Maguy Kabamba wrote: "The state is like the telephone in Zaire. It exists but does not work."[61] In political terms, the state imploded and was reduced to a "black hole of power."[62] One can say that, paradoxically, the state was in reality a small political elite of *dinosaurs* who formed the personal coercive regime's domestic structure of repression. It only existed through its initiation of illegality. This illegality spread from the center to broader layers of society, according to a dynamic which increasingly escaped the mechanisms of state control as such, and also involved an international network that surpassed by far the national Zairean "mafias" then in power. These mafias were and are active in the arms trade, the diamond and gasoline traffic, the laundering of narcodollars and other similar activities. Unlawfulness, arrogant arbitrariness and illegality thus became the only elements to make an increasingly fictional "state" evident and visible. For most people, the state has become the looting soldier's nocturnal knock on the door, "turning the house upside down" (*soda unatumbula na ndako*), as Kinshasa's Hindubill, a Lingala argot, powerfully puts it.

Fallen victim to the political instability and the capitalist banditry that it nurtured itself, the State thus turned into a chimera. As such, it no longer had the actual power or means to produce an authoritative historical master narrative reifying its own emergence and hegemonic presence as "integral state," as it had once tried to generate within the ideology of Recourse/Return to Authenticity, the neologistic cultural doctrine that was so characteristic of the Second Republic. With this official doctrine of the Return to Authenticity the nation's pendulum swung to the "traditionalist" side of the catch-22. The Return to Authenticity ideology was structured in opposition to the former colonial masters and the West. It was spun around a whole reality of more deeply rooted ideological and symbolic referents that drew from a pool of precolonial metaphors and images, pertaining to the office of traditional sovereign paramounts. Many of the traditional symbols and values related to sovereign paramount rulers, such as royal paraphernalia (the leopard skin, the staff, the flywhisk, the throne, the praise-name) or notions of kinship, lineage, family, power, authority and legitimacy, were selectively manipulated and subverted in order to give form to the aims of the Mobutist regime. They were meant to legitimize the Guide's status as "Father of the Nation," and to manifest his right to power as an ancestral right.[63] The reinvention and perversion of traditional elements to back up and touch up the violent realities of naked power were thus (more or less subtly) made use of to instill respect, awe, fear and subservience to a personal coercive regime. The Return to Authenticity ideology did not outlive Mobutu.

Faced with the collapsed state, the increasingly blurred boundaries of the state apparatus provided people on the local and urban levels of Congolese society with the opportunity to penetrate this "black box," this political space previously occupied but now abandoned by the state and the regime. As a result, everybody could "work politics" in Congo. "To do politics" (*kosala politique*) is an activity which is not considered dishonorable but it constitutes, rather, a prerogative to survival. It means "looking for opportunities," or "making deals" (referred to in Kinois speech as *kosala cop*, a derivation from "cooperation"), even though that is often synonymous with "scheming" or "being corrupt." The more elitist *kosala politique* has a populist counterpart in the "fifteenth clause," *article quinze*, an imaginary article of the constitution that refers to the system D of the common man: *débrouillez-vous*, help yourself, survive by adapting to the predatory rule of the street.

With the collapse of the state infrastructure, the state lost its monopoly and control of the political field. This naturally led to the implosion of the classic hierarchical state/society picture and to the creation of a new dynamic "model" of interaction, the contour of which is still only vaguely outlined today. This model was only partly captured by the emergence of multipartyism in the early 1990s. Instead, it is a model of interaction between multiple, dialectically interdependent, sociopolitical and cultural spaces and groups. These are linked to one another in constantly shifting hierarchies that are defined by the personalistic strategies of those at the top of the system and of other actors on the local, regional and national level, sometimes in but mostly outside of the spheres of formal politics. Within the Congolese context, the concept of the state has thus, in its quotidian practice, been reappropriated in terms of a great number of political strategies which cannot simply be described as forms of political "decay" or pathological dysfunctioning, for they constantly aim at the creation of networks and spaces of contact, cenacles of palaver, exchange, solidarity and complicity, enabling the circulation of commodities, money and wealth in people.

The splintering of the nation state's political arena was confirmed by the factual division of the country from 1998 onwards, as well as by the partial fragmentation of the nation state's "imagined community," or at least, by the state's incapacity to provide a leading and authoritative, monolithic and unified historical master narrative for the sustained construction of such a community (which continues to exist nonetheless: Congo is a country with remarkably little state but with lots of "nation"). As with the political space, where politics was quickly redefined in terms of new models of interaction generated "beyond the state," this partial vacuum gave rise to enormously varied and inventive processes of memory making and the invention of traditions in which the *temporality* of the nation state was replaced by something else. In

the absence of a canonized history, collective social memory was and is at liberty to annex more of the cultural space to develop its own, nonlinear, heterogeneous dynamics in which there is room for difference and openness. This is, for example, the space occupied by the popular genres of music, theater and painting. Hence Tshibumba, in a series of paintings depicting the history of Congo/Zaire, generates his own version of history, often taking great liberties with the historical "truth." Nevertheless, Tshibumba, and other painters such as the Kinshasa based painter Moke (whose portrait in this book was taken some months before his unfortunate death in September 2001) or even musicians such as Franco Luambo Makiadi in his "revolutionary songs" in which he wrote the history of the Mobutist revolution, still made attempts to create a linear historical chronicle, claiming to "represent what really happened,"[64] by capturing and freezing particular historical events within the frame of a canvas, and building up a chronology through a series of songs or paintings. Contrary to that, the collective social memory, as producer of "history," that is, differentiated yet collective experience, seems to evolve into something much more historically and chronologically dismembered and disparate today. This has opened up a process in which "history" becomes plural. As Kalulambi remarks, the straightforward historical narrative has "exploded"[65] into a multiplicity of histories, composed of fragments ripped at random from the pages of Ndaywel's history textbook, and interspersed with highly intimate personal recollections, memories, interpretations and representations. On the one hand, this disparity is a testimony to the resilience and creativity of the collective Congolese memory. It proves that the autochthonous collective imaginary was never fully domesticated by a colonial politics which aimed at disciplining and redefining the colonial subject and his mental worlds in terms of western models. On the other hand, the profound fragmentation of shared memory, and of the collective consensus concerning the representations of what constitutes historical "truth," is also symptomatic for the deconstruction of the social texture as harmonious memory environment. Whereas Tshibumba or Moke were still capable of fusing their own vision with a shared collective memory constructed in tune with the time of the nation state, painters such as Bodo and Pap'Emma are much more idiosyncratic. These painters tap into a newly emerging collective memory, in which the time of the nation is replaced by a religious temporality of a specific, eschatological kind, a dreamlike time of God (and of Satan). They replace a single historical flow of time with what Walter Benjamin called *Jetzeit*, a time which charges the past with the time of the now. Pap'Emma's famous 1991 painting, *The History of Zaire*, a vast canvas packed with superimposed elements of thirty years of Mobutism, stylistically illustrates the dissolution of linear historical "truth."[66] In Pap'Emma's visionary and epic worlds, the historical narrative dissolves into a

Isn't the city of Kinshasa bewitched?

painted landscape that highlights the construction of a highly individual mythical universe with outspoken religious dimensions, in which various pasts implode in the present, which itself is increasingly disconnected from "real time." The same goes for Kinshasa based preacher and painter Bodo, whose highly moralistic paintings, with their overt references to Bosch, place Kinshasa's history and daily realities against the backdrop of an apocalyptic space/time. It is here that history acquires oneiric dimensions and that the postcolonial historian emerges as oneirocritic of a disparately collective social imaginary and memory. It is in this specific dreamtime that Kinshasa reinvents itself today.

Garden of Delight.

DREAMTIME: IN THE REALM OF THE APOCALYPTIC INTERLUDE

TAXI CONVERSATIONS II [Kinshasa, April 2001]: On board a taxi-bus a preacher exercises his trade. Standing in the front of the bus, skillfully keeping his balance while the driver zigzags through the traffic on Avenue Lumumba, he holds one hand on his Bible and points his other hand toward the sky. With a thundering voice he preaches: "My Brothers and Sisters, the airplane of Salvation and Benediction does not land in your heart! And why does it refuse to land in your heart? Because the weather in your heart is bad. It is foggy in your heart because of all the sins that have accumulated there! That is why the Pilot does not land in your heart! Alleluiah!" Without much enthusiasm the rest of the packed bus responds with a mumbled Amen. At the next stop, near *Pont Matete*, another preacher from a rivaling church gets on the bus. He too starts preaching, trying to outdo his competitor. The first preacher gets upset and before long both start insulting each other, each claiming that this is his bus and his trajectory. Soon, the other travelers, with loud voices, start to intervene in the dispute. Some side with the first preacher, others with the second. One older man, wearing an old sun-hat, ill-fitting glasses and a short tie which makes one end of his worn-out shirt collar point upward, tries to calm down the two preachers who have started pulling and pushing each other. At the next stop, drawn by the tumult, a soldier gets on board. Theatrically, he unbuckles his belt and starts hitting the back of one of the preachers. Salvos of laughter and trickles of excitement run through the crowd that is watching the scene from the sidewalk.

A Saturday night in Masina, May 2000: In the *Mbuji-Mayi-Kananga*, one of the bars of the moment, beyond a sign that puts the place out of bounds for armed soldiers, a concrete stairway leads to a rooftop terrace. *Bana OK*, the heirs to one of the oldest Kinshasa based orchestras, Franco's *OK Jazz*, are getting ready for a late night concert. Bathing in a glow of yellow, red and blue lights, the *Mbuji-Mayi-Kananga* occupies the three levels of a storey building along the Avenue Lumumba in Masina, one of Kinshasa's most densely populated neighborhoods, also known as the "People's Republic of China" (*Chine populaire*). Around midnight, after a couple of tunes to warm up the audience, everyone starts dancing to the band's frenetic rumba rhythms. Holding back at first, the glistening bodies soon start to dance with more fervor in between tables and white plastic garden chairs. From the terrace, and much to the delight of the street children below, the electrifying sounds of the music drift out into the night, a tidal wave of sound rolling out over the endless sea of this vast *cité*'s corrugated iron roofs.

Downstairs, on the ground level, by the light of passing traffic and small kerosene lamps, women and girls hope to sell some groundnuts, cigarettes, firewood, and sometimes even themselves, to a never-ending caravan of passersby who are still trying to make their way home at this late hour. For lack of public transport and fuel, many will have to get onto *line 11*, that is, catch the "foot bus" and walk, often for hours, to reach home, while some of the more fortunate ones might get onto one of the open army trucks that *Mzee* Laurent Kabila put at the city's disposal to help solve the transportation problem. On these trucks, transport is for free (*ya ofele*), but due to the reckless driving of the conductors and the unsafe conditions in which the passengers have to make the ride, people have started commenting that only death is really for free (*okufi ya ofele*, "you die for free" on these trucks).

Upstairs, in the meantime, as on other nights, *Bana OK*'s play list consists of the songs that have come to form part of Kin's rich collective musical memory.[67] The band's songs propel the dancing crowd back into the sixties and seventies, a period which is now looked upon with growing nostalgia as a time when the future still looked bright, modernity's promises were still within reach, and *Kin-la-Belle* was still *Kin kiesse*, the city of joy, or *Kin makambo*, the turbulent city.

While listening to the music on that warm, effervescent Kinshasa night, my attention was caught by the orchestra's *atalaku*, the 'shouting deejay' who incites the dancing crowd with his slogans during the rumba-soukous' fast dancing part (*seben*). In his shouts I could discern a repeated reference to the number 666. In the context of contemporary Kinois urbanity, the city's typical rumba-soukous has always generated and represented an oneiric space of pleasure and enjoyment. In these arenas of popular culture, dancing, drinking, and ludic sexuality defined and firmly rooted the city's inhabitants into the excessive temporality of a neverending "now," a euphoric postindependence space *ivre de l'espoir des chairs et du sang*, "drunk with the hope of bodies and blood,"[68] from which death was firmly excluded. As Sam Mangwana, another legendary name of the Congolese music scene, sings in a famous 1960s song entitled *Zela Ngai Nasala* ("Wait, Let Me Work," released on the album "Festival des Maquisards"):

Ntango ya liwa mpo nayeba te oo.	When will be the day I die? I don't know.
Nalinga nalanda la vie ya liboma,	I want to live a crazy life
La vie ya sans souci na baninga,	A life without worry, together with my friends,
Ntango ya liwa mpo nayeba te mama.	I ignore when my death will come, mother.

In those days in Kinshasa, it was said that the crisis stopped at 8 pm. *Lobi pe mokolo*! [tomorrow is another day!][69] Today, however, this very same site of pleasure, in which death was totally crushed and obliterated and in which time was redefined in this moment of Eternal Now, this hedonistic site has become one of the main locales, along with the "enchanting" spaces of Christian fundamentalism, in which temporality and mortality are reintroduced. As such, Kinshasa reveals a fundamental part of itself in the bar and the church. These form the city's two main public spaces of appearance (and there now exists a considerable overlap between these two spaces, for many churches have their own orchestras who transform the sites of the religious gathering into a frenzied dance hall, using the rhythms of popular tunes but replacing the secular lyrics with more religious ones). It is through the increasing theatricalization of the city in both these spaces, also, that *fête* and *folie*, pleasure and psychosis, the ludic and the lethal, become interlocked and open up into the dimension which underlies all of Kinshasa's reality today: the dimension of death, long denied but now undeniable. Death has become omnipresent throughout the city: in the visible form of funeral wakes (*matanga*) that transform houses and streets into public sites of mourning and mercy, or in its more invisible form, that of the "second city," a shadow city which is constantly present as a parallel world of nocturnal and evil forces in the minds and lives of most Kinois.

As I mentioned above, the reintroduction of temporality, and thus of death, in contemporary Kinshasa is of a very specific, eschatological, nature and takes its point of departure in the Bible, and more particularly in the Book of Revelation, which has become an omnipresent point of reference in Kinshasa's collective imagination. The number 666 which was being shouted over the rooftops of Masina by the *atalaku* of *Bana OK* referred, of course, to the Beast mentioned in the Book of Revelation, 13:18: "This calls for wisdom: let him who has understanding reckon the number of the beast, for it is a human number, its number is six hundred and sixty-six." Not unsurprisingly, in the fundamentalist Christian traditions of the countless churches that have sprung up in the African urban locale and that bear witness to the luxuriant growth of millenarianism throughout Africa,[70] the Beast (the Antichrist) is commonly taken to be the *vicarius filii Dei* or the *rex sacerdotulus*, the Pope and the Church of Rome. More generally, the Beast refers to Satan and his demons. It is especially in chapters 8 to 19 of the Book of Revelation that Satan occupies an important place. The opening of the seventh seal ushers in angels and trumpet blasts that, together with vivid descriptions of terror, plagues, torment and great woes, symbolize hardhitting judgment messages, directed against Satan's system of things. Before the seventh and last trumpet calls forth great voices that proclaim the thousand year Kingdom of God and of his son Christ, there is a whole interlude describing the war between diabolic swarms and the hosts of heaven. In this interval judgments are executed against false religion (Babylon and its great whore) and against ungodly political systems and doomed unbelievers, symbolized by dreadful wild beasts, prototypes of the Antichrist. Satan is bound only to rise again after a thousand years in order to submit mankind to a final test, and will be finally disposed of and destroyed in a lake of fire, along with death, hell, his demons and any rebels on earth who follow him.

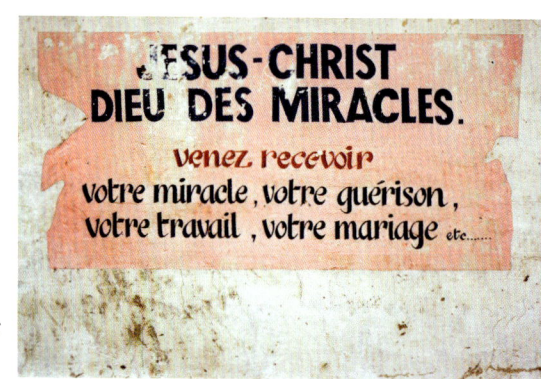

Jesus Christ, God of miracles. Come and get your miracles, your healing, your work, your marriage.

Jesus is the master of this compound.

By referring to the number 666, the musicians of *Bana OK*, from within the hedonistic site of dance and enjoyment, were thus producing the linkage between dance, death, doom and judgment. This linkage is also evident in one of Kinshasa's most recent dance crazes known as *la salle des morts*, the "Chamber of Death." This dance was launched by a small, Lemba-based orchestra, *Laviniora Esthétique* and its frontman "New Man" Dakumuda "Vieux Cellulaire." It has since been picked up by the city's biggest bands. In the "Chamber of Death" the dancers imitate the robot-like movements of zombies. Popular music culture thus opens up a space of death as well as an eschatological space, plunging the audience into the abyss of the end of times and linking the apocalyptic description in the Book of Revelation to the realities of everyday life as experienced by the inhabitants of Kinshasa today. In this collective experience of the Kinois, in which stress is predominantly put on the "death of the world" (*mokili ekokufa na l'an 2000*, "the world is going to die in 2000"), the current and very real hardships of life in the Congolese capital (war, violence, starvation, looting, social breakdown) are interpreted in the light of this end. In it, the lived-in time of everyday life in the city is projected against the canvas of the completion of everything, a completion which will be brought about by God and which, so far hidden, is already present with Him. As such the Book of Revelation is not only about doom and destruction, but it is essentially also a book of hope, a symbol of possible *recommencement*. As one Kinois put it: "the apocalyptic vision is a way to wash your heart and to start a new phase of life." This message of resurrection and entrance in the Glorious Millenial Reign is also a message that is strongly stressed by many of the churches. A Watchtower pamphlet (December 1, 1999: 9) which was widely circulated in Kinshasa under the title "Should You Fear the Apocalypse?" thus stated: "True, Revelation does contain judgment messages against the wicked. But in their public witnessing, God's servants focus mainly on the wonderful hope set out in the Bible, including that in the Apocalypse, or Revelation. Thus they

We are the ambassadors of Christ. Come and get your visa to heaven.

We serve out distributive food.

do not add to or take anything away from the prophetic words found therein. – Revelation 22:18,19."

And yet, the lived experience of most in the Congolese postcolony constantly contradicts these glad tidings which are expressed in the churches' creation of such geographies of hope. In the Book of Revelation, the judgment to come is announced by the coming of the Son of Man, in a cloud with great power and glory. His coming, though, is preceded by terrors, and by a magic interlude between his preliminary and his final victory over Satan. Life for most in Kinshasa situates itself in this interlude in which Satan fully reigns. For some others, the world has arrived at the end of the thousand year day of judgment and thus at the moment in which Satan is briefly released again. Thus, the popular understanding of the Apocalypse very much centers on the crack of doom and the omnipotent presence of Evil, thereby contributing to the rapid demonization of everyday life in Kinshasa.

As such, the Congolese experience is one in which the realities of the "in between" and the interstitial, which are so much celebrated by postcolonial theorists today, are constantly translated into mythical and prophetic terms as the *apocalyptic interlude*. Many Kinois seem to experience their existence as lived in an intermediate space in which salvation and doom, the revivalist moment and the presence of the Antichrist, or Saving and Condemnation, occur simultaneously. The temporal scope in which the dynamics of the apocalyptic interlude unfold is not that of real time. In this specific space/time the complex chronology between the various phases announced in the Book of Revelation (the first and second Coming of Christ, the presence and second release of Satan) has collapsed into a confusing present in which all of these moments somehow come together, collapsing in what is often a swirling conceptual and existential imbroglio, arising out of the explosion of the linear, though complex, narrative chronology which is outlined in the Book of Revelation.

A renewed vision for our Apostolic Church in Congo.
1) God; 2) The local church; 3) The body of Christ; 4) Collective work; 5) The world.

THE END OF THE WORLD AND THE GLOBALIZATION OF SATAN

When we enter the year 2000 the heavens will open their gates. Then, God will descend. He will come down and seat Himself on the royal throne. Jesus will sit down to His right and the prophets to His left (for example Moses and Eliah with the angels). The judgment will commence. After the judgment the good people without sins will rise to heaven. The sinners will stay on earth. Behind Jesus, heaven will close itself, and here on earth Hell will be established. There will be much suffering. Fire will burn everything. People will throw themselves into the fire. They will wage war. Those who are in heaven will experience delicious joys. No more suffering, plenty of food and singing, joy upon joy. After the first judgment Satan will establish himself in the world, and will start his reign. The world will transform into a Hell, and the Bible talks about the end of the world. The Bible tells us that when we come towards the end of the world wars start, the end enters, children no longer respect their parents. That is what we live today, that is why we see looting, wars, breakdown of authority. Then, afterwards, when we will have entered Hell here on earth, Satan will introduce a system with a stamp. The stamp will have the number 666. It is Satan's number. The stamp is like a *laissez-passer*, a permit. Satan will put a stamp with the number 666 on our arm. Without the number 666 you won't receive food. Without 666 you won't be able to buy things. Everybody with the 666 mark will be able to circulate freely and accumulate goods at will. Those who are saved by Satan with the number 666 will receive food for free. But without the number 666 in your body you will continue to suffer. Famine will be everywhere, things to eat will have disappeared. Suffering will be tremendous. Because of this suffering you will want to kill yourself. However, death will no longer be as before. It will no longer be the end of the world. The suffering of those who are not on Satan's side will be eternal. But those who accept to suffer and refuse to wear the 666 sign

Barbershop: Apocalypse at the nation's service.

Hell exists.

will be saved when Jesus will come down into this world for the second time, for at that moment he will proceed with the final judgment: "You, who were you?" "I was a preacher, preaching the word to my neighbors." "And I was a musician, I made people dance." "And I was rich, I helped the poor." At that moment, everyone wearing Satan's mark, the number 666, will be condemned forever. And then the world will be destroyed and Satan will be drowned in the water, under the earth. It will be like in Noah's time: God will destroy the world and create another one. And that is why we witness all these new things: the churches of spiritual awakening, the Kimbanguist churches, the church of the Africans and their God Nzambi a Mpungu. At the start of the year 2000, God will come down and destroy the world at midnight.

[Conversation with Vero, adept of the Eglise Evangélique Libre d'Afrique, EELDA, September 1999, Kinshasa]

Vero's account fully illustrates the contradictions and oscillations between the geographies and chronologies of hope and hell that I pointed out above. For those who refuse Satan's stamp, suffering will be eternal and yet they will be saved in the end. Although this account thus gives meaning to the current crisis in which most Kinois find themselves (those who suffer refused to sign a contract with Satan), it also squarely situates Kinshasa within the Devil's reign. As such, Kinshasa's collective social imaginary echoes the message of the fundamentalist Christian churches. A 1992 pamphlet of the Watch Tower Bible and Tract Society of Pennsylvania, which widely circulated in a French translation in Kinshasa in the late 1990s, further develops this theme: "Who Really Dominates the World?" Above this text the pamphlet shows a hand which holds the globe. On page three of the pamphlet, the answer to the question is revealed: "The leader of the world is identified. The Bible says: 'and the whole world is in the power of the evil one.' Moreover the Bible identifies evil in these terms: 'that ancient serpent, who is called the Devil and Satan, the deceiver of the whole world.' 1 John 5:19; Revelation 12:9." The message of the globalization of Evil (and jointly of God) which is propagated by Christian fundamentalism (and which, ironically, is the only form of globalization in which the Congolese, both as a target of and in praying against Evil, really take part and can claim a leading role), has become a popular theme which is further developed in the city's social imaginary. A recent work of art by a young Kinshasa based artist by the name of Pume Bylex, for example, forms a further elaboration of this theme.[71] His artwork, again a Boschian assemblage set in a small showcase, is entitled "Humanity taken hostage" (*L'humanité prise en ôtage*) and was described in minute detail by Bylex himself during an interview I conducted at his modest home in the Petro-Congo neighborhood of Masina, Kinshasa, in April 2001. Afterwards, he also elaborated in writing upon the meaning he tried to convey with this work:

Perspectives and visions of the artwork

— From left to right the vision of the Devil's special envoy: established as the Commander of the planet's unsettling. This Commander with his special braid is endowed with a redoubtable power.
— On the far right; the Devil, prince of darkness and in love with chaos, holds on to the planet with his grinding beak; to exercise all his power on earth. His grinding jaws also prevent him from losing his grip on the globe. With his vividly red tongue, he licks the planet to make it smooth and light; so that it can be transported easily by his Commander.
— In the globe's center, man is represented as the "master of the earthly realm." That is why he has a moustache, which denotes his authority. But now he is totally chained by the Devil, not capable of distinguishing neither the truth, nor reality.
— Actually, the Commander has been given a special grade; to underscore that he is fully licensed by his master. Secondly, his legs are arrowshaped to illustrate that he moves fast towards total disaster; that is to say, he wants to lead the world towards a total annihilation. His master is seated on his arms, which are shaped like wings and carry the globe. The master holds on to them tightly. The Commander's eyes are wide open as a result of the muscular effort of his uninterrupted howling. His teeth like daggers show that he wants, incessantly, to destroy all the barriers blocking his way. Moreover, the environment in which the Devil and his special envoy find themselves is marked by: radar fields which the Devil has invented to enter into contact with all of the planet's satellite networks.

The known perspectives of the Commander

Notes: the Commander, alias the master's disciple, is represented in three different guises:
1°. In the form of the **panther** with teeth-daggers. A panther with an antenna-horn (yellowish gold) which allows him to enter in immediate contact with his master (the Devil).
2°. In the form of the **migrating locust** which bespeaks his calling as a diehard looter (so to speak); that he terrorizes the entire world with his systematic looting.
3°. In the form of the **winged giraffe**. Here, the mighty and long neck of this giraffe enables him to snatch his meals (his victims) from a great distance. His sapphire blue, sacred wings reveal to us the ways he strolls through

the emptiness. And this chosen color which is blue proves beyond doubt his fidelity to the interdictions that are imposed by the master (Devil).

Different visions
  a) the metallic points that form part of the globe represent the world's different satellite systems.
  b) the image of weakened continents which fall off the planet.[72]

Again, the message of hope which lies embedded in the Book of Revelation is present in the artist's vision: in the very last line of his account he describes how the "weakened" or poor continents (in his view Africa, Latin America and Australia) drop from the globe. They are saved from the "Commander's" clutches, whereas the rich continents face total annihilation by the joined forces of Evil, the Commander and the Master. In the rest of his artistic production, Pume often appears as utopianist, giving body to ideas on architecture, industrialism, planification and social engineering, to create his own dream world, a world of perfection, placed in showcases behind glass, a fragile boundary between his utopian creations and the burlesque, dismantled world of Kinshasa which he thus tries to keep at bay. Despite this utopianism, the message of hope in "Humanity taken hostage" is but a small footnote to the meticulous and almost obsessive detail with which Bylex imagines, represents and describes the Forces of Evil. For Pume Bylex, as for many others in Kinshasa, the contemporary life world is continuously viewed as a "second world," an Armageddon, a place where the demons gather in their war against God (see Book of Revelation 16:16: "And they assembled them at the place which is called in Hebrew Ar-mà-ged'don.").

NOSTALGIA, BREACH AND THE "HERMIT'S CHOICE"

The dismembering of collective remembering of the historical past within the framework of the nation state, the constant religious transfiguration of daily reality, and the fragmentation of a collective consensus concerning the representations of historical truth is in itself a symptom of the breaking up of the social interweave as harmonious memory environment. The combination of all these elements also makes room for a mythologizing of the past (and the present) and this, inevitably, goes hand in hand with an increasing "synthetic nostalgia," as Marilyn Strathern has named the yearning for a shared past that seems to be irretrievably lost.[73] In Kinshasa today, this nostalgia seems to focus strongly, although, as I will show below, not exclusively, on the colonial epoch, "the time of the Uncles" (*tango ya banoko*),[74] the qualities of which, such as a certain sense of law and order, or a relative economic prosperity, are found to be lacking in the present. Surprisingly, perhaps, many in Kinshasa's streets call for a Belgian recolonization of the country. Increasingly also, this nostalgia covers the Mobutist period. In September 2003, in the streets of Camp Luka, children who have but a vague memory of the Mobutu period were singing: "Mobutu, Mobutu, ever since you are gone, all we eat is rice" (*Mobutu, Mobutu, banda okenda, loso na loso*). This kind of nostalgia is very selective; it is as much about forgetting as it is about remembering, omitting certain facts of colonialism or the postindependence rule, such as the issue of power, while foregrounding others, actively creating an imagined representation of the past. In this sense, nostalgia is symptomatic of a memory crisis, where memory begins when experience itself is irretrievably bygone.

For a minority in the Congolese postcolony, synthetic nostalgia does not foreground the colonial or Mobutist epoch but rather focuses on the antecolonial period. For this group of people nostalgia has become a *modus operandi*. Based in the neighborhood of Makala are the headquarters of "King" Misele, founder of a political formation and religious movement, the *Eglise du Christ en Afrique Noire des Apôtres du Congo* (ECANAC). Founded in 1955, King Misele's movement has become increasingly vocal about the king's attempts to restore an independent Congo state as it "existed" before 1491 (!). His political platform calls for cultural and political liberation, independence and unity for the Kongo people, including the populations of the Lower Congo, Bandundu and Kinshasa. They are rooted in a *ngunzist* prophetic religion which focuses on the Holy Spirit and which tries to unify all prophetic Kongo churches in an attempt to develop a truly African Christianity. For King Misele and his followers the post independence state is just a continuation of the colonial occupation of the ancestral land. Other church movements, such as the *Eglise des Noirs en Afrique*, founded by Simon Mpadi, share the same political and prophetic backgrounds. Many of these churches are active on the fringe of the official Kimbanguist church from which they tend to distance themselves since Kimbanguism, in their view, has drifted away from Simon Kimbangu's true message and has become a church which embraces "the God of White People" instead.[75] One of the most outspoken in its rejection of "white" colonialist Christianity is perhaps the movement *Grand Réveil Spirituel de Libération Africaine* (GRESLAF), also known as the *Union Spirituelle des Noirs*. Founded in 1990, as always after a prophetic vision, this church movement is based in Ndjili. In its religious and political meetings it blames "the white race which, through its introduction of Christianity, brought misfortune, misery and underdevelopment to the black race." In an interview that I conducted with a church representative in May 2001, this idea is further expanded upon:

The misfortune brought by the white race has many forms: sudden death, lack of intelligence, hunger, war, illness, the inability to invent, sufferings of all sorts. For GRESLAF this suffering began with the speech delivered by Belgian king Leopold II on January 12, 1883. He lied to us and cheated us. He sent missionaries to Congo to convert us, so that we would know the Christian God, but in reality they sent us Satan. From that time our misery began. We, on the other hand, pray to Nzambi Mpungu, the real God. He is the God of our ancestors and listens to us. Jesus came for the White People, not for us. Do you remember the song *Nakomitunaka*, "I ask myself," by Verckys? [Verckys, or Kiamuangana Mateta is a Kin based musician who rose to fame in the late 1960s and early 1970s with his orchestra Veve]. In this song he sings:

Ae nakomitunaka,	I ask myself,
Nzambe nakomitunaka,	My God, I ask myself,
Poso moindo ewuta nde wapi o?	Black skin, where does it come from?
Koko na biso ya kala ye nde nani ee?	Our ancestor, who was he?
Yezu mwana Nzambe ye nde mondele.	Jesus, Son of God, was a white man.
Adama na Eva bango nde mindele.	Adam and Eve were white people.
Basantu nyonso bango mpe mindele.	All the saints were white people.
Mpo na nini Nzambe?	Why is that so, my God?
Ae nakomitunaka,	I ask myself,
Nzambe nakomitunaka,	My God, I ask myself,
Babuku ya Nzambe biso tomonaka o,	In God's books we see,
Banzalu nyonso foto se mindele,	All the angels: their images are only white,
Basantu nyonso foto se mindele,	All the saints: their images are only white,
Soki zabolo foto nde moindo.	But the Devil, his image is black.
Injustice ewuta wapi o ah mama?	This injustice, where does it come from, oh mama?
Ae nakomitunaka,	I ask myself,
Nzambe nakomitunaka,	My God, I ask myself,
Poso moindo ewuta nde wapi o?	Black skin, where does it come from?
Banoko bakanga biso mayele boye,	The uncles [the Belgian colonizers] keep us stupid,
Bibeko ya bakoko bango baboyaka,	They refuse the statues of our ancestors,
Kisi ya bakoko bango bandimaka te.	They do not accept the fetishes of our ancestors.
Kasi na ndako ya Nzambe biso tomonaka,	But in church we see,
Tokosambela sapele na maboko,	That we pray with a rosary in our hands,
Tokosambela bikeko bitondi ndako.	That we pray to the statues that fill the church.
Kasi bikeko yango se mindele.	But again, these statues are white.
Mpo na nini Nzambe?	Why is that so, my God?
Ae nakomitunaka,	I ask myself,
Nzambe nakomitunaka,	My God, I ask myself,
Baprophete ya mindele biso tondima.	The prophets of the whites, we accept them.
Kasi ya bato moindo bango bandimaka te.	But those of the blacks, they do not accept them.
Mpo na nini Nzambe osala biso boye?	Why, oh God, have you made us this way?
Koko ya biso ya bato moindo azali wapi oo?	Where is our ancestor, of us blacks?
Afrika miso efungwani.	Africa has opened its eyes.
Afrika tozonga sima te (ah mama).	Africa, we will not go back (ah mama).
Ae nakomitunaka.	I ask myself.

The powerlessness of Africa comes from the fact that we belied our own nature.
> Instead of addressing our prayers to the God of our ancestors, we agreed to listen to the Christianity of the White Man. That is the source of our suffering. We disavowed our own God for too long. That is why we all die now. Before we didn't die like this, we were strong. So we have to break the chains and be delivered from the powers of darkness that were introduced by the Whites. The Bible that the Whites gave to us caused our disorientation, and so did their schools. And now they pretend to feed us because we are starving, but what do they bring: poisoned chickens, mad cow disease and all kinds of sick animals. *All these things caused us to lose our memory!*

In all of these churches' discourses *Nzambi Mpungu* stands in stark contrast to *Nzambi* as Christian godhead, that is, a more personified notion which was introduced by the missionaries and is actually a palimpsestual reinscription of the original *nzambi* concept as nonpersonal field of generative energy and vital life flow. *Mpungu* denotes knotting, bringing together, and thus the notion of *nzambi* as encompassing entity or force which unites and interconnects. In 1996 I carried out research in another church or healing community, a local branch of the *Dibundu dia Kongo* (DKK), the "Community of Kongo," also known as *Nzambi Mpungu*, the "ancestral God." The community of Dibundu dia Kongo is closely knit. Most members live together within a large villagelike compound,

referred to as *Mbanza Kongo*, the "City of Kongo," in which daily life is organized around the figure of a living prophet, present in their midst. As with Kungu (Kongo) Pemba the reference is a precolonial ancestral homeland, Kongo, and the church's ideology is distinctly opposed to everything that enters within the realm of the *mundele*, the "white," a term that includes not only the former colonizers, the present white expatriates, but also the representatives of the postcolonial (post)Mobutist State. As an island of (passive) resistance and indiscipline against these agents of modernity, the perceived ideology of a cultural colonialism, the closely knit community of the Dibundu dia Kongo tends to seclude itself totally from the outside world.[76] In a certain way, the community of Dibundu dia Kongo forms the perfect representation of what anthropologist Mary Douglas called the "hermit's choice," which implies a breach, a "voluntary withdrawal from society."[77] It is a breach which also neutralizes its political and revolutionary potential as a possible road towards self empowerment. In its daily practice, not unlike other religious movements such as that of Tata Ghonda's, the community functions as a time machine. It re-creates a time/space that propels one back into time, adopts the raffia dress of the ancestors, bans all kitchen utensils and foodstuffs that were introduced during colonial rule, and even prohibits the use of metal nails and other foreign items and tokens of modernity, such as soap, bottled beer, and wristwatches.

In sharp contrast to religious movements of this nature stand other church communities (certainly within the Pentecostal sphere of influence, groups such as "Full Gospel") that have opted for a radical break with the past. Contrary to the Dibundu dia Kongo, they offer their members the promise of partaking in a modernist dynamics *en route* to insertion into a globalized "modern" ecumene.[78] The underlying program here does not put the stress so much on the creation of a certain spiritual communalism, but on postnostalgic, individual self actualization through an active emancipatory process of self construction in which, to achieve fulfilment, one has to free oneself from past dependencies. As Giddens argues, modernity's moral thread of self actualization is one of *authenticity* (although not in the sense postulated by the Dibundu dia Kongo or, for that matter, the troubled trajectory of Mobutist nationalism). To be able to act "authentically" in the modernist sense means disentangling the true self from the false:

> As individuals we are not able to "make history" but if we ignore our inner experience, we are condemned to repeat it, prisoners of traits which are inauthentic because they emanate from feelings and past situations imposed on us by others (especially in early childhood).
>
> [Giddens, 1991:79]

Both the spiritual communalism of the Dibundu dia Kongo and the individualism Pentecostal groups evolve around the idea of breach. In the first case it is manifested as a break away from colonial and postcolonial frames of reference to return to the "authenticity" of the ancestors; in the second instance there is a rupture with precolonial and colonial worlds which are viewed as traditionalizing, backwards, and hence inauthentic and marginalizing, in an attempt to insert oneself *as individual* into the emancipatory evolutionist scheme of a globalizing project of modernity. Both thus adopt the same strategy, that of breach and a denial of the present, to escape the contradictions and the disjunctures of the postcolonial experience. Although both trajectories opt for different exits, I would argue, however, that they remain equally trapped in the catch-22 between communitarianism and modernity. The official Mobutist state ideology of Recourse to Authenticity, as a politicized version of the communitarianist position, that is to say, as a form of political retraditionalization and "Africanization," was embedded in a nationalist discourse which put forth the idea of a nation as an "imagined community" against colonialism. Hence it embodied a nationalist project, rooted in the (reinvented) past but geared towards the future (think of Mobutu's *Objectif 80*).[79] However, the "authenticity" option put forth by the Dibundu dia Kongo members excludes this link: for them the future is the past, that which lies before the grave of the (post)-colony. Hence the reappropriation by the members of this community of the figure of Lumumba, upon whose (absent) grave the Congo-Zairean postcolony was indeed constructed and continues to be constructed, especially after the murder of Laurent Kabila, day for day forty years after Lumumba's own violent death. Recently, the government erected a huge statue of Lumumba at Limete's *Echangeur*. The statue itself is a strange palimpsestual representation of a Lumumba who wears Mobutu's spectacles and has Kabila's waistline. The Dibundu dia Kongo, on the other hand, has turned a "bad death" into a "good death," by transforming Lumumba, the *évolué*, into a model ancestor, a super Kungu Pemba. The representations of Lumumba as Christ by Tshibumba and other painters are well known.[80] Lumumba-Christ, as redeemer of a Congolese modernity (which, as Bogumil Jewsiewicki notes, was confiscated twice, by the Whites during colonization, and by the Mobutist bourgeoisie afterwards), did not deliver his promise.[81] But Lumumba as Ancestor, and thus as spokesperson of *Nzambi Mpungu*, the Ancestral God, redeems the present (which in the Dibundu dia Kongo is constructed as ancestral past), the present/past, from the present as future, the present geared towards modernity.

Not surprisingly, however, the daily praxis of the Dibundu dia Kongo, as a performance of the idea of an unconditional return to the past, is continuously fraught with contradictions from the postcolonial "beyond the grave," and beleaguered by invading practices and representations deriving from the global postcolonial universe from which the community is trying to turn away. Apart from the obvious contradictions between the traditionalist discourse of the Dibundu dia Kongo and its nationalist references, Lumumba, Mulele and the (still living) Gizenga are not only reappropriated as model ancestors, but also turned into some kind of Holy Trinity. This does not only reflect a Roman Catholic, and thus "white" colonial influence in a community that constructs itself as "pre-white" (hence the criticism from even more radical groups such as GRESLAF who reproach the Dibundu dia Kongo for embracing Christianity), but also illustrates a process that is, as the story of Dr. Fontaine illustrated, typical of the elusive, shapeshifting postcolonial reality itself, namely that of the transfiguration of politics.[82]

In Zaire, as in the new Congo today, the ongoing transfiguration of politics was noticeable everywhere. It is a well-documented fact that Mobutu, from the early 1970s onwards, constructed around his person a religious cult which brought him in direct conflict with the Catholic Church. This cult is perhaps best exemplified by the famous clip on the Zairean State Television (OZRT) showing a Mobutu descending from heaven, aureole and all. More recently, the transfiguration of politics was best exemplified by two spectacular conversions from politician to prophet: the conversion of Dominique Sakombi Inongo, *éminence grise* of the Mobutist regime (who, combining the two professions, refashioned himself afterwards as one of the strongmen of the government of Laurent Kabila), and that of another politician, the *farceur du Seigneur* Bofossa.[83] Similarly, Tshisekedi, legendary leader of the opposition party UDPS (*L'Union pour la Démocratie et le Progrès Social*) or Monseigneur Monsengwo, the Archbishop of Kisangani, both of whom played a leading political role in the transition to multipartyism in the early 1990s, were alternatively addressed as Moses and/or Judas. In the same way Mobutu was referred to as "Noah" during the period after the 1991 lootings in Kinshasa, when he retreated to the *Kamanyola*, his cruiser on the Congo river. And when Joseph Kabila came into power after his father's assassination, Kinshasa's *Radio Trottoir* was quick to give these events a prophetic interpretation. Echoing many others in Kinshasa's streets, this is the view of Mr. Mapasa, a militant of a political party:

> All of this was predicted by the prophet Simon Kimbangu. He had foretold that the first president [Lumumba] would be loved. He was a gift of God to the Congolese people. The first leader will be wise and honest. He is a Christian. But he will be killed, he will not last long. His premature death is a punishment. The second leader [Mobutu] will be an Antichrist, a murderer. His reign will be long. All the wealth of the country will be stolen. He will make a pact with Satan and the forces of the occult. The soil of Congo will be stained with blood. This second leader is a punishment of God, a sanction for all the killing. His reign will be one of abomination, occultism and ignorance of God. But the people will fight back. They will repent and awaken spiritually. Churches will multiply. The third leader will die a horrible death.
> Seeing all this God will listen to the people and pardon them. He will send a third leader [Laurent Kabila], a leader close to the people, a leader close to our suffering. This leader will defend the national interests. He will revalue the people and return the power to them [a reference to the short-lived CPP, the 'committees of popular power' which Kabila installed in every neighborhood]. This leader will be assassinated. This will provoke God's anger in the same

> way he was angered when his first envoy [Lumumba] was killed. This is why the country was hit so hard with hunger, death, exploitation, war and shortages of all kinds. But the prophet Simon Kimbangu foretold that the country will heal with the fourth leader. This leader [Joseph Kabila] carries our hope. Like the second leader his reign too will be long but he will have the support of the people.
>
> [Kinshasa May 2001][84]

The Bible, as symbol of a *recommencement*, is continuously used in an attempt to change history, impose a new past and thereby remake a memory that replaces the previous one. "History itself," writes Mbembe, "becomes 'hope of history'. Henceforth, each death or defeat leads to a new appearance, is perceived as confirmation, gage, and relaunch of an ongoing promise, a 'not yet,' a 'what is coming,' which—always—separates hope from utopia."[85] Not surprising, therefore, is the fact that Laurent Kabila was addressed by many in Zaire as "Joshua." Like the other prophetic books, the Book of Joshua does not in the first place focus on the political history of ancient Israel, but provides a prophetic vision of that history. Paradoxically, however, each conversion makes history itself more elusive. The transfiguration of politics initiates a process that further attests to the explosion of a homogeneous, linear, "objective" history into a nebulous dust cloud of histories in which recent political history is immediately captured and transformed in and through biblical prophetic history, ancestral mysticism and fragments of individual life histories, as in Pap'emma's paintings.

The Dibundu dia Kongo's reference to a pure ancestral past is also fraught with other contradictions. For example, the church fills the ancestral time/space with images and references to the Caribbean Rastafarian movement, itself derived from early Black Zionism, which emphasized the meaning of the diasporic experience in African-American religious thought. Rastafarianism became generally known in Congo by way of the utterly globalized figure of Bob Marley, who is referred to by the Dibundu dia Kongo members as "the Higher Man." Similarly, the stress on living the ancestors' way translates into practice with the rule that within the community's compound people may not wear shoes, money or watches, a prohibition that one also encounters in other healing churches and which is actually inspired by a biblical reference (Exodus 3:5). In this way, one is continuously confronted with the paradox inherent in the community's attempt at mimetic reproduction of an "authentic ancestral" history which they have never, however, lived and which therefore has to be made and invented. Theirs is thus a synthetic nostalgia that denies and/or ignores its own syncretism and therefore remains a chimera, a fiction, a "hermit's choice" in which only a few can find refuge.

The option adopted by prayer movements such as Full Gospel (and other groups of the Pentecostal or charismatic renewal tendency) is fraught with the same contradictions. Here the mimetism is focused not on the precolonial but on a certain vision of modernity, a transnational world in which one can make abstraction of one's own local roots in order to become a world citizen, united with other world citizens by a shared faith in the Lord. Here the time machine does not take one back into time, but, rather, propels one forward in time, and at the same time away in space. The frame of reference is the imagined worlds of Brussels, Paris and New York. As such it translates the possibilities of the happy few, a rich urban elite, into the aspirations of an emerging lower middle class which sees its future to be in the elsewhere of the West's present, but for which these worlds remain largely inaccessible and out of reach, except in the imagination and through prayer, in which the notions of "heaven" (*lola*, the word used in the diasporic movement to refer to Belgium) and the West coincide. The individualism promoted here is thus directed towards a new idea of communalism, an insertion into an imagined global ecumene of high modernity which from an economic and political point of view, however, remains closed to the immediate experience of most. At the same time, the individualist aspirations in these prayer movements are contradicted by the social context which brackets them. The social reality in which these movements evolve does not allow for the kind of mercantile individualism promoted (as the link commonly made in Congo and elsewhere in Africa between successful entrepreneurship and the idiom of witchcraft testifies). Even more, these movements in and of themselves re-create older forms of communalism, defining, for example, the relationships between church members in terms of the vocabulary of kinship, as "brothers and sisters in Christ," a vocabulary that gives form to the members' social relations amongst themselves in the well-established terms of solidarity and reciprocity, thereby reintroducing the kinds of social pressures and exclusionist communitarianisms one is trying to escape from in the first place.

Other churches position themselves less radically in between the two exclusionist positions of the retreat into the past or the flight forward, two positions that share the same denial of the present. Many of these independent churches have been heralded for their capacity to bridge precolonial and colonial universes, and provide a religious synthesis between old and new, as well as a counterhegemonic model of resistance against colonial intrusion, the modern state and/or capitalist consumerism.[86] It seems to me, however, that in reality a synthesis is rarely reached. Instead, the syncretism encountered often offers a staggering reflection of fragmentation and disjuncture rather than a solution to these manifold ruptures. As in the two extremes, these churches are not capable of overcoming mimesis (reflecting as they do the actual social reality that brackets the churches' rituals rather than, as in our two previous examples, the mimesis through displacement of an absent model in the past or the future, in a precolonial space, or in the space of the West). Social memory is here presented in a palimpsestual overdrive in which one is confronted with an entanglement of layers upon layers of (pre)colonial memories and meanings, of hegemonic and counterhegemonic practices, contesting and conforming discourses, politics and antipolitics, change and continuity, up to a point where the social memory which is generated and which itself generates social and ritual practice, borders on meaninglessness. Meaning often becomes too diffuse, entangled, and saturated to be grasped fully, and whatever sense or meaning is generated gets lost and disseminated in the tumultuous, unfiltered noise of counter interpretations and of a multiplicity of plot lines that do not necessarily lead somewhere. What many of these healing churches illustrate is the collective struggle, but in the end, also, the incapacity of a late postcolonial society to break through the perpetuation of colonial violence. As Taussig has pointed out, this violence lay precisely in the organization of mimesis by means of a politics that disciplined and domesticated persons, space and, most importantly, time along the lines of western models.[87] In such churches, members fail mentally and practically to "imagine" and "remember," author and thereby "find" and institute society anew.

MEMORY, MEDICINE AND THE BODY

In recent years the social sciences have witnessed the implosion of the notion of history. Some have even declared the "end of history" (sometimes together with the end of the nation state) and "the future of the past." Anthropology's current fascination, even obsession, with memory and processes of remembering (and forgetting), topics which had barely been touched upon since Maurice Halbwachs, has mainly been aimed at producing alternative ways of taking the historical into account: memory as moral knowledge, as strategy to cope with the traumatic experiences of the past, as a local form of historical interpretation, as a form to deal with ancestors and with death, or as a way to shape attitudes toward power and contemporary public spaces. While some view memories of the past as providing a crucial discursive terrain for reconsolidating selfhood and identity, others have put the stress on "an *embodied* discourse of memory and forgetting which (respectively) asserts and denies social perdurance and cohesion," forming "the inscription and counterinscription of habitual practice in further practice."[88]

According to some, the contemporary focus on the body in the social sciences has emerged as a major manifestation of a crisis in the intellectual politics and epistemology of western thought, caused by, amongst other things, the erosion of historic forms of sociopolitical organization.[89] In this vein, Lambek and Antze, in *Tense Past. Cultural Essays in Trauma and Memory*, argue that the breaking up of familiar social weaves and worlds increasingly puts the burden upon the individual body to serve as the only remaining site of memory. As they point out, "medical discourse has reinforced and reified this state of affairs, individualizing memory, physiologizing it, and rendering it the province of a narrow body of experts."[90] Within Congo, however, access to biomedical healthcare has become problematic for most. Moreover, as master narrative for the etiological interpretation of and solution to physical (and by extension social) dysfunctioning, biomedicine, that powerful icon of modernity, has itself fallen victim to the deep crisis that characterizes Congolese society. Not only is the biomedical healthcare structure nonexistent in large parts of the country but the relationship between healthcare seekers and the healthcare services available has increasingly been marked by a basic distrust in recent years. People only go to hospitals to die, not to get better. The inaccessibility of hospitals and doctors, the pauperization and dilapidation of the public healthcare infrastructure that goes hand in hand with the privatization of healthcare in poorly equipped polyclinics which only a minority can afford, the lack of professionalism in the staggering number of pharmacies run by people without any medical or pharmaceutical training (the number of pharmacies in Kinshasa surpasses by far the number of bakeries, for example, and is only equaled by the number of churches)—all of these factors account for the dwindling prestige of the public hospitals and biomedical treatment as such. The imminent death of medicine is sometimes combined with a growing suspicion against biomedical praxis as hegemonic producer of death rather than of life. In September 1996, for example, a polio vaccination program in Kinshasa and neighboring provinces was boycotted by the population in many places, after rumors spread that blood samples would be taken, presumably to be sent to Switzerland or Nice to cure the ailing Mobutu with the blood of "his" children. Such anecdotes betray a fundamental distrust of the official medical healthcare services, which are often perceived as instruments used by the authorities against the population (in exactly the same way as many of the stories on the origin of Ebola traced the epidemic back to the State, the hospital and the mission).

Given the persistent crisis of biomedicine, as one of modernity's master texts to narrate and construct the body and thereby physiologize memory, what people are left with is their own individual bodies, as well as their own local practices, attitudes and discourses therapeutically or otherwise centering on the body and on body related individual and collective experiences of illness and misfortune. However, whereas ritual therapists and diviners are commonly and traditionally seen as those who restore relationships and heal the body by reinserting it in new generative relationships with the social body and the cosmos or the natural environment, thereby enacting and engaging in a praxis of "world-making," many of these local practices of healing and making whole, certainly in the urban context, have themselves been eroded and ruptured.

The symbolic regenerative sense of therapeutic ritual healing is often expressed in metaphors of "hatching out" or of "giving birth." This is perhaps most outspoken in relation to longstanding (precolonial) divinatory practices that continue to exist in Kinshasa's shantytowns as well as in the countryside. Such practices continue despite the growing competition of the many independent healing churches. Central African divination practice relates the diviner to his own ancestors, and through them to the source of life flow, which in the Central African context is often considered to be matrilineal. At the onset of the divination session, Luunda and Chokwe diviners, for example, shake their rattle "to awaken the world" while uttering an elaborate cosmogonic speech, known as "the greeting of the *ngoomb*" (Luunda: *kukoombidil ngoomb*) (the divination "spirit," object of an elaborate ritual cult, the knowledge of which is handed down within specific lineages who "own" *ngoomb*, usually from mother's brother to sister's son). In many respects this long speech mirrors the traditional political titleholders' ritualized enumeration of the royal genealogy in front of their ancestral shrines, but rather than referring to specific historical (political) events, the diviner's ritualized opening speech is situated to a much greater extent in a "euchronic" time, as a form of demiurgical birthgiving. In this sense, the act of divination does not recall a linear history of past battles and genealogies, but evokes the awakening of a regenerative flow, related in a rich and highly metaphoric language, performatively cast in strongly sensory and corporeal terms of copulation and orgasm. In fact, the Chokwe or Luunda diviner is to the divination basket as a husband to his wife; he passes the basket between his legs (Luunda: *kusilweesh ngoomb*) as if it were a female body and womb, to render it pregnant with meaning. The accompanying sound of the rattle awakens and rhythms the spasms of life transmission and life flow that are generated in this sexual communion, in tune with the cyclical rhythms of the world. Divining reminds the audience how much the uterine flow of life is a maturational process that escapes full agnatic and patriarchal dominion: life's inner and passionate impetus from the uterine life source vitalizes the social tissue that extends through the successive generations of uterine filiation.[91]

In this way divinatory and therapeutic praxis constitutes a culture's long-term memory.[92] Divination conjures up the ideologically important vision of the unchanging continuity of the cultural order in the natural and the social world (its divisions of labor, its gender relations, its intergenerational relations), against which the transformations of society, as it is lived in everyday life, may be measured. Although such longstanding, deeply-rooted, culturally and symbolically extremely rich divinatory practices continue to exist, they have become more marginal today. They are often supplanted by newer, much more hybrid forms of divination that seem to reflect (but not necessarily to heal) much better the sense of a changing, far less homogeneous order of the world in which the frames of reference of taken-for-granted habituses and memory environments are rapidly dissolving. Established etiological and causal frames of explanation no longer apply, for example, because witchcraft is increasingly disconnected from kinship. This struck me most strongly for the first time in 1991 when a group of young witch hunters (*ampeve*), who had left Kinshasa earlier that year to perform their witchfinding skills in the rural hinterland, descended upon a number of villages in a remote area of southwestern Congo in which I was then working. They started to point out witches, initially by making use of a divination technique that borrowed substantially from the more established divinatory traditions known throughout southwestern Congo. At the same time they were bringing in other frames of reference and discrepant voices and texts. They were strongly influenced, for example, by the vocabularies of trance and other practices as performed in the context of independent healing churches such as *Mpeve ya nlongo* (the Church of the Holy Spirit) which were on the rise in Kinshasa at that time, and which in themselves were already thoroughly marked by syncretism. The *ampeve* thus introduced a ritual setting full of dislocated images, which juxtaposed common divinatory elements, such as a mirror, with elements from a Christian tradition. For example, they replaced the diviner's ancestral tree shrine, with its symbolism of rootedness and belonging, by two sand sculptures representing Christ's bleeding heart and a giant vagina which simultaneously represented the grave not of a known ancestor but of the unknown "global dead." As such, the reinvented ritual space of divination recycled the notion of "birthing" but opened it up to different registers from external worlds. Thus, not only was this birthgiving practice disconnected from the familiar, ancestral dead and universalized through the figure of Christ, it was also disconnected from a place which makes the dead so that the living can exist elsewhere. As with older forms of divination such as the Chokwe basket divination common in that area, the *ampeve* started by calling upon the ancestors to "awaken the world." Unlike established forms of divination, however, where the diviner conjures up his own (matrilineal) ancestors, and through them the *ngoomb* divination spirit which is localized within and "owned" by the diviner's own matrilineage, the dead called upon in this instance were utterly deterritorialized, and belonged to more external, but very fragmented global "urban" worlds. In standard forms of divination, the elaborate traditional cosmogonic opening speech, uttered in a highly metaphoric, archaic and esoteric language, positions clients in an encompassing and social and cosmological environment, in unison with the rhythms of the world, with an ancestral beginning, and with a long, shared, sociocultural history. All that was replaced by short, broken sentences, spoken in a mixture of French and Lingala, full of disorderly and disconnected references. It was as if contact with the spirit world was made by randomly plugging into the distorted voices and fragmented dialogues of a radio telephone conversation or the transmissions of a short wave radio (imitated by the *ampeve* by means of short whistling sounds in between sentences):

> Hallo! Hallo! Mother, open up this cemetery, open me up in this cemetery. Hallo, mother Elisabeth, always, serve me, power, power, power. Behind the body, I haven't killed you for a reason, show me a person, lead me to him, other persons will pass you by. Hallo, Doctor Salomon. Hallo Madame Naminiata. Hallo Big Witch. Hallo Big Witch of the World. Hallo Big Mower. Open me up in your mirror. Hallo Moscow. Hallo Mister News. Hallo India. Hallo Paris. I am Master Benam, at your service. Hallo City. Nzofu [name of the village in which this event occurred], Hallo Nzofu City. Hallo White House.

In this instance, the dead called upon were no longer situated in a symbolic place that allowed for the living to create in the present their own place to be filled. By "opening up" the global dead in the diviner's mirror, the qualities of the mirroring itself between the living and the dead seemed to have changed. Here, divination no longer posited death, and therefore life, but, rather, unleashed the dead, and death itself as displaced, haunting presence, onto the living. Rather than being born out of death, in a movement of recycling that establishes intergenerational links between the ancestors and the living, one was being born into death, thrown into the world, the site of the living which is increasingly penetrated by and shared with the dead.

BODIES IN DANGER:
VIOLENCE, REMEMBERING AND DISMEMBERMENT

On the one hand then, postcolonial subjects in Congo seem to be cut off from biomedical texts and their potential to order memory by physiologizing it. On the other, they are increasingly disconnected from traditionally available discourses and practices of "memory" as produced, for example, in divinatory ritual, because of the palimpsestual reinscription and fragmentation of its original content, which dispossesses divination from its ancestral sources while breaking open the alien graves of a global cemetery. Robbed of the possibility of using these two available modes of inscriptive memory, people are therefore left with their own bodies as *locales* of culture (re)production and (political) power, and as sites of remembering and generating meaning.

Throughout Congo, local notions of health, life, fertility and well-being are commonly expressed by metaphors of tying, integrating physical, social and cosmological levels. Among the Luunda of southwestern Congo, for example, the body's knuckles and knee joints may be referred to by means of the term *munuung* (*kunuung*: to join, *kunuungin*: to connect, *kunuungijaan*: to be tied together). They form the "knots" or liaisons that connect the limbs to one another and make the body a whole (*munuung* is also the name of a tree, the substance of which is used to treat bone fractures). However, the metaphors of knotting, linking and tying are much more encompassing. The verb which denotes one's "being with strength" or "being in good health" (*kukasakan*) is formed from the stem *-kas*, "to tie" or "to bind." One's health and wealth-being, that is, one's "being well tied," not only bounds, defines and sets off one's individual corporeal health (*kukiindjik*: to block, to close, to be healthy) but also largely depends on one's being "tied" or knotted into the overall social and cosmological make-up of one's world. A sorcerer's attack makes one ill because it disrupts the interconnectedness and "ties one with cords or knots" into a disintegrative and negative bond that counters and undoes or unties the vital integration between the corporeal, social and cosmological fields. Being in good health is thus conceived as being "whole," in the sense of being knotted into this vital triple consonance. The Luunda verb *kusaanzuk* conveys this idea: it means to be whole as well as "to be in good health." The verb *kusaansumook*, on the other hand, is used with the double meaning of "being ill" or "being disrupted or fragmented" (derived from the verb *kusaans*: to cut up meat in little pieces). Similarly, one's own moral well-being is conceived of in terms of being "well connected." The Luunda use, for example, the verb *kwizaaz*, "to be at loose ends," to denote a state of being upset, uncomfortable or agitated. But these metaphors of tying, connecting and joining not only refer to individual physical health; the same metaphors are also used to refer, for example, to the continuation of the descent group, the joining and tying of male and female, or agnatic and uterine elements that enable the intergenerational transmission of vital life flow and the continuation and perpetuation of the community (the verb *kunuung* is used in this double sense of "to join" and "to continue"—for example, to denote the continuation, the "tying ahead" of the descent group [*kunuung kulutw*]).

What the above illustrates is that autochthonous notions of health and well-being start from and return to the body as main nexus of an integrative social and cosmological interweave. However, the body of the postcolonial subject seems itself to be in crisis. First of all, the long and spectacular break-up of the Zairean state, combined with the spillover from conflicts along its borders, most notably in Rwanda and Angola, opened up the spaces of violence even further, and contributed to the banalization of the material and symbolic usages of violence invented in earlier periods of the (post)colonial state. In the process of this swelling production of violence, bodies have increasingly become entities to be disrupted and dismembered. This is obviously the case in a growing economy of violence as produced through the machete and the bayonet. And when, in August

1998, Rwandan and Ugandan backed rebels invaded Kinshasa's streets, this brought the war to the heart of the capital. In the communes of Masina and Ndjili in particular, citizens, spurred on by the governmental nationalist discourse against the Rwandan "cockroaches," started to track down and kill the rebels. The technology of necklacing, which had already emerged a year earlier when Kabila's child soldiers walked into the city and the Kinois vented their anger and frustration at Mobutu's ruinous reign by molesting and burning some of his agents, became an inextricable part of Kinshasa's reality and imaginary.

Violence, of course, had diffused itself through the city's veins long before. Memories of the riots that swept through the capital immediately after independence have faded. More recently, however, in 1991 and 1993 two waves of massive and frenzied looting swept across Kinshasa and large parts of the country, devastating much of the city's economic infrastructure in the span of a couple of days. Around the same period the masked paramilitary death squads commonly known as *hibous* ("owls," because they usually operated after nightfall) became active in Kinshasa.

More generally, the militarization of daily life in Congo is illustrated by the increasing use of the military vocabulary in the church context where preachers such as Soni Kafuta "Rockman" refer to themselves as Generals of (often competing) church communities that are garrisons of God, armies of salvation, launching evangelization crusades.

The alternative space in which Kinshasa performs itself on stage, the popular music scene, has given rise to another kind of violence, grounded in the competition between different orchestras. Inevitably, the chronicle of Congo's music has always been also a social history of this turbulent city. Intimately linked to and rooted in the realities of the lives of the urban young, this music emerged together with the city in the 1940s and '50s. It formed the acoustic canvas of social and political developments, the rhythm of the times in which dance and disorder became increasingly intertwined. Against this social, political and economic backdrop, bands and orchestras emerged and split up, in an endless musical battle for public recognition. The history of the many meanderings and musical realignments of Kinshasa's competing camps and orchestras almost reads like a political anthropology of shifting patterns of schism and continuity, or fusion and fission. These range from the earliest generation of stars like Wendo, Bowane, and Kabasele, to Congo's fourth musical generation which emerged with a group of young musicians around the orchestra Wenge Musica in the late 1980s. In between is situated the rise and fall of Congo's popular music, from the coming of age of Congolese music in the 1960s with the generation of Tabu Ley Rochereau and, above all, the musical giant Franco, to the massive *fuite en avant* of Congolese musicians in the diaspora, mostly to Europe and West Africa. In Kinshasa, the second half of the 1990s was marked by the splintering of the original Wenge Musica into several rival orchestras. The most prominent of these are Wenge Musica *maison mère* and Wenge Musica BCBG, headed respectively by two of the original band's extremely popular lead singers, Werrason (nicknamed *mokonzi ya banyama*, the

King of the Forest) and J.B. Mpiana, also known as *Souverain 1er*, the "First Sovereign." Their music translates a whole imaginary of war, political power and ethnic violence into an embodied youth vocabulary and choreography. In and through dance, the juvenile

body thus appears as a subversive site, as a corporeal locus which reflects, and reflects upon, the violence generated by official cultural and political grammars that have been characterized by some as necropolitical, as the work of death.[93] At the same time, these bands not only express, interpret and symbolize the violence which exists in Congolese society at large, but their immense success, and the increasing starmaking that comes along with it among Kinshasa's youth has in turn given rise to a fanatic and often violent war between the followers of these two stars, especially in the neighborhoods of Bandalungwa, the home commune of both Werrason and J.B. Mpiana.

Kinshasa's youngsters have also been exposed to and familiarized themselves with other forms of violence. Throughout the 1990s, the major source of revenue for a large part of the urban young was the diamond traffic between Kinshasa and the Angolan province of Lunda Norte. Even today, large parts of the city's real estate and (in)formal economy, for example in certain parts of Bandalungwa, Ndjili's *quartier sept* and Masina, or in the residential areas of Salongo and Righini, thrive on money that is being injected into the city through the (mostly informal) *garimpo* diamond economy. As a result of this diamond "rush," many young Kinois spend some time in Angola in pursuit of diamonds. Upon their return many of them display the marks of their passage into Angola grafted onto their bodies: the marks of whiplashes (referred to as *ngonzi, ngondji* or *shingu de purata, kandambards*), bullet wounds, beatings and shell splinters, missing ears, cut off by UNITA (*União Nacional para la Independência Total de Angola*) fighters or MPLA (*Movimento Popular de Libertação de Angola*) troops, or the stumps which remain as a reminder of the limbs that had to be amputated after stepping on a landmine or a booby trap.[94] More often than not, the passage in and out of the Angolan diamond frontier constitutes a harsh initiation into the violent realities of the war zone:

> On May 10, 1993, I left Kinshasa in the company of two friends, heading for the Angolan border, some 1000 kms down south. Lacking money for transport we walked our way to Angola, where we hoped to find diamonds. Some 105 kms before reaching Tembo [a town along the border with Angola], one of us, Gilbert, became suddenly very ill. He couldn't walk any more, or carry the goods we had brought with us. We were in the middle of the bush.

not a village in sight. We built a little shelter and waited for Gilbert
to get better. On the third day, however, at 2 pm, Gilbert died.
We didn't know what to do. With a machete we dug a hole and buried
Gilbert, with his clothes on. At 4.30 pm we left that evil place. Some
15 kms further, we decided to rest. We prayed during most of the night.

[Interview with diamond digger, September 1996]

TAXI CONVERSATIONS III [Kinshasa, May 1998]: In a VW van I boarded at Kintambo Magasin, I overheard the following conversation between two young men. One had returned from Lunda Norte recently and was saying: "A young Congolese guy I knew had taken some cows across the border to sell in Angola. He slaughtered a cow and started selling the meat. His clients, both Congolese and Angolan, came to buy a piece of meat as usual. Since he didn't have a balance, smaller or larger pieces of meat were cut off. Each of these pieces had a fixed price. An Angolan paid for a chunk of meat, but started complaining that his piece was too small for the money he had paid. The Congolese boy added some meat but the Angolan still was not satisfied. After a brief discussion, the Angolan pulled out a knife and plunged it into the boy's abdomen. He died. Outraged, the Congolese bystanders killed the Angolan. Thereupon the other Angolans who were present started to attack the Congolese, who fought back. That day, they say, a hundred and ten people died."

In the summer of 1994, I, together with some 300 other Zaireans, was arrested in the Angolan diamond mining town of Cafunfo, during the time of the "War of Lunda" between UNITA and MPLA. The soldiers took us to the airport, where they made us line up. Among us was a young man of a slightly paler complexion than most of us. His name was Little Biblo. A soldier walked up to Biblo and ordered him to head for a corner of the tarmac, some 50 meters away from us, where many dead bodies were lying. There the soldier took his bayonet and drove it into the stomach of Biblo, who cried out: "*Nasali yo eloko nini?*" [What have I done to you?] The soldier drove the bayonet into Biblo's chest. I remember the latter was crying out: "Mama, I am dying!" The soldier nailed him to the ground with a third stab. Blood was coming out of the chest of Biblo, who was writhing on the ground, voiceless. Then he died. That day, twelve others were killed in the same way.

[Interview with diamond digger, September 1996]

We share our *mutsanga* [the sand hauled up from the river or dug up from an open mining site in order to be sifted] with the soldiers from UNITA. When we find a diamond in our part of the *mutsanga* we have to declare it to UNITA. If you don't and try to hide the diamond UNITA may kill you. They will lash you with a cord until your belly is swollen. Sometimes they whip you up to 200 times. Then they will start hitting you with a spade. I personally was whipped and then sent to "the hole" in the mine of Kanzu, because I tried to hide a diamond. UNITA digs a large hole, some five to ten meters deep.

They cover the top and just leave a small opening so that you can enter the hole. After having confiscated my diamond UNITA threw me in the hole where I stayed for a whole week. Fortunately, my friends brought me some cassava mush from time to time. To do that they had to bribe the *artivistes* [mine police], who then allowed them to throw the food down the hole. There wasn't any water to drink, though, or to wash yourself. There were many other people imprisoned in the hole. Every time some food was thrown down to us, everybody rushed towards it and started to fight. We had to sleep in our own feces. When I was there, two Luba boys died alongside me during that week. You can shout up to the soldiers all you want, but they won't come to help you. Only when someone comes to bring food you can inform them of the dead that are lying there. They then go to inform the friends of the dead person. His friends will have to pay money to the soldiers in order to be allowed to haul up the body. But sometimes the corpses are just left to decompose there together with the other prisoners who are still alive. When I finally came out of the hole I was taken to the home of one of the other members of my *écurie* [literally: "stable": small, and often ad hoc, co-operative units of young men in the frontier context of life in Angola. Usually these young men share the same ethnic or regional background, or have grown up in the same city neighborhood]. I had been beaten very badly, and after a week in the hole my health was very poor. My mates washed my wounds with hot water, and rubbed my body with VICKS [a pomade] until my health returned to me.

[Interview with returning garimpeiro, August 1998]

Kinshasa, December 30, 2003, Agence Congolaise de Presse: Hundreds of Congolese expelled from Angola's mining areas: Since last week hundreds of Congolese have been expelled by the Angolan authorities from the mining zones in the provinces of Lunda Norte and Malange. Sources mention that thousands of Congolese have arrived at the town of Kahungula, in the territory of Kahemba, since Christmas. They live in inhuman and deplorable conditions. Our sources also mention many cases of extortion and rape to which the Congolese were subjected during their expulsion. The only passage for returning to Congo which is authorized by the Angolans is the river Tungila. People were forced to swim across the river, and as a result many drowned. Many cases of death are also reported amongst babies, young children and ill persons. The town authorities of Kahungula fear that the meningitis epidemic which is currently ravaging the mining areas in Angola will also affect its own population [...].

Part of the trauma of the returning youngsters, or "children of Lunda" (*bana Lunda*) as they are commonly known, is due to an incapacity to envisage, or *remember*, meaningful relations that have been dismembered in the experiences of arbitrary violence and the construction of a culture of terror, in which the maiming of bodies aims at the creation of a maimed culture (including crucial frameworks of vital social knowledge) and dysfunctional social institutions.[95]

The individual pathologies of the traumatized returnees also translate into a social pathology. The logic of corporeal dismemberment is also present on the level of the collective imaginary. In the universe of diamond trading between Angola and Congo, for example, it is widely assumed that when one is the victim of misfortune (*mpiaka*), that is, when one does not dig up some diamonds after a certain period of time, one has been cursed or "pursued" by bad luck. In order to lift this curse, one "sells a finger" (Lingala: *koteka misapi*), a tooth (*koteka minu*), an eye (*koteka miso*), or one's vertebral column, by which is meant sperm (Lingala: *koteka mokongo*). Although I have personally met a number of people who had one of their fingers amputated or a tooth pulled out, and therefore have no reason to doubt claims that these practices do "really" occur, it seems to me that their importance does not primarily situate itself on this literal level. These practices and discourses are first and foremost significant on the level of a collective imaginary, desire and discourse which reflects the deeply felt *angst* experienced by the subaltern in a social reality that escapes or crushes him, and no longer seems to make sense. In using a discourse of the senses in which the actual boundaries of individual human bodies are dismembered and severed through symbolic or physical cannibalism or violence, maiming and torture, the *bana Lunda* express their more general experience (all too real in the Angolan and Congolese contexts) of a maimed culture emptied of "sense," and of an agonizing society in which the production and reproduction of social memory and meaningful habitus is jeopardized, and in which they themselves are under a constant threat of dispossession and dislocation of one's self.

The "selling" of one's vertebral column or sperm refers to a specific practice known to all who dig for diamonds in Lunda Norte. In order to assure success in the search for diamonds, one has to spend the night with (sell one's backbone to) an old, postmenopausal woman. Afterwards diamonds will find their way easily to one. The first diamond that is subsequently "captured" is given to the woman by way of compensation. Other informants mention incest between mother and son, or the sacrifice of the lives of one's parents, as successful ways of lifting the curse that prevents one from "capturing" diamonds and dollars:

A friend of mine, by the name of Mundelembongo [literally: "white man's money"], was told by a female sorcerer in Mwana Kafunfu, Angola: "If you want to make a lot of money, you should spend the night with your mother. Afterwards, come back to me and I will give you all the money and diamonds you need." Mundelembongo returned to Congo and explained his problem to his mother, who fled and never returned to her home. Because his mother was no longer available, he returned to Angola, where he sacrificed the life of his child. The child died suddenly in Kikwit, without having been ill.

In return for diamonds, the sorcerer will tell you to sacrifice your mother and father. If you can't do this right away, he will give you dollars and tell you: "Give this money to your father [by accepting it the father will die]. If your father refuses to take the money because he is a sorcerer himself, then buy a loincloth for your mother, that way, we will grab her life easily."

Diamonds and dollars, in other words, take possession of one and, as diamond traders repeatedly state, make one "mad." Diamonds are consequently described as "demons." In a movement of dispossession and disappropriation, they reduce the *mwana Lunda*, dominate and fragment him in the body, and thereby make him abdicate responsibility for his body and his acts, firmly locking him up in the world of the imaginary. Diamonds and dollars have a terrible effect on people: they make a person lose all sense of self-determination; they turn a person into a thief, a cheat and a liar; they "eat" or destroy people, for in return for stones one sacrifices one's manhood (symbolized by the tooth, the eye and the backbone, three key elements in the conceptualization of male personhood); they cause one to become an animal or a sorcerer, both of which are characterized by disruptive, incestuous or cannibalistic behavior. They break down the normal boundaries that characterize the cultural order of life, given form in the relationships between the generations, or between genitor/genitrix and offspring. By sleeping with an old woman who, being menopausal, is structurally not considered to be a woman anymore, or by "eating" one's mother and father (and thus one's own lifesource) or one's own child, the *mwana Lunda*, like a sorcerer, thus inverts the natural flow of the lifestream from ascendants to descendants.

In return for diamonds, one not only sacrifices one's own work power and productivity (finger), one's youth, strength and beauty (tooth) and one's own fertility and sexual prowess (backbone), but diamonds even make one "sell" one's friends (Lingala: *alekisi baninga na ye*) or family members. They totally isolate one and invert the normal ties of solidarity and reciprocity into the destructive internal mechanisms of redistribution by means of witchcraft.

THE LIVING DEAD: THE ZOMBIFICATION
OF THE POSTCOLONIAL "BEYOND THE GRAVE"

Through an attack on the senses, in severing the physical and cultural boundaries of the human body through the violence of extraction, maiming, torture and witchcraft, both the individual and the social body are "dis-membered," thereby occasioning a trauma which shows in the incapacity to forget the dismemberment, or to "re-member" what has been disconnected. First, the trauma is the inability, on an individual level, to "re-member" oneself as an integrated, healthy human being; second, it means the destruction of a habitus, a deeply embodied social identity. The trauma may thus also be seen as a "memory hole,"[96] as the incapacity to remember or reconstruct a social body, or social relations, in a meaningful way, for it is through the combination of subjective and objective, or private and public registers that memory obtains its discursive and performative power.

The production of physical and social dismemberment lies at the heart of crisis, for it inevitably also disrupts the essential social and spatio-temporal relationships between the living and the dead, the "tying ahead between generations" on which societal order depends in the end for its regeneration and the production of its social memory.

Mbembe, when defining the relationship between state and society in the postcolony, points to what he calls the "zombification" of both the dominant and those whom they apparently dominate. Geschiere, on the other hand, in his *The Modernity of Witchcraft*, mentions *Ekong*, a form of Cameroonian witchcraft of new riches, in which the witches do not eat their victims but steal their bodies from the grave, transform them into zombies and put them to work on invisible plantations. In the context of high postcolonialism as provided in Congo, the zombification of social reality reaches even beyond the political and economic realms. It encompasses the sociocultural world in its totality, thereby creating a general atmosphere of connivance, familiarity and interchangeableness between the living and the dead.[97] Dismemberment turns the living into "living dead," while the dead, with disembodiment, increasingly seem to expand their presence into the realm of the living. The living, in short, have become near dead, whereas the dead have become near living.

The theme of the "living dead" is very much alive in the minds and experience of most Kinois. In April 2001 I visited a friend in his homestead near Lemba Terminus, a crowded and seething market square where young *cambistes*, illicit money changers, await their clients. On one of the garden walls in my friend's compound, somebody had painted a black square serving as a blackboard. On it, one of my friend's little nieces, fourteen year old Mimi, had just written out a draft of the essay she had to prepare for school. The topic she had chosen for her essay was the following:

Topic: 'the dead are not dead'

In the history of this world, ever since its creation until today, the life of Man ends with death. Man is alive when he lives, but dead when he no longer lives. However, in analyzing today's topic we will comment upon this fact: the dead are not dead, they are active in the "second world." According to the Bible they are not dead until the Last Judgment. In the next few lines we will elaborate upon this thought. The dead are not dead due to their preceding actions that have made them immortal. As we have illustrated above, a person's acts will never be forgotten. And by connecting this logic to the Bible, we will see that the dead will be judged according to the acts that they posed before their death. These acts never die, in a way. This also illustrates that the dead are not really dead. They are somewhere while waiting for a judgment of their previous acts.

Mimi in person

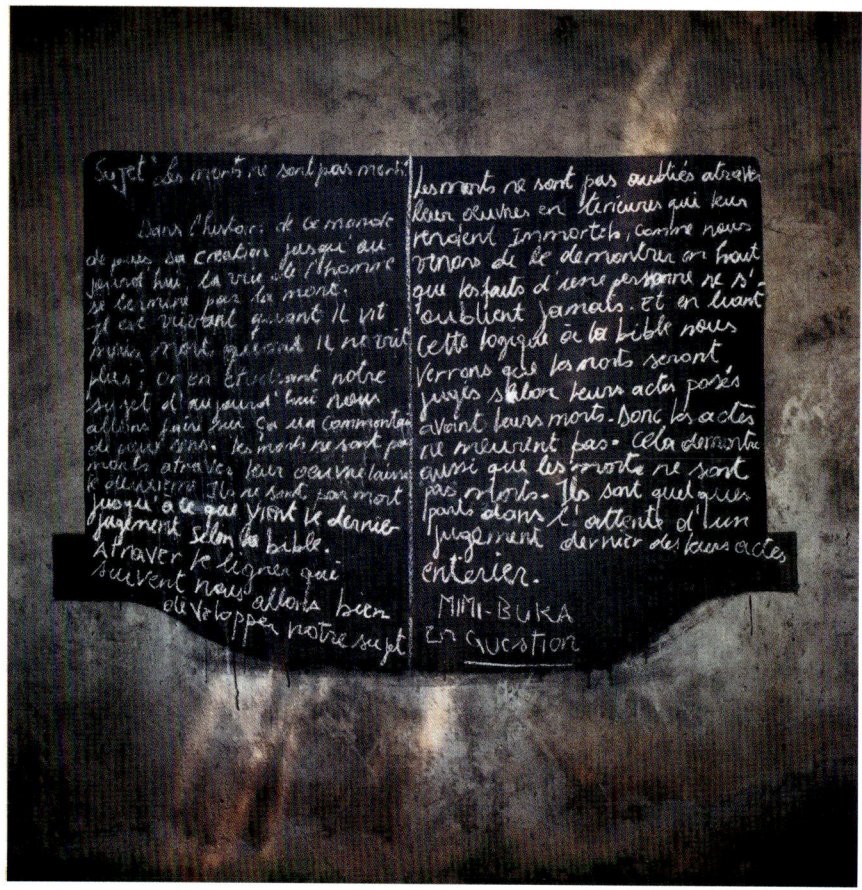

One of the Bible passages Mimi was referring to is John, 5:28–29: "Do not marvel at this; for the hour is coming when all who are in the tombs will hear his voice and come forth, those who have done good, to the resurrection of life, and those who have done evil, to the resurrection of judgment." Similar passages that are frequently quoted include John, 11:11–14, on the resurrection of Lazarus, where Jesus compares death to a deep sleep; Acts, 24:15: "[...] having a hope in God which these themselves accept, that there will be a resurrection of both the just and the unjust"; Isaiah, 26:19: "Thy dead shall live, their bodies shall rise. O dwellers in the dust, awake and sing for joy! For thy dew is a dew of light, and on the land of the shades thou will let it fall"; Daniel, 12:2: "And many of those who sleep in the dust of the earth shall awake, some to everlasting life, and some to shame and everlasting contempt."

The new churches and prayer movements have contributed a great deal to the growing interchangeableness of living and dead by constantly focusing on these messages of resurrection as framed in the specific religious time frame that pervades Congo today. This religious zombification can be witnessed in all the revivalist churches, where accounts of returnees from death abound, as illustrated by the following excerpts from a 1998 interview with Mama Nsasa, a schoolteacher and member of the church CADC (*Communauté de l'Assemblée de Dieu au Congo*). Mama Nsasa tells us how she died and returned to the living:

> In the compound in which I live there are many tenants. One day, everybody had gone off to a prayer campaign. I was home alone. Children were playing outside. Towards the evening I put my chair outside, near the door. The doors and windows of the other tenants' rooms were closed. Nobody was there but me. Then I heard a voice who called me three times: "Don't be afraid. It is me, God, who is calling you. Go inside the house, lock the door, kneel and pray." I did so and prayed for a long time. Then I heard God's voice again: "Don't be afraid. It is me, God. I want to put you to sleep to make you see things. I will take your breath [your life]. Afterwards your body will remain. The living will sing and pray for you. Tell them before not to mourn you, not to bury you, you will return to life. Tell your landlord and the director of your school. Tell them not to search for you if you go missing for two or three days." When I heard His voice who told me about this coming event, my spirit was no longer of this world. My spirit was gone, my voice muted. The next day I went and told the people what had happened to me. Everybody said this was the work of God.
> [...]

Days later, I was anxiously waiting for the event to happen. I gave my watch and my shoes to a woman who leads the prayer group, for these things no longer belonged to me. Then I saw a light. It guided me to the church. It was packed with people and everybody was praying. I saw them pray but I could only hear their voices very vaguely. In which world am I? In which world are they living? I fell asleep on my chair while contemplating this light. Then prayer halted and at that very moment I heard someone call me three times. I replied three times: Jesus, Jesus, Jesus. I fell onto the ground immediately. At that moment I was dead, but my breath was still there, as if I didn't yet have a visa to leave. The preacher and the deacons rushed towards me. They massaged my feet, my arms, my head. They tried to move my body but it had become rigid. I couldn't answer them because my voice had left me. When they asked whether they should pray for me I nodded my head. They prayed, and when they uttered a final "Amen," my breath was interrupted and I was dead.

After a lengthy account of her passage in heaven, where all the "images" [*bilili*, s. *elili*: shadow, but also image, photograph, portrait, symbol, reflection] of all the people of the world are stored, she returns to the world:

From heaven I saw the whole world beneath me. Two days had passed since they had taken me, and my body had become cold, as if somebody had put me in a refrigerator. The people standing around my body touched me and only felt the cold, and the women started to cry and beg God to let me return in the world. They were ready to close the lid of my coffin. Then a preacher who lived in Ngaba [a neighborhood of Kinshasa] arrived on the spot. He was guided by the Spirit. He ordered people to start praying to bring me back to life so that I could bear witness of what I had been shown in heaven. In the evening of the second day, God liberated me and put me back in the world. On my way back I crossed groups of dead people with chains around their arms, their neck and their ankles. They were dressed in black, as in mourning, while they descended to Satan. I was still dead but my voice was freed, I could speak. I started to speak about my voyage and the preacher wrote everything down what I told him. When I finished I was dead again, and the preacher started to pray to God to return me for good to the world. And finally, on the third day, God worked a miracle and resuscitated me. I moved an arm first and then a leg. The preacher said: "Let us pray, for she is returning." When they ended a prayer with "Amen!" my ears were unplugged. And with the second "Amen!" my eyes opened. On the third "Amen!" I stood up. A disgusting odor came out of my body. Everybody fled away and watched me from a distance, but the preacher ordered the women to lead me into

> a nearby house and wash and clothe me. They gave me some water to drink and blessed some food which they gave me also, and which I swallowed with great difficulty. While I was dead the blood and the water in my body hadn't circulated, my intestines had become hard, but slowly I returned to life and started to give witness of God's miracle.

The changed place that death occupies in the experience of many Congolese is embedded in the diffuse time scale of the apocalyptic interlude. As Vero expressed it, not only is death no longer as before, it is no longer the end of the world either. Depending on one's interpretation of the apocalyptic time scale, the Day of Judgment is either about to happen (for example, on the first of January, 2000 or, according to some today, in 2050) or lies already behind us, meaning that the world now lives in the grip of Satan. In the first case, salvation is near for those without sins. Said Bibiche, a 20 year old student, during a conversation:

> There will be a flood. Water will be plentiful, everywhere. And then we'll all die. There will be an eternal night. Those with a clean heart will resuscitate. Those with sins will go down in the water forever. Heaven will fall down upon us, and we won't recognize each other any more. This will be the century of our death. Sinners will die, those who committed adultery, those with AIDS, those who drink, those who dance to worldly music ("the tunes of the country," *banzembo ya mokili*). More than 500,000 men will die, and 3 million women. All those who won't obey the Word will die. Before Christ's Second Coming, wars will be fought everywhere, we will live in hunger and famine, the churches of false prophets will multiply and the witches will encroach upon us. All of these things can already be seen in Congo today.

In the second case, one already lives in this drowned world, in the grip of the forces of Evil (and indeed, Bibiche's description of war, famine, religious fanaticism and witchcraft sounds true enough in the Congolese context). Here, however, hope is not entirely absent either, because one can still be saved in a distant future, when Christ will descend for the second time and rescue those without Satan's stamp: the 666 sign. For many Kinois, who seem to be caught between a vision of a (nearby or distant) New World (*mokili ya sika*) and the constant intrusion of a second world of demons and devils, both time scales seem to coexist simultaneously.

But it is not only in the religious realm that death has acquired new meanings. In daily life, death is distributed in new and often shocking ways — not only through warfare but also through illness:

> Kinshasa, August 23, 2001 (APA): Travelers coming from Bandundu informed us that a "Mwana Lunda," a diamond dealer who is suffering from AIDS but is not otherwise identified, revealed that he slept with 85 women and girls at the Hotel Lendu of Bandundu City when passing through that city the last time. The young man (over forty) bought boxes of dried salted fish which he stocked in his room. The news quickly spread. Women and girls of easy virtue came running to the young diamond dealer in great numbers to offer their "services." When the latter finally moved out of the hotel, he left a list of the addresses of all the women he had slept with behind on his bed. It did not take long for this scandal to be known throughout the whole city. At this point, a staff member of "Doctors Without Borders" remembered that someone who corresponded to the description of the Mwana Lunda visited him to obtain AIDS treatment. Some families have been left with three, even four, victims.

Here, death reveals itself as a different form of violence, and it is embedded into yet another, different order of invisibility. The geography of urban social life emerges through a new cartography of suffering and illness that often remains invisible and only surfaces now and then through the intermediary of the sufferers and the way in which they navigate through the urban space. AIDS, this weapon of mass destruction, draws intersecting but highly invisible, immaterial lines of contact between people. These lines run throughout the city like veins filled with contagious blood. The *mwana Lunda* referred to above is, in a very real sense, a living dead. Death has here become a contaminating illness. The intersecting of these invisible lines of contact determines individual life itineraries and defines the connections between sufferers and the groups of people around them. On this level, the city can be read as a map of entangled biographies and trajectories that inevitably lead to the terminus of the cemetery, where death is finally made visible. It is the cemetery that is connected with all the sites of the city. The cemetery forms the ultimate point of mooring for this urban cartography of invisible death.

The omnipresence of death has also turned it into a model for social and political action. On March 9, 2000, in eastern Congo, the women of the occupied Kivu province declared a four day "mourning" period to protest against the daily realities of violence and poverty in which they had to live, after rebels buried an unknown number of women alive. On the first day the women stayed at home, weeping, lamenting, and refusing to eat. For the next three days they dressed in black, covering their heads, a sign of sorrow. A month later, on the sixth of April, 2000, thousands of kilometers to the west in Kinshasa, Etienne Tshisekedi's UDPS opposition party announced, for the nth time, a "dead city day" (*journée ville morte*) to protest against the continuing warfare in Congo. In this country where, for many years now, political action has been translated in the creation of a "dead city," and where funerals and mourning ceremonies (*matanga*) have become the motor of social and political criticism, Kinshasa has sometimes been described in the local press as a necropolis, a cemetery city (*cité cimetière*), the term playwright Nzey Van Musala has coined for the capital of this "thanatocracy" that Congo has become, a country the citizens of which are more dead than alive, while its cemeteries are overcrowded and corpses are simply abandoned anonymously at the entrance of mortuaries. Not only has death thus become a metaphor used to speak of certain areas of daily life in Kinshasa, but the country in its totality has become a place in which one constantly inhabits two worlds: "that of the dead and that of the not-so-alive [*pas-tout-à-fait-vivants*],"[98] or "a place and a time of *half-death*, or, if one prefers, *half-life*."[99] That is why RDC (*République Démocratique du Congo*) is called, in popular speech, *Rdécès*, the "deceased" or "dead" Republic of Congo, where, people say, *on répare même les cadavres*, "even corpses are repaired." In a sense, one could argue that death is the only tangible kind of "democracy" (some call it "demon-cracy") that has been installed in Congo so far.[100] Papa Nova, a shopkeeper in one of Kin's suburbs, has painted onto the wall of his small pharmacy-shop: "Rich and Poor Equality in Death-Cemetery" (*Riche et pauvre égalité à la mort-cimetière*).

Death has also become embedded in altered structures of solidarity, of kinship and of relations of gerontocracy. This is illustrated by the changing position of the *noko*, the maternal uncle, whose authority has greatly diminished in the urban context, and most notably in matters related to death. Said one informant, during a mourning ceremony in Camp Luka, a popular neighborhood of the commune of Ngaliema:

Today, in the white man's village [the urban *cité*], things have changed. In the village where we come from, the maternal uncle was a chief. If a problem arose in the family, people called on him for advice and guidance. Today, the uncle has lost that status. In the city, the uncle has become a useless thing, considered by many as a sorcerer, especially by all who pray and for whom things traditional are satanic. Before, when we buried a dead body, it was the uncle who addressed the family, and when we returned from the burial place, it was the uncle who "lifted the palm branch" [formally ended the mourning period]. The uncle was the "owner of the dead person," he was the first responsible. Today, the uncles have multiplied. There now are three "uncles." The actual uncle is considered a nuisance. People flee him for fear that he will ask a contribution to the funeral. He no longer addresses the family. Instead the preacher has become the uncle who speaks and directs the mourning ceremony. And the third uncle is *Cataphar* [from *catafalque*, funeral chapel].

> Before, the uncle received funerary gifts from the attendants during the funeral. Now these gifts mainly go to the preacher and to *Cataphar*, for the payment of the location of the draped chapel. The preacher and the funeral chapel have become the new uncles, whereas the real uncle now hides during funerals for fear of being accused of the deceased person's death.
> [Fieldnotes, September 2000]

Once again, the "multiplication of the uncle" in this mortuary context points to the changed place accorded to death itself. Whereas burials and funeral wakes (*matanga*) have always played a tremendously important role in strengthening the social network, they no longer seem to be able to fulfill that role completely. In that respect one can point to the "pillaging of death" in the emergence of a new funerary ritual called Ekobo in Kinshasa's streets in the early 1990s:

> Following the beliefs of certain tribes, Ekobo was originally conceived as a means to preserve and protect persons exposed to the attacks of returning dead from evil, as well as a means to finance the burial payments within the family. Ekobo has become, however, the practice of delinquents who stop innocent people in the street to extort money from them, which they say will be used for buying coffee, sugar and firewood during the funeral wake. [...] In case one refuses to pay up, these youngsters throw dirt at one, or physically harm one.
> [Elima newspaper, 21–22/9/91, *Halte à la pratique illégale et dégradante du rite mortuaire "Ekobo,"* Stop to the illegal and degrading mortuary ritual "Ekobo"][101]

The changed character of funeral rituals is partly due to the fact that, for an increasing number of people, death occurs outside of a kin based network and has therefore lost its capacity for implacement. In a state which is itself adrift and in which many people are on the move, displaced for economic and political reasons, it has become increasingly difficult to posit the dead. The dead have often become anonymous, buried hastily, mourned by few. As Kin-based playwright and novelist Yoka Lye Mudaba remarks in his novella *Le fossoyeur*, "The Gravedigger":

> Our dead from the peripheral zones are real dead. When they are buried, they are forgotten. And when one remembers them, one forgets the location of their graves. Our dead are peripheral, our cemeteries are peripheral, and our salaries are peripheral![102]

During the 1995 Ebola outbreak in Kikwit, funeral ceremonies were already drastically deconstructed from collective events to lonesome burials in which dead corpses were no longer washed by relatives, but put in plastic bags by strangers and dumped in anonymous mass graves. Shocking as this was to most of Kikwit's community, it also paved the way for an increasing banalization of death, the production of brutally gratuitous death, which has continued in other locations since, as we all know from watching the television images coming from eastern Congo.

As Bataille once put it, sacred things are established through a labor of loss.[103] An often heard remark in Congo's cities, however, is that "there aren't enough tears left to mourn all the dead," for they have simply become too numerous. Invaded by an ever increasing number of dead that cannot be put to rest, the society of the living has stopped mourning or remembering them and in the process, death has been desecrated:

ATTEMPT TO BURY A WOMAN IN A USED COFFIN DUG UP IN ONE OF KINSHASA'S CEMETERIES. KINSHASA, 01/10/2002: In the night of December 31, 2001, in Bwanga street 21, Mikondo neighborhood of the commune of Kimbanseke, Kinshasa, a young man, aged 27 and not otherwise identified, brought home a used coffin, which had apparently been unearthed in a local cemetery, in order to bury the body of his wife, who died at the age of 17, after childbirth in Kinshasa's General Hospital. [...] The next morning, according to our informant, the members of the bereaved family were getting ready to go to the morgue to prepare the corpse for burial. Much to their surprise they noticed that the coffin brought along by their in-law was old, broken in several places, and covered with red earth. Inside, the cloth used to embellish the coffin was torn and dirty. Asked to provide an explanation as to the state of the coffin, the widower fled, in an attempt to escape from the wrath of the youth of the Mikondo neighborhood, and the penalty awaiting him for having desecrated a grave. Our sources indicate that the coffin is presently kept at the police station of Jumbo in the Mikondo neighborhood. An official investigation has been started. According to some, this event is linked to a criminal network of youngsters which specializes in unearthing and reselling used coffins. The deceased woman was buried on Sunday, January 6, 2002, in the cemetery of Siforco, located in the commune of Masina, Kinshasa.

[ACP press release, January 10, 2002]

In return, however, much like the troublesome postwar ghosts of Mozambique, Zimbabwe and an increasing number of other places throughout Africa, the desecrated dead have become increasingly restless, and no longer remain silent in their peripheral graves. Numerous rumors relate, for example, how coffins, carried by family members on their way to the cemetery, start to jump and shake uncontrollably, dragging their carriers after them; how a brother, a friend, a husband was buried at home but was later spotted digging diamonds in Angola by friends and acquaintances who informed the family upon their own return from the Angolan *terra morta*. Listening to the rumors and stories of *Radio Trottoir,* or to the witness accounts in churches, one realizes just to what extent the dead are active amongst the living. In sects such as that of Ebale Mbonge, a former Mobutu official and another case of political transfiguration, dead people foretell coming political events through the mouths of mediums. Everywhere, it seems, the dead themselves revive and multiply. At night, they attend concerts to dance to the popular tunes of Kin's orchestras. Places such as *Rond Point Victoire*, the center of Matonge, are said to be so crowded due to the numerous dead who are attracted by Matonge's nightlife. At night, also, road blocks are often manned by soldiers from the second world. Although the deceased sometimes also return to protect and as-

sist the family members they left behind, more frequently their interventions are less benevolent. At best the dead are just annoying. For example, an increasing number of husbands and wives are reported to be visited at night by their deceased partner, who is literally unable to "liberate the apartment for the living." Often, though, the wandering dead try to take those that remained behind with them into the second world which they inhabit and from which they operate. For lack of money, many people are not able to buy a tombstone to put on the grave, which would help to obstruct the return of a deceased family member.

But the living do not leave the dead alone, either. When Mobutu finally fled Congo in May 1997, the periodical *Jeune Afrique*, in a box entitled "Ancestors," reported:

When leaving what was known as Zaire, Mobutu is reported to have exhumed the remains of his ancestors to take with him. What a strange funeral procession in which the dead form the cortege of the living. Imagine the difficulties a normal mortal (if one may use this word) would encounter when passing the Customs with such a load. "Nothing to declare?" "No, sir... uh, yes: my deceased grandfather and grandmother."
[*Jeune Afrique*, issue 1899, May 28 – June 3, 1997]

In the end, in the postcolonial *beyond*, we no longer find *pre* or *post mortem*, no past and no future, no memory and no oblivion, no dead and no living, or rather, only "fake real dead" and "real fake living" (just as the *vrais faux dollars* or *faux vrais passeports* of Congo's informal economy). Locked together because of their incapacity both to remember and to forget, the living and the dead have become trapped at the end of history's cobwebs. Beyond the grave there lies no peace, only the shuffling along of severed souls, dead or alive.

INVISIBLE CITIES II
OMBA SHAKO
THE STORY OF A STREET KID

Omba Shako is a twelve year-old boy who left Kananga to come and live with his mother's brother in the neighborhood of Kimbondo, which is located in the vast commune of Mont Ngafula, on the outskirts of Kinshasa. While still in Kananga, Omba was believed to be bewitched by Mister Tshimanga, a neighbor. Little by little Omba in turn became an important witch, a "boss of bosses" (*patron des patrons*) in the realm of the night. Confronted with the "true" nature of Omba after a couple of incidents following his arrival in Kinshasa, his uncle decided to send him to a charismatic renewal church. In September 1997, during an evangelization campaign, Omba revealed his story to the churchgoers:

One day, when I was still a little boy, I took our red plastic gourd and went down to the source to get water. While I was walking through the village on my way to the river a man called me into his house. This is what he told me: "My child, come over here, I have to tell you some good news." I was eager to hear what good things he wanted to tell me so I followed him. He said: "What are you standing there for at the door? Go inside the house." He gave me a chair, and after I was seated he brought some *fufu* cassava mush and cassava leaves. He told me to eat because he could see that I was very hungry. The food was exquisite, like sugar in one's mouth. The *fufu* was of good quality, and the leaves were prepared with good vegetable oil. I ate everything.

After my meal I continued my way to the river. While I was filling the gourd I could feel my stomach vibrating. This was strange! Why did my stomach vibrate like that? "Maybe it was the *fufu* that I ate at Papa Tshimanga's," I told myself. "What else could it be?" After a while I felt like vomiting, but nothing came out. I hurried back to the village but I didn't tell anyone about this, not even my father or my mother. I kept everything to myself, buried at the bottom of my heart. My father had noticed, though, that I didn't feel well. He asked me why I was sitting down as if I was suffering. I denied that something was wrong.

During the night Papa Tshimanga came. It was already very late. He said: "Omba Shako, I have come to take you with me, let's go to my house. You have eaten my food during the daytime, and now you will eat my food during the night." When we approached his house he repeated once more: "Look, you accepted the *fufu* I gave you during the day, and now you

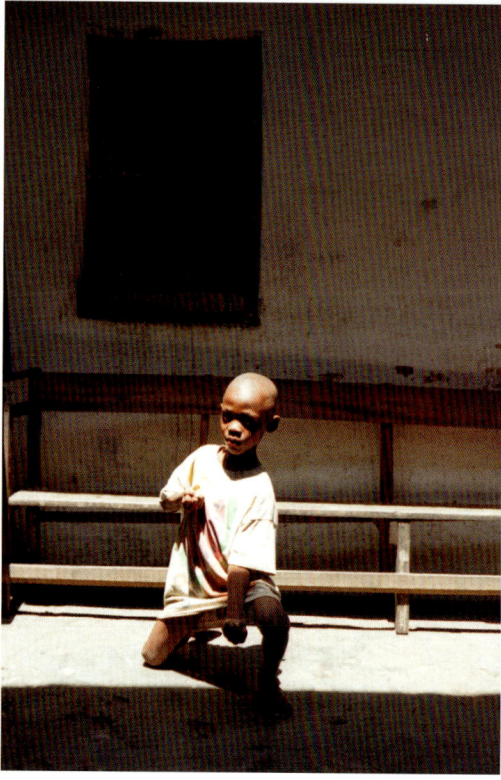

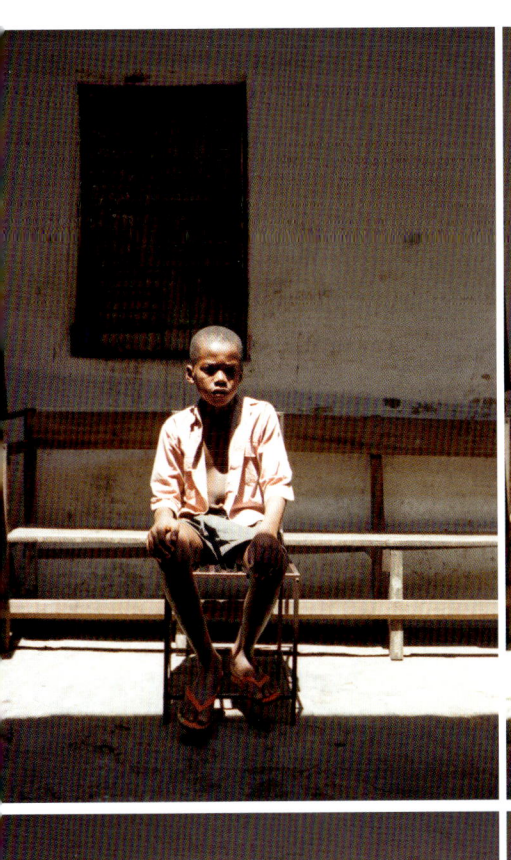
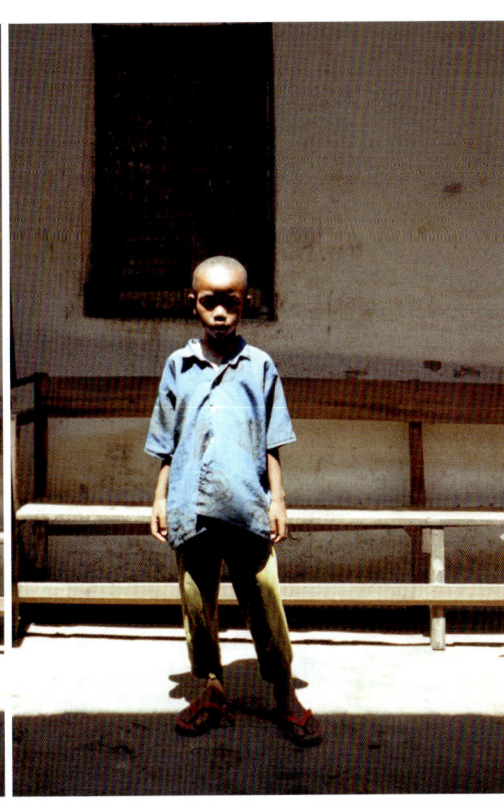
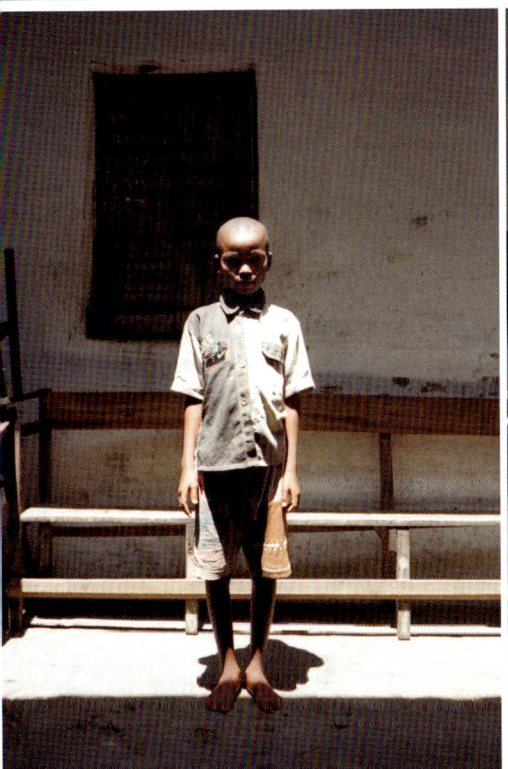

have no choice but to accept my things of the night. This is the situation:
As from now on, you and me will work together every night. Where I will take
you, you will learn to see everything in a very clear way (*pwelele*). You will
understand that the things that I gave you during the day come from the
night. Once we arrive at our workshop you will remain calm. Do not fear
anyone. My friends, the chiefs of the night, will arrive in big numbers,
but do not feel afraid of them, they all have their own work to attend to.
Do you understand me? Let us go then." As soon as he had said that
we were at the cemetery all of a sudden.

I saw a big bonfire burning in the middle of the cemetery. Many people
had gathered around the fire, but we passed it and sat down at a second fire
nearby. Here people were less numerous. There were only three men sitting
there: Papa Chief, who was also the Cook, Papa Butcher, and Papa Killer.
All three addressed me: "Hey, you little child, now that you have come to our
village, you should know that this is a place of leisure. It is a village of 'give-
give' (*donnant-donnant*): 'Give and you will be given to, and when you are
given something, you should give back' (*pesa bapesa yo, bapesi yo, yo mpe
pesa*). You ate from our things during the day, the good things that Papa
Tshimanga gave you. Now you are about to eat our things during the night.
Afterwards you will start paying your debt to us. You will enter our group
of the night. If you consider escaping, know that we will eat you. Do not be
afraid. Sit over there and wait for us while we go to search for today's meat."

I waited as I was told. Other people approached and asked me: "Who are
you? Where do you come from? How did you find out about this nocturnal
village? Who brought you here? Have you already eaten the food of the night
before? Here you will eat like you have never eaten before. In your village
people can't afford to eat meat, but here, really, here we have everything
we need. This is a village of leisure and pleasure. You will eat so much
that you will grow tired eating. But the food will eat you too."

After a long time the three men came back with a huge amount of meat.
It turned out to be a big, fat man. They put the body down. Papa Butcher
started to cut the body into pieces. First he severed the head, then the legs,
then the arms, the stomach and the intestines. He ordered me to go and wash
these in the river. The intestines looked like any animal's. Upon my return
they were all drinking blood. I was given some too. Then they started singing:

When you drink blood, drink the secret too
The one who drinks blood
Also drinks the secret
Over there [in the world of the day] the one who
drinks blood does not have a father
He does not have a mother
He does not have an uncle
Drink the blood, drink the secret
Keep the secret in your heart
Close your heart like a box
Become like the heart of a boa.

We did not have a cooking pot. We did not have a mug. We did not even have a spoon. They cut off the corpse's head and then emptied and pierced the skull. Now we had a cooking pot! They put all the meat inside the skull. Then they started making a spoon from one of the hands and the forearms. One ear was turned into a mug to drink from. The legs, the arms, the head, the ribs: everything became a tool. In the beginning I did not really know how to use these utensils. But I learned quickly.

The whole night we continued eating. I started to think that life in our daytime village was nothing compared to this. Compared to life during the day, when food was scarce and meat was absent, the nocturnal village offered a lot: plenty of meat, *fufu*, plantains, rice...

We finished our meal, and then we got on board an airplane to return to the village of the day. This airplane was made from a small basket. Papa Tshimanga put some drops from a small bottle onto the basket and spoke: "Basket, be light, the airplane of our ancestors." Then he mounted on board. He himself was the pilot. When we got to our village Papa Tshimanga saw me to my house. All of this appeared to me as in a dream. My brothers who share the same bed with me didn't notice my absence. I slipped back into bed before they woke up.

We started going to the nocturnal village at regular intervals. I was told: "Now that you have been given and know many 'things of the night,' you should give us the life of one of your family members. Give us either your father, your mother or your uncle. You can choose yourself, we don't care which one of the three it is."

I reflected upon this for a long time. I did not know what to do. I said to myself: "If I give my father that is bad, and if I give my mother that is bad too, and it would still be bad with any other member of my family. But if I don't give them a person they will kill me instead. I already know too much about their village and their ways of the night. I have already eaten too much of their nocturnal food. What should I do?" I turned this question over and over in my head, and finally I decided to take my uncle's child. His name was Didier. I still thought these things weren't serious and that no real harm would befall Didier. A couple of days later, however, I saw them arrive with Didier's corpse.

I look at Didier.
I look at myself.
Tears are starting to fall from my eyes.

I started crying. When the others saw that I was crying they said: "Look, this is the village of the night. Here one doesn't cry! Here we do not feel sorry for the person that we kill. In the village of the people with two eyes [the diurnal world] you keep your secrets to yourself. Even if we kill your mother or your father you will not denounce us! Even if we kill your child, you will have to keep it a secret from your wife. And if people accuse you of having killed somebody you will have to deny it. A witch never confesses. Even when you feel guilty, never accept the accusations. A witch does not feel any pity for his victims. To him they are just like animals. We eat humans. It tastes better.

Stop! Anti-witch. Fights against witchcraft. Neutralizes witchcraft and fetishes and all problems of bewitchment and illness.

We do not eat pigs, chickens, goats, or sheep. All of that is food for the 'people with two eyes.' But we, we have four eyes. But let us eat first and then we will teach you the knowledge of the night."

When we finished our meal they took me to a tree. The name of this tree was *mbota yikulu*. It was a tree around which people gathered to discuss things. Every witch knows this. When an "airplane" arrives, this is the spot where it will land. The tree is like a runway. An airplane which doesn't land on this tree breaks the rules. The pilot will be judged by the others and will have to pay a fee with either his airplane, money or a human life.

From there we went to another tree that had fallen down. We sat upon its trunk. Papa Opener, the one who opens one's eyes [initiates one into witchcraft], took some herbal medicine and rubbed it into my eyes and onto my neck. Instantly, I started seeing, not only through my old eyes, the eyes that everybody has, but also through a pair of new eyes on my back. I started to see everything in two ways. They told me that from now on I had two pairs of eyes.

We were still sitting on the tree. Then came another Papa Opener, the one who opens the belly in the world of the witches. He took some herbal medicine and rubbed it on my belly and my backbone. He said: "From now on you have two stomachs, one in front and another one on your back. That way, when you eat, you will really be able to eat enough and contain it all."

Papa Tshimanga, who was responsible for having taken me there, called me and said: "Now you have become the King of Kings, the Boss of Bosses: You may eat, you may kill, you may even start to construct your own nocturnal village. Look how beautiful things are in our village of the night! Lots to eat, lots to drink, plenty of meat... When you will return to the village of the day, which we call the village of the animals, you will see and understand everything that goes on there. Nothing will escape your attention. You will also recognize your fellow witches. You will see that they live miserable lives during the day, lives of crisis. But enough for today.
There remain a lot of things that you will have to learn. We will show you how to build an airplane and how to fly it. We will also show you how to build a television, and a radio transmitter. In order for you to access this knowledge, however, you will have to give us the lives of two people. For each piece of information we request the life of a person. But for now, enjoy your meals with us. Visit us regularly. We will teach you how to cut the 'animals' into pieces, how to distribute the meat, how to sell it. You can sell the meat

for money, or you can give it away in return for another person. When you barter with meat, you should always get a whole person in return. If you give away the meat of a doctor or a businessman to another witch, he should repay you with a whole doctor or a businessman. If he is given the meat of a pregnant woman, he will have to reimburse with a whole pregnant woman, not just parts of her. If he is given the meat of a small child, you should receive a child in return. Even if he only takes a finger, he should pay for it with a whole person."

This is a list of things to remember: In the human body, everything has its use:
 — The blood is fuel, diesel, kerosene and red wine.
 — The water that the body contains is motor oil, brake oil, perfume, drinking water, kitchen water, medicine to drink, medicine to rub onto your body.
 — The backbone is a radio, a cell phone, a radio transmitter.
 — The head is a cooking pot, the glass from which a boss drinks, a swimming pool, a bucket which you can use to wash yourself.
 — The eyes are a mirror, a television, a telescope.
 — The hair can be used to make mattresses, or to fill the sofa for the living-room.

Papa Tshimanga also told me: "When you cut the meat into pieces, don't throw anything away. If you throw something away you will have to pay for it later with a human life of the same value as the one from whom you threw a piece away: the head of a family will be paid for by the head of a family. If the person had three children, you will pay for him with someone who was equally father of three children. Another rule: If you give our nocturnal food to someone in the village of the day, you will have to bring that person with you in the night. Finally, don't watch other witches while they are eating. Everybody is free to eat in his own way, in the manner that suits him best."

Let us continue the list of things to remember about the human body:
 — The skin serves many purposes: It can be used to make a *patron*'s blanket, or to cover his sofa. It may also be used to provide the rug upon which the *patron* will sit.
 — The body's slime is like Vicks pomade, or like shoe polish.
 — Sperm is like the grease that one uses to maintain car parts. It can also be used to cure someone who suffers from impotence, or who has broken his back.
 — Other body liquids also have their use. They can be used to put in the radiator of a car or an airplane.

I am an important witch. I am a boss among the witches. I am talented and initiated. I have opened my own village of the night. During the night we eat well. We have lots of money. We feel sorry for the people in the village of the day. We own an airplane that allows us to circulate everywhere in the Republic of Congo. At night we travel to Bandundu, Lower Congo, Mbuji Mayi, Kananga, Mbandaka and other places. I live in Kinshasa but friends from all over the country come to visit me. I also visit them. I also return home, in Kananga, where I work: I go to the market and sell my meat. I also sell human bones. They are used as spare car parts. When your car breaks down you can replace the broken part with a human bone. When I am not working like that I kill "animals" and I eat.

There is one setback though. At night there are a lot of night soldiers around. These are all the soldiers that Mobutu left behind when he died. They don't know what to do for a living. They are angry and do not like it when airplanes other than their own land in Kinshasa at night. They do not want to see other witches sell their meat in the markets of Kinshasa. In Kananga our nocturnal market was outside of town, but here in Kinshasa the market is in the middle of the city, in Camp Tshatshi, the garrison where the soldiers live. The soldiers want to monopolize the market in Camp Tshatshi. At that market all items are very expensive. We are very unhappy about the way in which the prices keep going up. We only hope that the soldiers will eventually flee, since their Boss, Mobutu, is already dead.

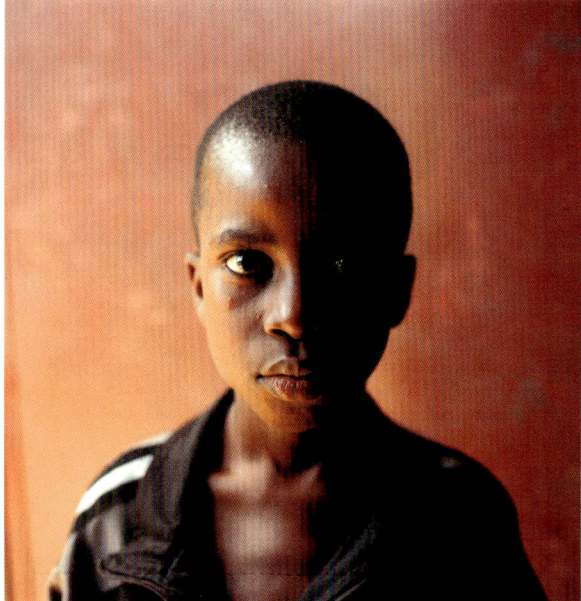

PORTRAITS

I. I am living in the church because I became a witch. We went to the Kalamu river to wash ourselves, and then we became witches, my sister Shako and I, after having eaten a zucchini that my friend Amidi gave to us. That night I saw Amidi in my dream. She asked me for the life of my older sister Godee. My sister died four days later. We ate her.

II. A woman of my neighborhood turned me into a witch. She gave me a *nsafu* fruit to eat. I am in this church together with my little sister. She was initiated in the things of the night not by this woman but by her friend. But this woman visited us often during the night. She took us both along on her nocturnal journeys. We frequently traveled to South Africa at night. We left at midnight and returned by dawn, around 4 am. Our airplane consisted of the shell of a groundnut. This woman wanted the life of my other sister Anto, who was twenty-six years old. She also forced me to eat parts of Anto's body. But it took a long time before we made her die. She suffered for three years. She died in the year 2000. And then my mother had a dream. That dream revealed that we were witches. That is how I was found out. We also created some major problems at my father's work. As a result he was fired. But I was always opposed to the idea of killing him. Our parents were not angry with us but wanted to help us. They brought us to this church in order to be delivered from the powers of darkness. The woman has now stopped following us.

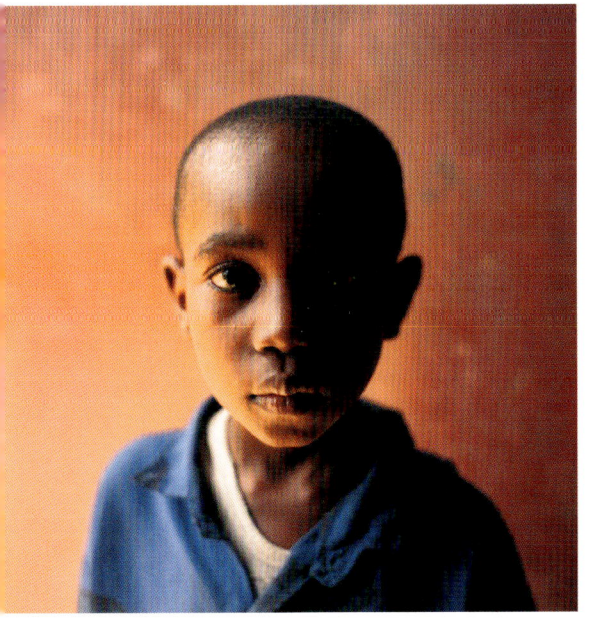

III. I am here because I want to put all things related to witchcraft behind me. People discovered my true nature. My mother had a dream about my brother Jonas. In the dream Jonas was biting her in her legs. In the morning she questioned Jonas about this, and he confessed everything. He also told her that he was not alone, but that he worked together with his sister and his brother during the night. That is why our mother brought us to this church. We are here together. I was initiated by Ya Taty. She wanted the life of one of our other sisters, the one who goes to school. We killed and ate her. We made another sister of ours ill, but later we felt sorry for her and made her better again. Since we are here, the witches have abandoned us. Today our father came to see us. He told us that we could go home next Monday.

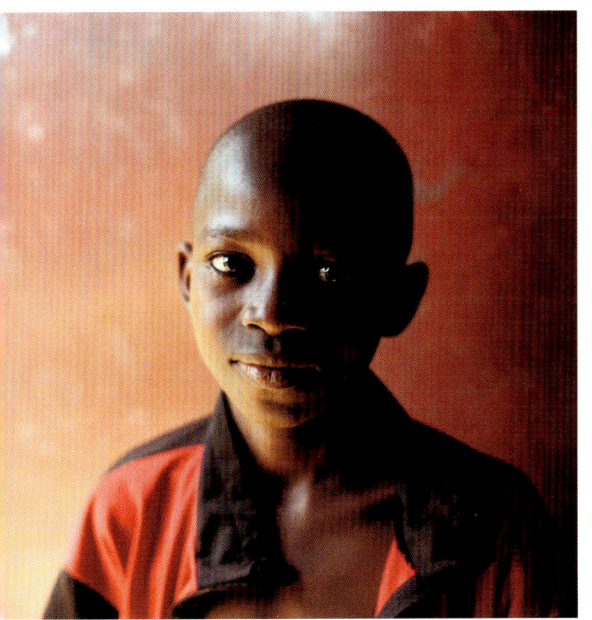

IV. My name is Arnold, I am ten years old. I am here because of my grandmother. She turned me into a witch. Now I am here together with her. She wanted me to kill first my mother and then my father. Before that she wanted my younger brother. I refused. My father used to be a taxi driver. But because of all this, my father lost his job and his house. He doesn't have a place to stay anymore. I personally never ate anyone. I am just staying here until my father finds a new home. Then he will come and take me home. I never recruited someone else to be turned into a witch. My younger brother Claudy, who is seven, is a witch too, but he was contaminated by my grandmother, not by me.

V. My grandmother turned me into a witch. One day I accompanied her to visit one of her friends who was making *chikwanga* [a cassava paste, wrapped in leaves]. She bought me and my brothers one *chikwanga* and we ate it. Starting that day, she asked us to provide her with the lives of people. My mother intervened and brought us to this church. I had told my mother about what was going on. My brothers have spent more time here, I have just arrived. My brothers and I would travel together at night, but we always refused to kill a person, despite my grandmother's insistence. And now we have become good Christians. We are only waiting for our father to pay the preacher so that he will release us and that we can return home. My father owes the preacher a bag of cement for each of us. My brothers and I, we are four here, so that makes four bags of cement.

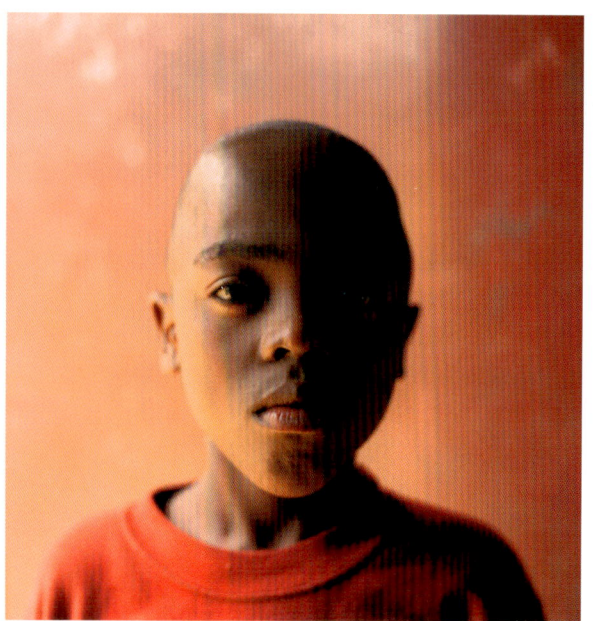

VI. My name is Touckys. I became a witch because of my maternal uncle, my mother's older brother. He gave me some bread. He lived with us, but when it was found out my family chased him away. He turned me into a witch when I was eight years old. My eyes were opened to see in the night when I was nine. I am thirteen years old now. My older brother was also in the second world. He and I would meet regularly during nocturnal gatherings. We would set the date to kill and eat a person. My brother started killing people before I did. Since I became a witch I have only eaten one person, a girl. She wasn't a relative of ours. In the second world I am married. My wife's name is Helena. She only exists during the night. Together we have two children, a boy and a girl. I arrived here five days ago. Everybody at home is praying for my sake.

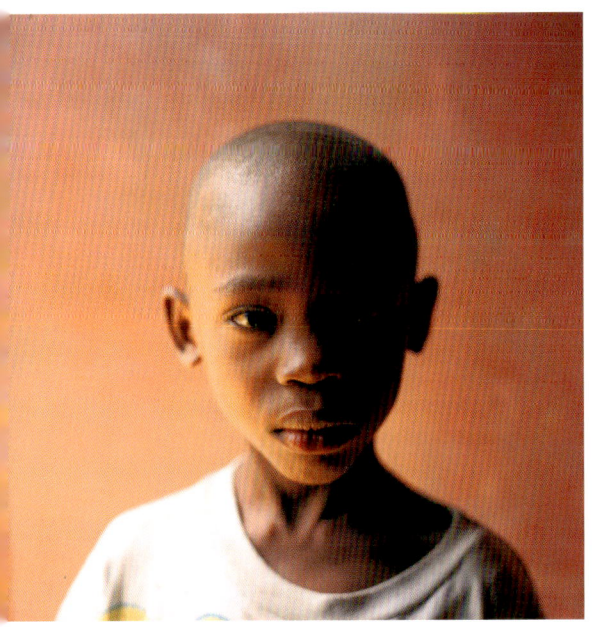

VII. I am Jonathan. My sister Naomi used to walk through the night. My father is in Equateur province. Our mother is in Kenya. Both are soldiers. We used to live with our grandmother, the mother of my dad, near the OUA building in Kintambo. My parents left us behind. When they left they did not inform us. Here we have been for two weeks. I never killed anybody, so I hope that I will be delivered quickly.

VIII. My name is Caro. I am five. I live in Bandalungwa, and I am Luba [one of Congo's ethnic groups]. I am here because I am a witch. My mother turned me into a witch. She gave me dried salted fish to eat. The preacher discovered my true nature. My parents are no longer together. My father visits me every day. My mother never comes. My mother wanted me to bring her the head of my father. I refused. My mother used to beat me a lot in the second world, while we were roaming about together. We used to fly around in our airplane. My mother was the pilot. In the world of the night I am married. The name of my husband is José. I have a daughter, Nadine, and a son, who is named after his father. But I no longer want to meet them. I never ate human meat. One day my mother scratched my father's face with her nails, but that was during the day. My father is a boxer. When he discovered that I was a witch he started hitting me, but then the preacher came and stopped him from doing that. I was still very little when my mother made me a witch. My father told me repeatedly to stop these things. He told me that witchcraft was wrong. I will never go back to my mother again. If I start living with her again I risk becoming a witch for the second time.

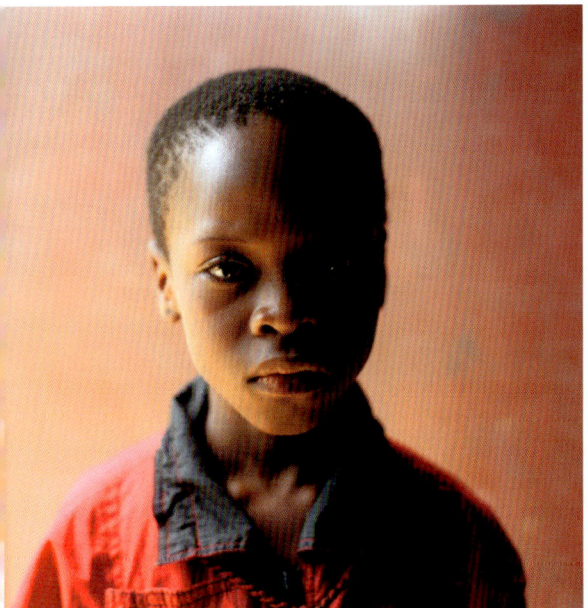

I turned my little brother into a witch as well. He is still at my father's. Before, the two of us used to live with my mother. Then my father came and brought me here, in the church.

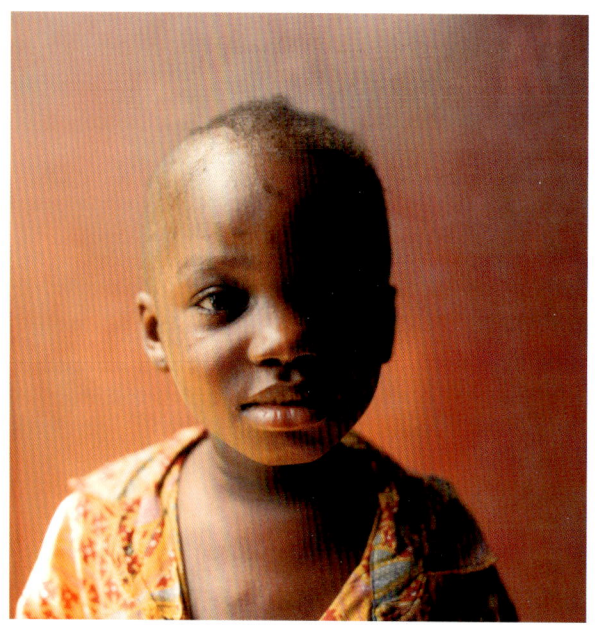

IX. I am Vany and I am three years old. I was ill. My legs started to swell. And then they started saying that I was a witch. It was true. The preacher confirmed it. He also said that my problem would be over soon. He would deliver me. I became a witch when I was still very little. My aunt gave me some groundnuts. She made me wash her laundry in the second world. And then my hair started falling out and my legs and my head started to swell. My aunt lives in Lubumbashi. My daddy is a teacher, here in Kinshasa. I have been here two months. I am waiting for my mother.

X. Mama Lolo taught me witchcraft. She gave me a biscuit. I know her well. She is a neighbor. Then she requested the life of one of my uncles. I said no. And I immediately informed my mother about this. She brought me here. My father died when I was still a baby. Here in Kinshasa I live with my grandmother. I have been here for four days. I have not been delivered yet. Even last night Mama Lolo visited me. She took me to a nocturnal meeting where I drank some blood. I threw up afterwards. During the night I am much older. I am married to Crispin. We have twenty children. I see my children every night. They live in Kintambo, in the house of Mama Lolo.

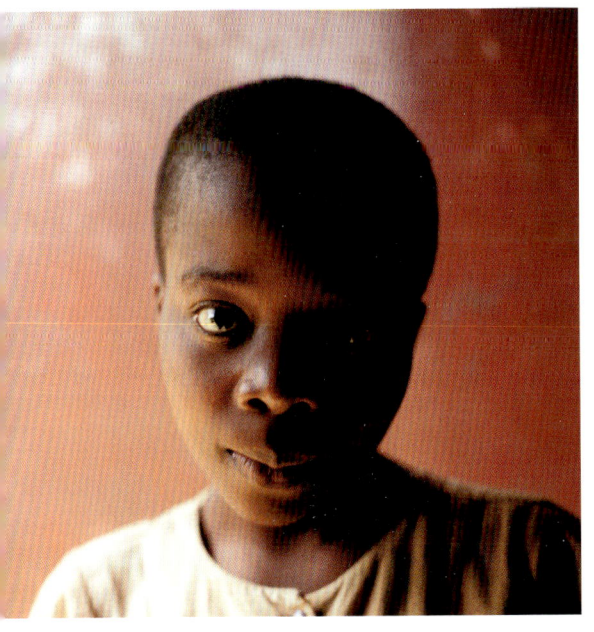

XI. I used to sell cigarettes for my father's younger brother. I would put them on a little table in the street, next to a small shop of a man who is known in my neighborhood as a sorcerer. He is the one who contaminated me. He gave me biscuits that contained witchcraft. I started to lose weight from all the night travel. I traveled in spirit, by dedoubling myself. During that time my father's younger brother suddenly died. My dad started asking questions. Why was I suddenly losing weight like this? I replied that I didn't know. One day, the preacher visited my father in our home. He declared that one of his children was carrying an evil spirit. That evening my older brother beat us, the younger ones. My father called another preacher and he pointed me out as a witch. I have always denied this. The preacher lied to my father about me. But I was sent to the church and this is where I still am. There was also something else. After I had already been sent from home to be treated in the church, a woman from our neighborhood told my father that I was responsible for the illness of my little baby-brother. My parents wanted to take the baby to the hospital but this woman declared that there was no point in taking her to the hospital because she was dying. The whole family was present when the baby died, except for me. Everybody blamed me for the baby's death and I ended by confessing everything. It was I who had killed my father's brother, together with the shop owner. And then he wanted a second person from me. Above all he wanted my father, but my father was too strong. He escaped thanks to the strength of his prayers, and the same with my mother. They couldn't save the baby, however, no matter how hard they tried, because I had already given my little brother in the second world. Now I have been delivered thanks to the good services of the preacher. My parents come to visit me here now, which is a great comfort to me. They also treat us well here in the church. They only beat us when we do not listen.

ON BEING SHEGE IN KINSHASA
CHILDREN, THE OCCULT AND THE STREET

Isn't the city of Kinshasa bewitched? [Bodo, painter and preacher, Kinshasa, May 2001]

BAR OBSERVATIONS I [Bandalungwa, May 2001]: In the labyrinthine darkness of the *Maisaf* club, along one of Bandalungwa's main streets, girls are dancing with themselves in the mirrors that surround the small dance floor. The white shirt of a solitary customer and the triangular lines of phosphorescent red paint on the black walls reflect the light of the TL tubes that are attached to the low ceiling. The whole place breathes an otherworldly, bluish, atmosphere of suspended reality; and everything in this space suggests the familiar promise of some as yet undefined and unknown thrill that is laying ahead, waiting to happen. Or maybe not. In the darkness of the rooms body and mind undouble themselves. (Stronger, though, and more unexpected than the tension of erotic awareness that this time/space of suspense and suspension generates in me, the atmosphere brings back long forgotten childhood memories. Every summer, during the Great Brussels Fair near the *Gare du Midi*, the pleasantly creepy tours in the inner labyrinths of the phantom and horror palaces used to have the same thrilling effect on me.) Swaying their bodies on the captivating rhythms of the rumba, the dancing girls are totally absorbed in their own reflection, with expressionless faces, like mechanical dolls, perfecting the same moves over and over again. And endlessly reflected in the opposing mirrors, rows of identical girls, all moving simultaneously on the music's beat until the images fracture in the corners where the mirrors meet.

"SITING" THE IMAGINARY

In Congo, as elsewhere in Africa, there has always lurked, in a rather unproblematic way, another reality underneath the surface of visible reality. Movement and stagnation, social or physical reproduction and death, the diurnal and the nocturnal, have always existed in and through each other. "More precisely," states Mbembe, "the invisible was not only the other side of the visible, its mask or its substitute. The invisible was in the visible, and vice versa, not as a matter of artifice, but as *one and the same* and as external reality simultaneously—as the image of the thing and the imagined thing, at the same time.

In other words, the reverse of the world (the invisible) was supposed to be part and parcel of its obverse (the visible), and vice versa. And in this capacity to provide a basis for, and to state the inseparability of, the being and non-being of persons and things—that is, the radicality of their life and the violence of their death and their annihilation—lay the inexhaustible strength of the image."[104] Witchcraft is one of the mechanisms in which this inseparability and simultaneous multiplicity most clearly comes to the fore. "The efficacy of defensive fetishes and aggressive sorcery," notes Devisch, "relies on the principle of the subversive capacity of 'catastrophic retroflexion' (cf. *pli-catastrophe* [...]), otherwise described as the homeopathic reversal mobilized in the 'floating signifier' [...] proper to residue, detritus, or excretion. Maleficious sorcery is replete with imaginary exploits in a no-man's land of vertigo and fascination in which the forces of floating signifiers, reproduction and death, daring and delirium intersect [...]. Imprints, crushed leaves, ash, traces of blood, and feces all serve as the residual locus of delirious contamination or reversal between attack and immobility, between the eroticism of engendering life and the inebriation in the face of death and corruption."[105]

Setting out from a recent but widespread phenomenon, that of "witch-children" in the capital of Kinshasa, this chapter intends to discuss the changing nature—should we call it crisis?—of the imaginary, or better: of the qualities of junction and disjunction, of the equilibrium in the mechanisms of reversal between the imaginary and the symbolic, and, ultimately, of the epistemological breach that results from these alterations in Congo today. This breach is basically appearing in what is a growing indiscernibleness between the first and the second world, or between reality and its double.

In his insightful chapter on the "thing" and its double in Cameroonian cartoons, quoted from above, Achille Mbembe remarks upon exactly "the new experience of speech and things" which I have hinted at. He nevertheless assumes that despite the scale of the transformations and the discontinuities, an imaginary world has remained. More generally, the "imaginary," a notion with a complex genealogical tree which includes Lacan, Sartre, Barthes and Castoriadis, has become the social scientist's catchword to capture the ways in which a general subconsciousness, with its autochthonous networks of meaning, is related to the ruptures and constant alterations of a hybridized postcolonial urban (and increasingly also rural) landscape. Appadurai, for example, developed the concept of the imaginary, or more broadly, imagination, as an organized field of social practices in new global cultural processes. In the same vein Bayart, while discussing the cultural dimensions of political action, describes the imaginary as the dimension out of which emerges a continuous dialogue between tradition and innovation.[106] The imaginary is primarily, he adds, interaction: interaction between the past, the present and the projection of a future, but also interaction between social actors, or between societies, the relations of which are selectively shaped by their respective "imagining consciousnesses." The mediating qualities of the imaginary turn it into an institutionalizing social force through which a society confronts and absorbs changes and mutations, and thereby defines and authors itself anew. With the dissolution of more traditional anthropological locations for research,[107] the imaginary, as an alternative field site, therefore presents novel opportunities for more detailed analytic scrutiny of the multiple transformations that African society is currently undergoing.

One of the leading questions throughout this chapter, and indeed throughout this book, though, points in a different direction: what happens if the very nature of the imaginary as a flexible but organized field of social practices has become disorganized and has lost, at least to some extent, its localizing force and its capacity for creating continuity, producing sociality? The imaginary is the dimension of the invisible, but what if the invisible becomes, or takes over, or pushes aside the visible? What if the imaginary is no longer the socially productive phantasmagoric but constantly crosses the boundaries and invades the real in an unmediated, non-symbolic way? What if the imaginary is no longer the *irréel* but, as Gilles Deleuze states, the *indiscernibility*, the incapacity to recognize the distinctness, between *réel* and *irréel*?[108] What, in other words, if the dual and therefore nonalienated relationship with the double which until recently certainly existed in local Congolese experience, most notably in relation to the witch, is becoming problematic and leads to alienation instead? If death, as the double of the living, belongs to the realm of the imaginary, and if the imaginary thus operates the disjunction between life and death, what then does it mean for a societal constellation when that distinction ceases to exist? Can we say that Congolese reality seems to be losing its capacity to dedouble itself easily into multiple others to (re)institutionalize itself through this act?

In dealing with the widespread phenomenon of witch-children in Kinshasa, I propose to tackle these questions by looking at the relationships between the growing presence of death, the notion of the double in the articulation between the imaginary and the symbolic level, and the forms in which continuity, exchange and gift are spelled out in Congolese towns and cities, and particularly in Kinshasa, today.[109] In these urban worlds the frenetic construction of local modernities goes hand in hand with the expectations and promises of a millennial capitalism that finds its sometimes fanatical expression in the thousands of independent churches operating and proliferating in the urban context of Congo and elsewhere in sub-Saharan Africa today. It is in these locations that the social and cultural imaginary in Bayart's sense, as interaction in time and space (between heritage and innovation, between past, present and future, between rural and urban realities, or between Congolese and the global world) is most strongly active. More and more, children and youngsters emerge as, and form the crucial sites of, identity, in which all of these interactions take place. Children and youngsters appear as the ultimate focal points of the contemporary Central African imaginary. Children, as *opus operatum* and as *modus operandi* of crisis and renewal, form the identity locations in which the ruptures and faultlines of an African world in transition become manifest. As part of a wider transformation of the sociocultural, political and economic architecture of the urban landscape, children and youngsters thus are at the heart, or better still, the *frontier* of the reconfiguration of geographies of inclusion and exclusion, or private and public. They have the capacity to fracture public space, and reinvent or even bypass it, in the same way as they often bypassed the nationalist projects of the Zairean state in the past. What constitutes the internal dynamics of young people's lives in Kinshasa? What is their view of the good life? What are their cultural politics and in which geographies, ecologies and subjectivities are they located and imagined? Which are the collective fantasy spaces which children and youth erect for themselves, how is their social imaginary constructed, and how does such a construction inform us about their outlook on life, their understanding, interpretation and formation of the worlds in which they live? How *do* young Kinois today live, at home or in the street, with the ruptures and breaches in their lives, brought about by historical processes of colonization and decolonization, warfare and the mechanisms of global capitalism? How do they integrate disruption and fragmentation into their own lives? How is memory work generated in children and youth? How do they relate to tradition? Which are the social "theaters" in which potential moments, points and places of renewed ritualization, identity formation and (re)invented, reintegrating rites of passage are being shaped?

    Children of the street have always existed in Kinshasa, but in recent years their numbers have swollen dramatically. One phenomenon that has greatly contributed to the growing presence of the street child, variously referred to as *phaseur, moine* (monk), *moineau* (swallow) or *shege/chegue*, is the changing pattern of witchcraft accusations which may currently be observed in the capital. The incessant reinvention of the Central African urban lived environment is not at all marked by a Weberian *Entzauberung*. It is, on the contrary, enacted and produced most strongly, not only in the "enchanting" spaces of Christian fundamentalism, but also in the frenzied and often obsessional production of discourses and practices surrounding witchcraft. Both are, of course, intimately related. Overall, observers have remarked upon the general increase of witchcraft accusations in Congo over the last decades.[110] Although this remains to be proven, it is clear that the dynamics of witchcraft themselves have

undergone some dramatic changes over the past years. One of the most disconcerting phenomena that highlights this evolution is the central role that children are nowadays given in these newly developing witchcraft discourses and practices. In contemporary Kinshasa, thousands of children are implicated in witchcraft accusations, and often end up in the street as a result of this.[III] Then, they find themselves at the heart of one of the most disturbing transformations in the Congolese societal *multi-crise* (*Le Potentiel* newspaper, 4/9/2000), namely the changing relationship between the world of the visible and the invisible, between life and death, or between reality and its double. Commonly described as a "dead society" (*société morte*), Kinshasa's street children, who to a large extent live during the night and often sleep, eat and live in places such as cemeteries, have come to embody the growing alienation of the order of the visible. They constitute a fulcrum between the processes of doubling and dedoubling and fully exemplify the permeability and interchangeableness of the borderlines between day and night, living and nonliving, public and private, or order and disorder.

Children and young adolescents have never before occupied a more central position in the public spaces of urban life, whether in the popular urban music culture, the media, the churches, the army, the street, or the bed.

Occupying such a prominent social position, children are not only victims but have also become active impact factors in and on Congolese society.

The newly generated, central but ambivalent, societal status of children seems to have crystallized most clearly around the figure of the witch, which is the materialization of a cultural imaginary of crisis on the intersection among, for example, money, power, kinship and sexuality.

Secondly, "new situations demand new magic." Due to the increasing impact of global media and of globalization *tout court*, the newly arising tensions between traditions and modernities are being defined, and sometimes resolved most powerfully, in the field of witchcraft. First of all, the heritage of colonialist modernity as embodied by the postcolonial state is sometimes perceived to be a source of witchcraft and evil in and of itself. As one preacher of a healing church explained:

> The late Mobutu brought witchcraft from the village to the city. Now everything is destroyed in Congo, not because of the incapability of the Congolese, but because of witchcraft. Our country has been sold somewhere. It has been sold to a mysterious world (*monde mystérieux*), to museums abroad, even in France, Egypt, Morocco and the United States. These are strategic places of evil. And this witchcraft even brought us the war. All of this because our leaders and our government touched fetishes in India and elsewhere.
>
> [Interview, September 1999, Church of Beth Shalom, community of Masina, Kinshasa]

In this interpretation, the postindependence state, the heir and propagator of a certain colonialist model of modernity, but also the forces of globalization (from France to India) are at the origin of witchcraft. On the other hand, as I have pointed out before, there is not only the witchcraft of modernity. Witchcraft practices in Africa have also been reformulated gradually to come to represent one of the major gateways to "modernity," in a rapidly developing space of "expectations" and desire in which an "economy of the occult" has become the means to win the "war of dreams."[112] This nocturnal economy of power and desire, which forms the hyphen between a fast growing local economy of violence (including the violence of the new moral economy imposed by the churches) and the violence of a penetrating global economy, is also increasingly being accessed and shaped by the young. Children have started to occupy a more central position in the public realm. Here they appear also as major societal players with access to these new global economic fields, and often in direct opposition to the generations that precede them.

Thirdly, the austere living conditions of Congolese urbanity have caused a profound transformation of existing idioms of witchcraft. The ever increasing poverty of the population of Kinshasa, and other cities and towns throughout this vast country, is being accentuated by the war in the east of the country and adds to the pressure that existing structures of kin based solidarity are currently undergoing in the urban context. Undoubtedly, the linkage between children and witches is related to a profound de- and restructuring of the notions of motherhood, gerontocracy, authority and, more generally, the field of kinship itself. These transformations are themselves grounded in an even more profound crisis that punctuates urban life: that of the logic of reciprocity and gift as the most constitutive part of the basal structure that underpins the field of kinship at large.

Finally, the crisis of the gift, in its Maussian sense as total social fact, also embodies the crisis of the symbolic, the increasing impossibility to "site" the imaginary in an unproblematic way. The crisis of the (structuring of the) symbolic, the capacity to symbolize, reveals itself in the unraveling and tearing of two interdependent levels: the level of the symbolic, the first world, the reality of reciprocity, contract and representation, and the level of the imaginary, to which the second world also belongs, and which informs the social logic and the symbolic as internalized social structure.[113] Because these two levels no longer operate as two sides of the same coin (hence the *mystique*ness of the Congolese world, the awareness of "displacement," the experience of the world as dislocatory presence which evolves from a more general rupture between signifier and signified, or from a change in the ways in which the floating signifiers operate), the imaginary is no longer simultaneous with, no longer underpins and legitimates reality. Typical for the Congolese postcolonial reality, that is increasingly acquiring and marked by an oneiric dimension, ever larger chunks of the fields of kinship, reciprocity, money, market, sexuality, power and violence are thus pulled out of the symbolic realm back into the imaginary.

WITCH-CHILDREN IN THE STREETS OF KINSHASA

The rather anonymous peripheral and transitional zones, like Kinshasa's many public administration buildings and places—neglected and filled with refuse—seem to breathe lawlessness and the inert violence of a social order that excludes more and more people from the progress that they expected a school diploma or migration to Kinshasa would ensure. These spaces of promiscuous transit [...] are the areas where bands of youngsters, either escaping or excluded from their social or familial context, retire after midnight on pieces of cardboard. Here it is strikingly apparent how few groups have actually taken root in the life of the city, and how much the State and its public institutions, which once claimed to provide access to modernity, are adrift. Each quarter of the city secretes, as it were, its own peripheral zone, primarily in rundown areas near large junctions or transport terminals. Anonymity and mixing appear to overwhelm any semblance of personal relations and obliterate any ethical point of reference. Rather, one goes there to both "seize a stroke of good luck" and "deflect any misfortune" away from oneself and onto another.

[René Devisch, 1995: 611]

BAR OBSERVATIONS II [Barumbu, April 2001]: An expatriate *mundele* is sitting on the small outdoor veranda of the *Libulu ya Metro*, a modest bar along the crowded Avenue Kasai, the center of Barumbu neighborhood. Night is falling abruptly. In the short twilight zone that marks the equatorial rhythm between day and night, the shadows lengthen and then fade out suddenly when the sun begins its precipitate descent, as if it were pulled down by some strong force into the Congo river's underworld.
One by one more men trickle in and seat themselves on the veranda, looking forward to a cold beer after the day's heat. Facing the road, two giant loudspeakers on each side of the veranda vomit soukous music into the street. The music mixes with the metallic sound of the muezzin's call for evening prayer, his voice rising from the minaret of the white-and-green mosque which is located a couple of blocks further up on the Avenue Kasai.
The Avenue itself finds it hard to live up to the ambitions of its name. It is narrow, overcrowded, barely leaving enough place for the open gutters between the road and the houses, bars, telephone *boutiques* and shops that line the street on each side. A ragged group of street kids floats past the bar's veranda, and stops to listen to a song, while screening the bar's customers. When they see the expat, they put on their most miserable faces and start to beg for a beer. The expat calls out to them: "If you want money you will have to dance for me first." The kids start to execute their dance steps to the sound of Koffi Olomide's *ndombolo*. When they finish, however, the expat chases them away without giving anything. The other customers roar with laughter while commenting upon the incident.

My name is Mamuya. I am fourteen years old. I became a witch because of a boyfriend of mine, Komazulu. One day he gave me a mango. During the following night he came to visit me in my parents' house and threatened that he would kill me if I didn't offer him human meat in return for the mango he had given me earlier. From that moment I became his nocturnal companion and entered his group of witches. I didn't tell my mother. In our group we are three. At night we fly with our "airplane," which we make from the bark of a mango tree, to the houses of our victims. When we fly out at night, I transform myself into a cockroach. Komazulu is the pilot of our airplane. He is the one who kills. He gives me some meat and some blood and then I eat and drink. Sometimes he gives me an arm, at other times a leg. Personally I prefer to eat buttocks. I keep a part of the meat to give to my grandmother who is a witch too. Komazulu is a colonel in the second world, and he has offered me the grade of captain if I sacrifice a person. That's why I killed my baby brother. I gave him diarrhoea and he died. With our group we have already killed eight persons. Our victims haven't done any harm to us. Sometimes, though, we judge them. If they don't defend themselves well, we kill them. Sometimes when a man is buried in the cemetery, we go there and say a prayer. That prayer makes the dead person wake up and then we eat him. Now I have come out of the world of shadows thanks to the prayer of the preacher who treats me in church. But the others who are still in the second world keep pulling at me. They want to kill me now for fear that I betray them.

[Interview in the Church of the Holy Spirit, Selembao, Kinshasa, September 1999]

In 1994, I accidentally came into possession of a videotape which triggered my interest in witch-children. The videotape featured three Congolese children between the ages of eight and twelve. They were being cross-examined by a number of Congolese adults and two Belgian men, members of a Pentecostal prayer movement in the Congolese diaspora setting of Brussels, Belgium. The three children had recently left Kinshasa to come to Belgium. The tape shows how the three children are accused by the adults of the death of a number of their relatives in Kinshasa, one of whom is the mother of one of the accused boys. During the (at moments rather violent) cross-examination, of which the tape offers a one hour-long summary, the three kids acknowledge that they indeed "ate" a number of people in Kinshasa. In a story that much resembles Mamuya's or Omba Shako's, they explain in detail how they exited their bodies and flew to Congo in a "helicopter," which they had made out of a matchstick. In Kinshasa they had been helped by older witches and nocturnal friends, and most prominently among them the grandmother of one of the three boys. Finally, the three give a morbid account of how they killed their victims, chopped them up, and distributed the body parts amongst witch friends to "eat" during a nocturnal feast in which the grandmother participated, dancing naked around the victims' houses. The taped testimony was later sent to the boys' relatives in Kinshasa to corroborate the existing suspicions.

In 1999, such stories had become part and parcel of the daily life in a city like Kinshasa. In fact, there are now so many children involved in similar rumors and accusations that even international press agencies have started to report on them.[114] One immediate effect has been that the city streets have started to abound with ever growing groups of street children.

A distinction is to be made here between children of the street and children in the street. The former are those children who have nowhere else to go and who live, work and sleep in the street on a permanent basis. A much larger group of children is forced into the street for reasons of economic survival. They find food and money in the street by working the streets shining shoes, running little errands, carrying around *ligablos*, little portable shops made from cardboard boxes and containing cigarettes and other small merchandise such as chewing gum, cola nuts, hardboiled eggs and *tangawisi* roots. Contrary to children of the street, the latter return to their parental homes on a regular basis.

Until recently this phenomenon of street children restricted itself to the more important traffic-arteries of areas such as Gombe which are part of "La Ville," the central "white" colonial heart of the city where embassy personnel and other expatriates still generally live today. Today, large groups of children live and roam through some of the public spaces within this area, such as the pavilions on the central market (referred to in the language of the street as *Mozambique* or *Pékin*), the space around the post office along Gombe's main boulevard, the square in front of the railway station, abandoned government buildings or the cemetery of Gombe. Other popular places amongst street children are, amongst others, Camp Impela (Stade des Martyrs), Yamaka (ex-Pont Gaby), Stade du 20 Mai and Funa, the eucalyptus forest at the entrance of Ndjili, the BKTF compound (Masina), the "Indou" market (Kingasani ya Suka), Bar Opika (at the crossroads between Kabambare and Bakata), Rond Point Victoire (Matonge), abandoned railroad tracks, the beaches of the Congo river and many more. Most of these spaces are linked to specific activities and therefore only occupied by these children during specific moments of the day or specific times of the week in their sometimes highly nomadic existence. During the day, many live on top of the market pavilions, which are referred to as "planets" (*planète*) or *Golgotha*. There they sleep and let "their body and their sex rest." For most, the market is a space of opportunity, "a hole of money" (*libulu ya mbongo*), a place "similar to Tshikapa" (a Congolese diamond-mining town in Kasai province). Others, especially boys, have little jobs carrying goods or buckets of water for merchants and market customers, or running errands for the shopkeepers. Some beg or look for anything they can pick up from the street to sell or eat, while others work as thieves (*tsifer*) and pickpockets (*kobeta deux doigts*: to "beat" two fingers, a pickpocket technique), and fill their afternoons with *donker* (looking for a money opportunity) and stealing (*koyiba*, *kokota tarmac* [to enter the tarmac], *koluka* [to search] or *attaquer* [to attack]). Says twelve year-old Trésor, "Stealing is my profession. I steal from everybody: From the White Man and from the Black Man. I even was able to send my brother to Europe by means of the money I stole in the street!"

Towards the evening, when the market empties, children start to become more active: boys gather, wash themselves in the open market gutters, referred to as "the river" (*la rivière*), and start moving to other places where they meet to cook some food, to play (a popular game amongst street children is *mpinda*, a simple game with a coin), and to spend the money earned during the day on clothes, tickets for the movie theater or a soccer game. More regularly still, street children spend their money on alcohol (beer, *lotoko* or *herwa*, locally brewed alcohol), drugs (mostly Valium, marihuana [*nwa, diamba, likaya*, either in the form of powder (*pimbo*) or as leaves (*pelouse*)] and glue, but increasingly

also heroin and, to a lesser extent, cocaine). In an article of the July 27, 2001 issue of the Kinshasa-based newspaper *L'Avenir*, journalist Bibiche Muzeke quotes from a report by the organization *Assistance Contre la Drogue*, in which 301 selling points of cannabis are identified throughout Kinshasa, as well as 32 selling points for heroin, two for cocaine, and 128 for *lotoko* and other illegally brewed alcohol. Very often children mix Valium, cannabis and other substances into their food. Drugs play an important role in street life. Street kids consider that one needs between thirteen and eighteen pills of Diazepam "to make the spirit [of the street] enter." They prepare one for the street and make one tough. Street children, like child soldiers, state, "When you smoke cannabis it gives you 'thirty-six rages' [it makes you very angry], and it turns you into a war machine" (*omeli bangi, omipesi 36 colères, okomi machine de guerre*). Above all they help one to sleep, to "efface problems from one's head," to "chase away shame," to "make one's heart bad in order to steal," or "to give one a healthy appetite" and become strong. More generally, drugs also serve another purpose: They enable children to become "drunk" (*kwiti* from French *cuite*), which is seen as a means to "think" (*kobouler, kokanisa*), "reflect" (*mpo na kokotisa idéologie, mpo na kokotisa mayele*: literally, "to make ideology or wisdom enter") and be "calm" and "aware of oneself," or have *double face* ("dedouble" oneself, as if you leave your own body to observe yourself). Also, drugs "make memory come back" (*kozongisa mémoire*).

Girls, some as young as five or six years, often work the streets and prostitute themselves (*koroder, rodage*) after nightfall, for "the body is a shop, it is money and merchandise" (*nzoto eza magasin, eza mbongo, eza lokola marchandise*). A local newspaper heading reads:

PEDOPHILIA GAINS GROUND. A tour of the city's more turbulent neighborhoods during the evening reveals to all who wish to see the scale of the evil in our city: "Sodomy," "abomination," desolation, decay on all levels. Prostitution in general is an acceptable activity for those in need of money. For street children, though, and especially the *shege* girls who spend all their time in the street, it seems to have become an obligation. Touring the commune of Gombe, and more precisely around the beach Ngobila area, near the Onatra building and the BCDC [a bank] we have seen for ourselves the impudence of the *phaseurs*. Girls, aged between five and eleven have routinely become the victims of sexual violence. In search of a shelter against rain and mosquitoes, numerous are those girls who accept everything their occasional benefactors ask in return for a night in a bed. Many of these girls are also under contract with night watchmen, who authorize them to spend the night in a house or a room in return for carnal pleasure. On the boulevard du Trente Juin [Kinshasa's main boulevard] one can witness quite a spectacle as well. Barely dressed to attract the hunters of female beauty, minors expose themselves in public. Their ultimate goal is to be taken care of by the Don Juans that one may find throughout Kinshasa every night. Near the Memling hotel we were not in the least surprised to encounter a thirteen year-old, highly pregnant, adolescent girl. God only knows what will become of this pregnancy and of the young mother, for the only ones she can count on are no older than she is.

[...] [*Le Satellite*, April 9, 2001]

Several categories of street girls are being distinguished: *fioti-fioti* (little little one, or "dancer"), *nionio* (girls with firm breasts; *nionio* is the word to denote very small grains of diamond), *makoma* (girls with large breasts, named after the successful religious family gospel/pop band Makoma, whose female lead singers are second generation Congolese teenagers living in the Netherlands), *mabata rouges* ("filthy" prostitutes, literally "red ducks"), *mabata verts* (green ducks), *ancien de Saio* ("old," "worn out" prostitute, after the veterans of the Force Publique, the colonial army, who fought in the Ethiopian town of Saio during World War I), *kamoke* (little one). Often very young girls, *bakamoke*, act as an assistant to an older girl. If the latter considers that the money offered by the customer is not enough, she may recommend the younger girl for the job.

In recent years street children have become a familiar aspect of street life not only in areas such as Gombe, but in all parts of this vast city, whether it is around the football stadium, under bridges, or in shacks and cardboard boxes, referred to as *baguesta* (from "guesthouse," in reference to a colonial hotel of that name which still exists in Gombe), along railroad tracks and rivers.

Many of these children were forced to take to the street after being singled out by family members in a witchcraft accusation. Such accusations against children within one's own family have become a common occurrence that transcends all rank, class and ethnic divisions and differences that characterize Kinshasa's urban context. Increasingly, children between age four and eighteen are being accused of causing misfortunes and mishaps, as well as the illness or death of other children and adults in their family and neighborhood environment. The following is an account given by a thirty-year old AIDS patient, a mother of three children. At the time of my interview with her, she was being treated in a healing church together with her four year-old daughter, Nuclette, accused of witchcraft:

> I have suffered a lot in my life. I sold vegetables at the market. The father of Nuclette was deeply in love with me but now he has left me. I was responsible for this separation: All of a sudden I could not return his love anymore.
> One day, I noticed that my market money had disappeared. People told me that Nuclette had stolen it, but I wouldn't believe them. But then, Nuclette began to be suspected as a witch by our neighbors. Apparently, Nuclette had tried to bewitch a woman who lives in our neighborhood. Nuclette had changed herself and appeared like an adult woman when she went to harm this neighbor. One day, when I was out, that neighbor came over to our house and started complaining to my mother: "How can you accept to live together in one house with the same witch-child that has tried to bewitch and kill us in our home? We are no family of yours. We didn't know that this child is a witch. Why does she try to harm us?"

My mother and I decided to take the child to a prayer session at *pasteur* Norbert's. That evening I washed my two other kids, and we all went together to the "prayer control." The preacher started to prophesy and it was affirmed that Nuclette was a witch but that the two other children were not touched by this evil. Then the *pasteur* asked me where my husband was. I told him that he had left our neighborhood and was now living in a different area in the city. I didn't tell him my husband's name, but he cited it and said: "It was Nuclette who caused your marriage to break up. She made your husband leave. And when you were sleeping in your bed at night, she came with other witch-children and injected you by means of a diabolical needle with contaminated blood." This is how I started developing AIDS. I became very,

very thin. People started saying that I had AIDS. Thanks to the preacher of this church, we now know that the AIDS is diabolical. I have been here in the church for over a month, and the preacher has purified me. I was dying when I arrived here, but now I am cured of AIDS.

[Interview in Selembao, September 1999]

In other cases little girls are suspected of transforming themselves into stunningly beautiful women to lure their own fathers and uncles into their bed, to snatch away their testicles or penis, and to cause their impotence or even death. Illustrating the fact that Congo's current societal crisis is, to an important degree, also an etiological crisis (an aspect to which I will return later on), children are also believed to be at the origin of madness, cancer, or heart attacks amongst their relatives and parents; other kids appear to be three or four year-olds in the first world, but in the nocturnal, second world they have themselves already given birth to many children. These in turn become witch-children roaming through the streets of Kin. Others still are believed to transform themselves into "mystic" serpents, crocodiles or *mami wata* sirens. In each of these cases, the "real" self of these children is invisible to others. In the politics of invisibility that characterizes the second world, as product and as practice, the self has been separated from its external sign, the face.

Most of the time, all the hidden suspicions and open accusations erupt into a violent conflict within the accused child's family. Often the child in question is severely beaten, in some extreme cases even killed, by family members or neighbors:

[Field notes, Mombele, May 1997] A man frequently dreamed about the thirteen year old son of his landlord. The landlord and his family lived in a separate house in the same compound. In his dreams the boy harassed and threatened to strangle him. Soon everybody in the neighborhood was informed about these strange dreams. One morning some young men, all neighbors, gathered in the compound and started throwing stones on the corrugated iron roof of the owner's house. The boy was inside. When they started throwing the stones, the boy appeared. People started to stone him. A stone hit him on the head. The child fell down, bleeding profusely. Some men put a tire around his neck and set fire to it. When the boy's parents arrived, their child was already burning to death. The parents did not interfere for fear that they would undergo the same fate.

Although such forms of extreme violence are by no means the rule, most of these children, though, are disowned and repudiated. Displaced, disenfranchised, but feared by most, the alleged witch-children (called *sheta, tsor* or *tshor*, from French *sorcier*, witch) end up in the street, where they often team up after a while with other abandoned children. Children thus form their "stable" (*écurie*), usually a group of up to seven persons. These gangs have a varying life span (from some weeks to some months, rarely longer than a year). Often, several of these stables associate to form a larger, more loosely knit group. Witch-children are believed to adopt the same form of organization in the world of the night. Stables of witch-children also fashion themselves after a military army model. In their nocturnal army, witch-children accord grades to themselves, from sergeant to general, and one climbs in rank with every victim that one has killed and "eaten."

Most of the gangs in Kinshasa (amongst the best known are United States [*Etats-Unis*], Jamaica [*Jamaïk*], and Bad Times [*Temps Mauvais*]) are organized around age and gender, with clearly separated groups of older and younger boys and girls. Mixed groups with boys and girls together are quite uncommon. Each group constitutes, in varying degrees, a cooperative unit: the members often share the money they made, the goods they stole and the food they found during the day. Group members roam around together. They defend and protect each other against outside threats, and borrow money and clothes from each other. Most male groups have strongly established hierarchies, with a clear pecking order and a recognized "chief." Hierarchies in street gangs are also established through the "bravery" and "daring" which one shows, for example by "stealing" the girl of your best friend: *ozali makasi, linga mwasi ya moninga*, "if you are strong, make love to your friend's girl." Many of the girls' groups, usually smaller, are organized around a slightly older girl who is called mother, and who often acts as what one could describe as "pimp" towards the two or three younger girls under her care. Although there often is a great solidarity amongst members of the group, there is also a lot of social pressure, control and intimidation. Boys, for example, say: *omoni oyibi*, "if you see me steal, steal as well," that is, don't denounce me, or else you will have to suffer the consequences. One of the unwritten rules amongst members of an *écurie* is, "Don't harm or intimidate your friend" (*mutu, abangisa moninga te*). But at the same time it is said, "What is yours is yours, what is mine is mine" (*ya yo, ya yo, ya nga, ya nga*). It is extremely important not to be seen as weak, as a *fopaner* (a poor thief, who only steals during the daytime), a *mbakasa* (someone who is afraid and who doesn't know how to find money) or an idiot (*yuma*). One should rather be a *yanké*, a strong person, or an *actionnaire* (a capable thief, who also enters people's homes at night), someone who has *face* (who is street wise) and has the heart or the spirit of *zembe*. One should also be without fear, be someone who is not afraid to confront policemen or soldiers. Most important, one has to possess "whiteness," that is, be with good luck (*lupemba*). This is also why street boys refuse to wear underwear, for it blocks good luck (*caleçon ekangaka lupemba*). For the same reason children shave off the hair around their private parts and cut their nails.

The interaction between the gangs as well as between members within the same group is often rather violent, ranging from fist fights and beatings to physical mutilation (often by means of pieces of glass and razor blades) to sexual violence, rape and even gangbangs by older boys on younger girls and boys. Frequently, the intra and intergroup violence is related to initiatory moments as well, in which violence is used by way of *baptême* to make the street spirit (*zembe*) enter your body and teach you how to endure, how to be hard, patient and without pity. Initiation into magical knowledge related to the street equally involves forms of violence. In order to be able to find money, for example, a ritual specialist makes six burns on one's left hand, and ties a red cord around one's left forearm, a ritual practice called *mbetenge*. When one touches these burns at midnight money will come to one easily. In the same way, street children are also initiated into fighting styles (*bilayi*, a term inherited from the Bills in the 1950s) that come with specific ritual knowledge.

Although pregnancies occur frequently in the street, and girls often have a *mukukule*, a special street boyfriend with whom gifts, love and friendship are shared, the existence of nuclear street families is quite rare. Oftentimes the children who end up in the street, whether or not as the result of a witchcraft accusation, previously occupied a structurally marginal position in their own family environment. Kazadi, for example, is an eighteen year-old who has been living in the street ever since the age of eleven. His mother died when he was ten. His father remarried, which provoked a dispute between him and his deceased wife's sisters. One day his older brother was sent by their father to the market to buy some goods. On the way he lost his father's money and for fear of being punished, the boy decided not to return to his parental home. Kazadi soon followed his brother into the street, because his "father's new wife didn't feed me properly and generally treated me very badly." Says Tabuki, a sixteen year-old girl who has been in the street for a year where she prostitutes herself:

> My mother died, and my father is in Bukavu. I came to Kinshasa because of the war with my paternal uncle. In 1997, when Kabila entered the city, I was still in school. My older brother was a Kabila soldier who lived in Camp Kokolo (a military garrison). After a while my paternal uncle stopped feeling responsible for me. He refused to give me any more money and sent me to my brother in Camp Kokolo. My brother, though, was often absent. Sometimes I stayed in his house on my own for two days or more. That is how I started seeing "husbands." One of them, a petty shopowner, paid my school fees. When my brother heard about this, he beat me up. Out of fear for what he might do I ran away and started living in the street.

[Interview, Selembao, April 2001]

Due to the AIDS epidemic and other causes related to the poor living conditions in Congo, many of these children were orphaned at a very early age. Others were abandoned by their mothers, often teenagers themselves, and grew up amongst, sometimes distant, relatives: (classificatory) grandparents, uncles, aunts, cousins, or one of their father's co-wives. When one or both parents are still alive (and average life expectancy for the total population in R.D. Congo is less than fifty years and as low as forty-seven for men) they are often absent, an absence which is increasingly due to patterns of displacement, migration and diaspora under the pressure of economic factors, political instability and war.

CHURCHES AND CHILD-WITCHES

The spiral of violence that erupts in the kinship group because of the pattern of witchcraft accusations directed at children, is partly countered by the church and prayer movements that are flourishing everywhere. As I have argued, fundamentalist churches, and foremost amongst those the Pentecostal churches and apocalyptic movements that may be found throughout sub-Saharan Africa nowadays, devote a lot of attention to the figure of Satan, to demons, and the struggle between Good and Evil. Beyond any doubt the churches' contribution plays a crucial role in the ceaseless production and increasing centrality of the figure of the witch in the collective imaginary of Congolese society, which is itself being restructured in terms of an Armageddon, a second world in which demons have gathered in an all-out war against God (see the Book of Revelation, 16:16).

Paradoxically, then, the *Verteufelung* of the figure of the witch in the discourse of these churches makes the witch itself more omnipresent in the social field. Therefore, the position of the churches in relation to evil, straightforward as it may seem at first sight, nevertheless produces contradictory tensions in the social field. The churches' role with regard to the child-witch phenomenon is an equally ambivalent one, which makes them both part of the witchcraft problem itself as well as of the local solution to this problem. On the one hand, the space of the churches is one of the most prominent sites in which the coincidence of the figure of the witch and the child is produced. During the masses and collective prayers, children are urged to make a public confession in order to reveal their true natures as witches and confess the number of victims they attacked (see further below). Rather than being a perversion, the naming of the witch offers an opening to solve the crisis, as it has always done in more traditional settings. Before this public moment they have usually been sniffed out or recognized as witches by the church leaders and *pasteurs* during more private consultations. In these meetings more "traditional" divinatory

models are often blended in with the church discourse to create a ritualized moment of witch-finding. As a consequence of these denunciations, however, international aid agencies and NGOs such as *Save the Children*, in their struggle against the marginalization of children, accuse the church leaders and *pasteurs* of child abuse. These organizations usually treat the problem of witch-children in Kinshasa as a humanitarian problem of street children, while choosing to totally disregard the cultural implications of the witchcraft aspect. And yet, one could argue that the churches, in providing and authorizing this type of diagnostic, offer an alternative to the violence and conflict that occur in the family as the result of a witchcraft accusation. The church leaders do not usually produce these accusations themselves, but merely confirm and thereby legitimate them. In doing so, the space of the "healing" church enables the relocation and reformulation of the sometimes extreme physical and psychological violence that the accused children have to undergo within their kin-group. The child is removed from the threatening family context in which its place has become highly problematic, and is left in the care of a *pasteur*. Here, the often equally tough treatment starts with an initial period of seclusion and quarantine, either individually or collectively with other child-witches. As I have observed myself in recent years, some churches take in up to a hundred children a week. The period of seclusion, during which these children usually live in rather poor conditions in terms of food and hygiene, may last from a couple of days to some weeks or even months, depending on the seriousness of the case in question.

During their seclusion, the children are subjected to a period of fasting and ritual purification. The lavish administration of laxatives and emetics aims at cleansing the witch-children's bodies from the meat of the victims that they ate. Undigested pieces of meat or bone, but also objects of all kinds which are found in the children's vomit and feces will be used as corroborants during their public confession before the assembled members of the church. During the period of seclusion, the children are regularly subjected to interrogations, sometimes alone, at other times in the presence of one or both of the child's parents or other related adults if the latter are willing to cooperate. Many adults, though, are too afraid of their children to maintain close contact with them. During these more private sessions that evolve between the child and the preacher or one of his or her assistants, there slowly emerges a narrative of disruption and descent into evil which will also help to structure the "outing ritual" of confession in the public space of the church later on. This period is a crucial point in a whole process of emplotment which helps to shape up the imaginative task of modeling an experience of crisis and drawing a rather standard and stereotypical narrative configuration out of a simple succession of illnesses and deaths. As part of a therapeutic narrative process, which eventually leads to the children's story of confession, the emplotment that takes shape here gives the experience of crisis a direction. It mediates disruption and promotes self-healing, even though the children themselves are not, or only in certain ways, free in their choices of how to plot their narratives.[115]

During or after the moment of public confession, a relative of the accused child usually addresses the church gathering. In this way, Omba Shako's uncle asked permission to speak after his nephew's confession (see Omba's story):

> My Brothers and Sisters in Christ! It is truly the Spirit of the Almighty which pushed me to bring this child here during the church's Evangelization Campaign! Praised be the Lord! This child is my sister's child. He lived in Kananga with his parents. He came to live with me in Kinshasa not longer than two months ago. But I am far from pleased with this child's behavior. He does everything with a jealous heart. It is easy to see that he is a sorcerer. I brought him to this church to make sure that I was not mistaken. At home he has already provoked numerous conflicts between my wife and me. One day, my wife and I had gone out. We had left our three year-old daughter, Rebecca, in the house. As soon as we had gone, Omba went into the house and opened the room where we store our food. He took a cooking pot which contained *pondu* [prepared cassava leaves] that my wife had made earlier that day. We would have eaten this upon our return home in the evening. Omba, however, took the cooking pot, opened it, looked left and right to see if nobody had seen him, and then he urinated in the pot. When we came home in the evening, my wife noticed that the pot was filled with a strange liquid. It smelled of urine. She wondered who could have done this. Little Rebecca informed us that Omba had urinated on the food. She said, "He took the cooking pot, opened it, looked around to see whether someone could observe him and urinated. He did not see me, but I could see him. Don't eat from this food, father!"
>
> This event caused me a lot of problems with my wife. We did not eat and everybody went to bed feeling hungry. Many people in the neighborhood had already told me that Omba was a witch. If we keep him with us any longer, he will kill either me or my wife. One of the children died recently. Omba is the one to blame. He gave my child to the witches. I have listened to everything he confessed today. I no longer want him in my house. Let him stay here in the church. Tell him that he abandons his witchcraft. Tell him to repent!

After his uncle had spoken, Omba fell down, got up again and started to cry, while singing: "They refuse to listen, they will not give up witchcraft" (*baboyaki koyoka, kindoki batika te*). Then he fell down again, got up and began to pray in a loud voice. Punctuated by biblical references to the story of Noah and his wife who were saved during the Great Flood, while all the sinners repented too late and perished, he prayed:

Oh Lord
I am your child
I come to you with all my heart
to you my Father
Oh Father of Love
Father, don't leave me behind in the hands of my enemies
I had forgotten you
I killed people
I ate the meat of my fellow brothers
I turned them into animals
They became like animals of the forest
But now I give myself to you
I am your image
Father, take my heart
You are the strongest

Some days after the crucial moment of such a public confession the preacher proceeds by organizing a number of exorcizing moments, referred to as *délivrance* (deliverance) or *cure d'âme* (soul healing). This ritualized exorcism is often carried out collectively in prayer groups under the guidance of female church members known as "interceptors" (*intercesseuses*). The child is placed in the middle of a circle of praying, often trancing, women who regularly lapse into speaking in tongues, a sign of the Holy Spirit's presence. The child, the focus of this powerful praying ritual, is then repeatedly subjected to exorcizing prayer and the laying on of hands. Usually one woman takes the lead in prayer while the others sustain her by regularly punctuating her preaching with religious songs and hymns. Depending on the type of church, these praying sessions unfold in collaboration with the child's mother or some other relative in the hope of facilitating a reintegration of the cleansed witch-child within its family. In many cases though, parents are not very collaborative and such reintegration remains problematic. The child's parents and other members of the kin group often remain too afraid to accept such a child again in their midst. It is usually in those all too frequent cases that the children are subsequently forced to take to the street.

ESTHER'S "SOUL HEALING"

The following text is a translated summary of a deliverance session, originally in Lingala, for a six year-old girl, Esther, formerly known as Falone, who looks as if she is only three. This fact was interpreted as a clear indication of her *mystique*ness. When I met Esther, she lived with her maternal grandparents. As her grandmother explained to me, Esther's mother had traveled to Angola to try her luck in the diamond traffic there. Her father had been a soldier in Mobutu's army. When Kabila came to power in 1997, the father was arrested and sent to Kitona, a reeducation camp in the Lower Congo. He never returned to Kinshasa. One day the grandmother found Esther in the street where she had been beaten up by the neighbors on account of her being a witch. The grandmother, however, continued to care for Esther and even took her to several hospital centers after Esther became ill. No clear diagnosis of her ailment was ever given by any doctor, but Esther herself had started to look "like a seventy year-old woman" and had completely stopped speaking. In one hospital, and with the financial support of some European nuns, Esther and her grandmother stayed for nine months of sustained treatment but to no avail; Esther did not get better. Finally the grandmother turned to prayer. During one intensive prayer session at home, Jesus revealed to her "the thing" in Esther's body. During the same period, the grandmother had started to dream that Esther and her witch friends were trying to kill her. At this point, the grandmother decided to entrust Esther to a preacher for more professional prayer help. With his assistance, the whole terrible truth about Esther slowly started coming out. Also, many of the misfortunes that had recently befallen the family suddenly began making sense. It turned out that in the second world that Esther was inhabiting at night she was an adult woman with a husband, a certain Papa Bukafu, with whom she had eleven children, six "to the right" (boys) and five "to the left" (girls). Esther and her witch family lived in a river under water. At night she transformed herself into a *mami wata* siren. Esther became a witch after having received a piece of dried salted fish from a neighborhood woman, Mama Losiya, at the marketplace. Afterwards this woman started paying nocturnal visits to Esther. They started hunting together, both in Kinshasa and abroad, in Europe. During these voyages Esther walked around with a stick she used to kill people.

It also appeared that Esther had apparently "blocked the way" (*kokangisa nzela*) of her mother and her two maternal uncles who were "hunting" for diamonds in Angola but had met with no luck so far. When news got to Kinshasa that one uncle had been killed by an Angolan (UNITA) soldier, his death was quickly attributed to Esther as well. Similarly, she was believed to have "blocked" another maternal uncle who held a university degree in economy but still hadn't found a job after two years. In the meantime, her grandfather who had worked all his life as a warehouseman at Ndjili, Kinshasa's national airport, was fired. When Esther's mother finally returned empty handed from Angola and found that her daughter was the source of her misfortune, she almost killed her. In the meantime, Esther herself had started to look like an old woman and had totally stopped speaking.

In September 1999 when I met Esther and her grandmother for the first time, they were still deeply involved in deliverance sessions. Thanks to the "soul healing" during which she had also received her new name, Esther had regained some of her former looks, although she had not grown at all. Therefore she was still closely monitored by the church community who feared that she might collapse back into the world of shadows. Each week her grandmother brought Esther to the church to participate in a session of deliverance led by an older woman who acted as the preacher's personal emissary:

In a vision I see a big river, like an ocean. Some trees are long, others short.
> This water holds a lot of power. In this place there is a whirlpool, a big river, I say, with black water. And I see a snake who sits where Mother Mary is, a snake which is fixedly looking her in the eyes. And I also see a little girl with untidy hair. In one of her eyes, there is a white spot, while the other eye is totally white as if she were blind. This child's name is Falone. We have given her the name of Esther. She has the power of the water in her. She moves powerfully and calls herself *mami wata*. Summon all the compassion that you find in yourself and pray for this child. Open your eyes for she has a strong power residing inside her.
>
> [*Speaking in tongues*]

This other woman, they showed her a snake. The snake is her witchcraft. There is
> a woman who sells on the market. She is the one who gave fish meat to Esther. The powers of the water come from a man who is their neighbor. On his land there is running water coming out of a stone. There is a spring. In this river a white man used to wash himself. Let us pray for God's grace for He is the only One who is King and who can save this child from the powers of witchcraft and magic.
>
> [*Speaking in tongues*]

Stand up! Destroy! Cursed be the day this child received the meat out of this woman's
> hands. That the bewitched meat she ate remains without effect! In the name of Jesus Christ! Her grandmother tells us this child travels to Europe. In her hands she holds a stick, a stick to kill people. God's grace! You, you are mothers, you know how to give birth; you know the pain of childbirth; help this child; block the path of the devil; and tie all the persons who wish this child harm and who visit her at night. Block the path of Mama Losiya; destroy her in Jesus' name. Let us pray now for the weapon she uses to kill people. Disarm her in Jesus' name.
> The spirit tells me that Esther is communicating with other witches through her little finger at this very moment. Cut all communication lines,

all the radars, all of her signaling with her arms. Close down the place where
Losiya is. Block all evil in heaven and on earth. Close all roads. Block Esther's
eyes and ears. Let the devouring fire descend to annihilate all the military
grades she received from other witches. Destroy her airplane so that she can
no longer fly away. Oh, heavenly fire. They say He is fire, and when Saul had
the fire, he fell down. Let us raise our arms in Jesus' name. You, who are a
mami wata, go into the water and disappear in the water. Where do you hide
like a queen with long hair resembling a siren's and with long nails? The siren
destroys and causes accidents and stirs up evil spirits in the middle of the
water. Holy Spirit, take possession of her. Where are you? Grab her; take
her with you. Victory is in Christ's blood. So, out of the depths of our faith,
because she is still a child, because of my faith and yours, raise your hands
so that the blood of Christ may engulf this child and the powers of the night
can no longer enter her body. Esther, repeat after me: I refuse Satan; I refuse
witchcraft; I refuse *mami wata*; I refuse to live in the water. Save me so
that I can become your humble servant. I refuse the works of Satan.
[*In French*] Oh Eternity, Almighty Father, Great God, I lift You up, You have
given us this child, Eternal Father of Israel. Hallelujah! You deliver, You break
the chains; You, my Eternal King, have delivered this child from the powers of
darkness and from the power of sirens. Jesus, we ask for a sign. Let her grow!
She is six years old now. We want to see how she will have grown
a month from now. Let her regain her health; let her grow normally.
God has told me: shave her hair; buy some new clothes; and throw
the old ones away.

CHILDREN AND THE GEOGRAPHIES OF INCLUSION AND EXCLUSION

BAR OBSERVATIONS III [Matonge, April 2001]: The night is falling. Marie-Françoise
and I are sitting in the *Vis-à-Vis*, an open-air bar opposite Matonge's legendary
La Crèche night club. *La Crèche* is an imposing three-story
building which looks out over *Rond Point Victoire*. Big spotlights light up
the large yellow Primus sign on its flat rooftop. The yellow contrasts sharply
with the black of the night. Modestly mirroring *La Crèche*, the *Vis-à-vis* club
recently reopened its doors. A couple of years ago, this bar converted into
a church but for some reason it shifted back into its former shape.
Three young girls with tight mini skirts, heavy make-up and wigs, *sapeurs* in
fake Gaultier outfits, groupies of tonight's local band, A.C. Milan: a colorful
sample of Kinshasa's night life characters is trickling in, one by one occupying
the tables around the central *piste*, the dance floor, which is slightly higher
than the rest of the bar's floor space and covered with enameled bathroom
tiles. Earlier in the evening someone must have deposited and then forgotten

a pile of plastic garden chairs in the middle of the dance floor. Looking up from our table to the walls of the compound and the night sky above, I notice the radiant eyes and white smiles of numerous street children. Like expectant bats, *bangembo* as they are called here, they are seated on the wall and the rooftops of the neighboring houses, trying to catch a glimpse of tonight's concert. When I turn my head back to the dance floor, I notice how a little street kid has installed himself on top of the pile of plastic chairs, totally oblivious of the crowd around him, looking inward, royally resting after a long day.

The standard European and northern American interpretations of children and youngsters usually view them as dependent, not fully grown and not yet ready to act in a responsible way. The social space to which children are relegated is that of the family and of school. This conceptualization is so pervasive that children who do not correspond to these definitions are immediately perceived as potential victims in need of help. Within the sub-Saharan African context, on the other hand, few children are familiar with the luxury of the protection offered by parents, school and state in the West. In the urban African context the local sociocultural construction of children certainly is radically different from the cultural politics of childhood that applies in the realities of the West. Viewed from such a western perspective, it is indeed not difficult to document how children are often reduced to victims requiring help due to the political, economic, sociocultural, psychological and sexual violence

Soldiers are not allowed to enter the bar in battle dress, with guns, bayonets or grenades. Orders from headquarters.

that pervades the African continent today. Some even speak of a generalized African "youth crisis."[116] To deny the realities that correspond to this general victimizing discourse with regard to children would be very shortsighted. Yet children, especially in the oftentimes extreme living conditions in which they grow up in Africa, are not only vulnerable and passive victims, *subjected* to, or "made and broken" by, the socioeconomic and political processes of the African reality, but they are also active *subjects*, "makers and breakers" of that reality. Children in these worlds often have the capacity to act strongly on the worlds in which they live, in both positive as well as negative ways. In line with more local notions of agency, children and youngsters in such African contexts are often not regarded, nor do they regard themselves, as future or proto adults but as social actors in the present with a marked role and presence in the very heart of the societal context. As such, children and youngsters appear as Janus-like figures and thereby embody a frontier dynamics of mutation, which has become one of the most essential qualities of the Central African postcolonial space.[117]

On the one hand, then, children in Kinshasa are increasingly relegated to sites of exclusion (chased onto the street, expelled from the kin group, secluded in the churches). On the other hand, however, children have never before been so prominently present in the urban public space. Firstly, there is the very real and violent power "from the barrel of the gun" which child soldiers (*bakadogo*) have come to represent. In 1997, when these child soldiers (some of whom were no more than ten years old) made their entry in Kinshasa as Kabila seized power, this was a totally new and rather shocking fact for most of the capital's inhabitants.

Economically as well, young adolescents occupy a more central position than ever before. Throughout the nineties, large numbers of Kinshasa's youth became "children of Lunda" (*bana Lunda*) and trekked *en masse* to the Angolan province of Lunda Norte to gain access to dollars and diamonds. Upon their return, these youngsters had often acquired a financial power that exceeded that of their parents by far and that allowed them to access versions of a modern lifestyle from which their own elders were excluded. In Kinshasa today, it is said that the one who possesses *lard*,[118] money, is a *patron* or a *mwana ya kilo*, "a child with weight," regardless of his or her age. Together with these youngsters' financial independence (and responsibility) thus came social power. This newly found power most tangibly demonstrated itself in the context of family and kin and, inevitably, also gave rise to intergenerational, diamond-related, witchcraft accusations triggered by disputes over the redistribution of the newly accessed wealth. In relation to this diamond witchcraft, rumors abound about "witch-children of Lunda" (*mukishi mwana Lunda*) who have sex with their mothers or kill and "eat" their fathers and uncles in return for diamonds and dollars. In these contexts, the empowering witchcraft idiom of eating, formerly the prerogative of elders, fully illustrates the nocturnal possibilities of immediate access to the fruits of modernity. As twelve years-old Omba Shako explained in response to the question, "why he professed to like eating human meat":

> In the human body, everything is useful. The blood is fuel, diesel, kerosene and red wine; the water that may be found in the body is motor oil, brake oil, perfume, drinking water, medical syrup, and other medicine like pomades to rub your body with. The backbone is a radio, a satellite telephone, a radio transmitter; the head is a cooking pot, the glass from which the *patrons* drink, a swimming pool, a bucket which you can use to wash yourself in; the eyes are mirrors, a television, a telescope; the hair can be used to make mattresses, or a sofa for the living-room. The skin serves many purposes: It can be used to make a *patron*'s blanket, or to cover his coach; it may also be used to provide the carpet upon which the *patron* will sit. The body's slime is like Vicks pomade, or like shoe polish. Sperm is like the grease that one uses to maintain motor and car parts. It can also be used to cure someone who is suffering from impotence or who has broken his back. Other body liquids also have their use. They can be used in the radiator of a car or an airplane.

Another boy, Mabela, who is twelve, expresses his fascination for modern technology through the vocabulary of the occult:

> Our nocturnal airplane is fabricated with the bones of dead corpses, preferably the bones of the arms and the legs. The motor of our airplane is made from a skull. We do not take the bones from just any dead corpse. One needs the bones from an old man, someone who has lived for a very long time, say seventy or eighty years. This old man that we use, he must be someone with authority in his village, or in his family. (In case there aren't any bones available one can always use a plastic airplane toy.) We use the dead corpse's blood as motor oil. The urine and the water in the corpse will be used as kerosene for the airplane. The electrical wiring of the airplane is done with the dead person's veins. Finally, one needs the eyes of a cat or an owl for the airplane's headlights.

Here the nocturnal consumption of one's elders gives straight access to, and is quite literally an incorporation and ingestion of, modernity's technology and its spaces of consumption. In this sense, the space of the street and the time of the night is the time/space for the creation of multiple alternative or parallel modernities. According to some, the word *chegue* originated when

Kabila's child soldiers walked into Kinshasa resembling small rebels or *Che* Guevaras. A more frequently heard explanation is that *shege* refers to Shengen, the town in Luxembourg where European Union member states signed a treaty to abolish the inner frontiers and create a free and open European zone which can be accessed in its totality by means of one single visa.[119] For Kinshasa's *bashege*, for whom traveling to Europe is not an option, the street is viewed as an alternative Shengen territory: It is the space where food, freedom, sex, drugs and money can be freely accessed. To them the world of the *cité*, which is referred to as *Belesi* (derived from *Belgique*, Belgium, the name of one of Kinshasa's neighborhoods during colonial times), is a world of constraints, a backward world which belongs to the past. Significantly, the modern housing style in the streets of Kinshasa was also referred to as *Belesi* during colonial times because living in these durable brick houses with their corrugated iron roofs was perceived, no doubt with some irony as well, as accessing the colonialist modernity as it was thought to exist in the metropole. In contrast to this, Kinshasa's street children now consider the street to be modern and exciting. The street and the night form the spatial and temporal zones in which the young generate themselves in self-invented processes and narratives of globalization. Simultaneously, their material horizon, the singularity of their space, and the social geography of their lives, often only extend to the corner of the street or the borderline between one neighborhood and the next.

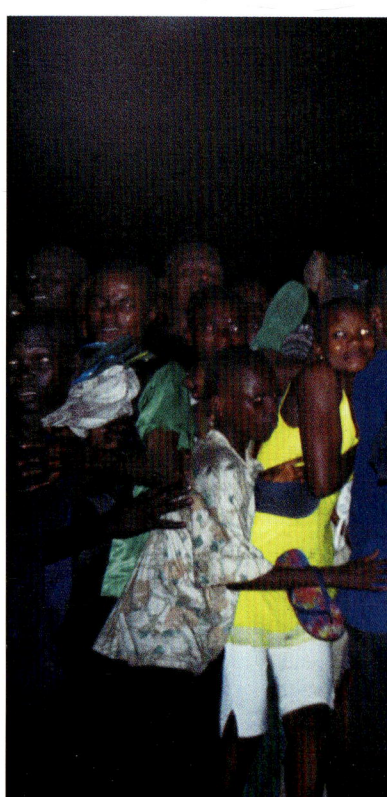

Thirdly, in popular urban public culture as well, children and young adolescents have again, often literally, started to appear before the footlights. In the lyrics of recent songs of Congolese superstar Papa Wemba, the same street children (*shege*) who are stigmatized as witches have been given a prominent place. They are frequently invited onto the stage, in what is a bit of a public provocation, to sing along with Papa Wemba and his orchestra Viva La Musica. On a 1995 hit record entitled *Pole Position*, the *atalaku*, or shouting DJ, of Papa Wemba's band stirs up the audience with the slogan *Shege chance eloko pamba* ("street child, fortune, happiness, is a small thing," that is, it is also within your reach). Even more recently, the same Papa Wemba, in a 1999 record entitled *Fula Ngenge*, launched the phenomenon of the *bafioti-fioti* (kiKongo) or *bakamoke* (Lingala), literally "the little little ones," which celebrates "little girls who love to dance" (*bafioti-fioti balingi babina*). On stage, twelve year-old girls have indeed replaced female dancers in their late teens and twenties to entrance the audiences of Kinshasa's major orchestras with their dances and sexual radiation. In the process, the sexual attractions and dangers of little girls, the female counterparts of the male child soldiers, have developed into a widespread urban mythology in which the figure of the *kamoke sukali*, "the little sugared one," appears as ultimate *femme fatale* and man-eater. In weekly issues of locally produced comic strip serials, which are in many respects the printed equivalent of *Radio Trottoir*, Kinshasa's powerful rumor machine, the narrative figure of the *kamoke sukali* has become a central character. The best known in this genre are the comic strips of "the enigmatic philosopher of the realm of the informal" (*l'enigmatique philosophe de l'informel*), Papa Mfumu 'Eto 1, also known as "the uncontested high-priest of African mystico-religious-secret painting" (*Le grand-prêtre incontesté de la peinture mystico-religio-secrète africaine*). His weekly issues of comic strips, extremely popular though of poor technical quality, are sold at crossroads and bus stops throughout Kinshasa.[120] As Esther's and other similar cases attest, the *kamoke sukali* is often related to the *mami wata* siren, a relation that most fully embodies and realizes the linkages that exist between sexuality, gender, age, death, access to modernity's materiality, and the second world.

Similarly, children have become central actors in the media. Not only do private, often religious, TV stations in Kinshasa stage regular shows during which individual children are produced and publicly denounced, but the new constellation of meaning that is being shaped around children and witchcraft is also modeled by more global media. Influential in this respect are the soap series and films produced in Nigeria and Ghana, videos and audio adaptations of which circulate in Kinshasa. These films often bring narratives constructed around the adventures of spirit children (echoing Ben Okri's acclaimed *The Famished Road* in which the leading protagonist, Azaro, is equally a spirit child). They are frequently broadcast on popular religious TV and radio stations such as the RTMV (*Radio et Télévision Message de Vie*, Radio and Television Broadcast Message of Life), which is owned by one of Kinshasa's most successful preachers, Fernando Kutino, founder of a church named the Army of Victory (*Armée de Victoire*).[121] These films, originally in English, are translated live into Lingala, and some of the translators, such as the well-known José de Jésus, have become stars in their own right. In Kinshasa today, the most popular of these films is undoubtedly *Karishika*, a Nigerian production by Ifeanyi Ipoenyi.

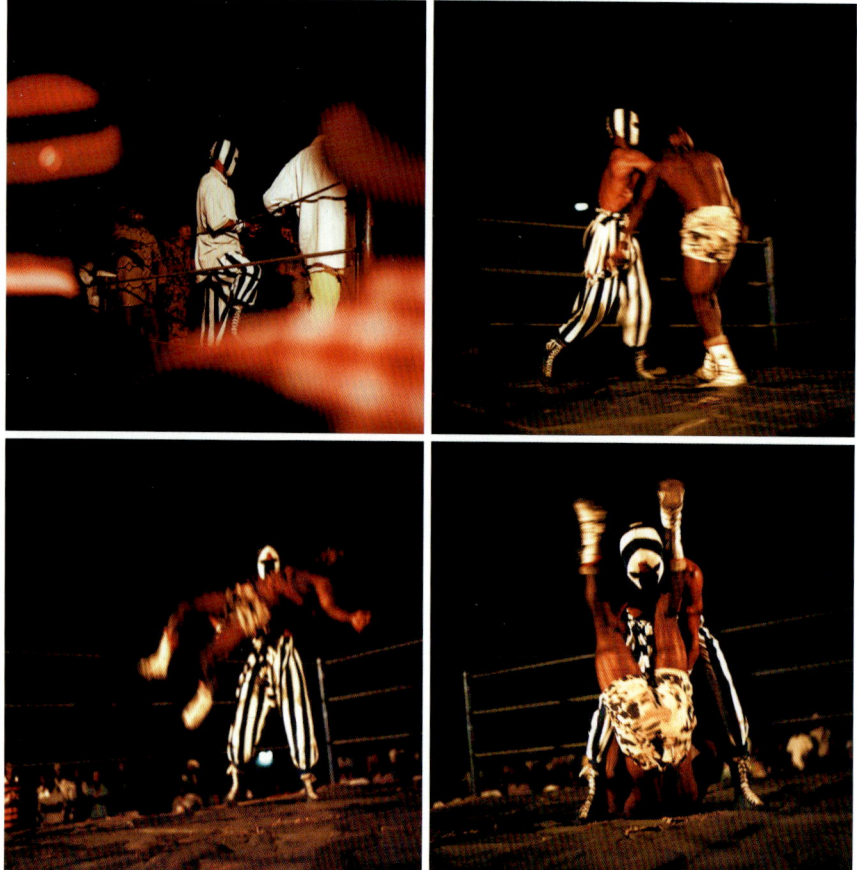

This 1998 feature film, starring the Nigerian actress Becky N. Okorie, tells the story of a young girl, Karishika, the queen of demons. The end of times is approaching. Seeing that everybody has started praying in the charismatic churches, Satan is concerned that hell might depopulate soon. He therefore sends his emissary Karishika from hell to the world to come and win souls for him and possibly destroy the whole world. Karishika sets out and starts winning souls by seducing men, but she does so in such a brutal and dangerous way that God becomes annoyed with the devil and his helper and starts a counterattack. In Kinshasa, the figure of Karishika was immediately seen as yet another incarnation and transformation of the basic *mami wata* persona, like the figure of the *kamoke sukali*, or the seductive but dangerous and unpredictable Dona Beija before that. Together with her lover Don Antonio, Dona Beija, a young female character from a Brazilian soap series that was popular in Kinshasa in the early 1990s, even gave her name to the unreliable and quickly devaluating New Zaire or "heavy Zaire" (*zaire lourd*) bank notes that were introduced by the Birindwa government in 1993 to replace the old Zaire currency and curb rampant inflation. The new notes, however, quickly lost much of their financial weight.

Films like *Karishika* and its Congolese counterparts (such as the series *Jean 10:10* by *Le Groupe évangeliste EJCN*) squarely position the world of children and youngsters in the religious realm. And, indeed, nowhere are children more centrally present on the public scene than in the space of the churches, and more precisely during the crucial moment of public confession and witnessing. As it appears from the excerpts of the cases which I presented above, it is at moments like these that children are in a position to demonstrate the real power they possess. In their testimony, they in turn may implicate the adults who allegedly initiated them in the world of witchcraft: a market woman such as Losiya, who offered food to the child in order to link her to the nocturnal forces of evil; a father, mother or relative who offered a glass of water to the little friends of their son or daughter, but expected a nocturnal counter gift in human meat in return. In many cases, these public accusations have severe consequences for the adults whose name is mentioned in the children's testimonies. Frequently it sets in motion a violent reaction of relatives or neighbors, and leads to the beating up, lynching, necklacing and burning of the accused adults.[122]

In this way, children may use their narratives and their status of "witch" to settle certain scores with some adult relatives or neighbors, or more generally, to remove themselves from parental or family control and thereby create their freedom. As Barry points out in an interesting article on street children in Ouagadougou, a prominent but scarcely debated motive for children to take to the streets often also is a longing for freedom.[123] Street children in Kinshasa express it as follows: "At home it is 'cold-cold' [*malili-malili*], but the street is where one is free (*place ozali libre*); if you feel like stealing you can steal; if you feel like fighting you can fight; if you feel like lying, you can lie; if you feel like smoking you can smoke." One often hears: "To stay at home is wrong" (*ndako eza faux*), or "at home, eating is an uncertain and difficult thing" (*na ndako koliya manoeuvre*), whereas the street is experienced as a space where life is indeed hard and filthy and one has to be tough (*yanké*) and "sign a contract with death" (*kosigner liwa*). At the same time, it is also perceived as an almost oneiric space of diversion, possibility and promise, where "your body belongs to yourself" and you can "dedouble yourself," dance, drink, "dream" and "have fun" (*rêvesser*). The word *rêvesser* has particular connotations in the street children's vocabulary. No doubt derived from the French *rêve*, and making allusion to the oneiric qualities of the nocturnal life most children lead, it means: passing time in a nice way, dropping defenses and letting yourself go in your "hidden life." Paradoxically, the public space of the street is to some extent experienced as a space of quality time, of dream time, and of greater privacy and intimacy than the family household can give. It is not that many of these children have no family, home or relatives to turn to, or that they are no longer taken care of. Rather, they have made the decision to willfully "uninsert" themselves from their family context and from the responsibilities, expectations and futures that lay embedded within a normal family life. In Kinshasa, becoming a witch is certainly a way to attain such independence, to challenge parents, public authority and the established order, and to inscribe oneself into a specific temporality. It is a time perspective that is certainly present in Kinois culture as a whole, but that is lived most fully and recklessly by street children: the timeframe of the moment. On a more immediate level the street is perceived by many children as a space of opportunity where they may escape from the poverty (*bozangi*) of their family home and calm their consumerist dreams by buying clothes, shoes, and other luxury items with the money earned in the street.

A CRISIS OF KINSHIP MODELS AND PRINCIPLES OF SENIORITY? ADOLESCENT STRATEGIES OF SELF REALIZATION

All of the above only becomes possible in a context of communal turmoil and complex societal shifts and changes. These are partly realized in and through the fundamental crisis *and* restructuration of common models of kinship. If, as Geschiere has stated, witchcraft is the shadow side of kinship,[124] then the generational shifts within the idiom of witchcraft, as well as the partial disconnection of witchcraft and kinship which occurs especially in the urban context (and here the marketplace, for example, becomes a dangerously contaminating place where strangers such as Losiya skillfully intrude into one's life), are indicative of profound transformations in the field of kinship and the ways in which it was structured until recently.

Just as the unfolding urban dynamics in the West have contributed to the creation of a world of simultaneity in which the existence of time and chronicity are denied, so the ceaseless spread of modernity has led to frantic changes and ruptures in the collective memory work of the Congolese. These transformations are also reflected in a collectively shared sense of loss and irreversible change manifested, for example, in the crumbling of the patriarchal gerontocratic order, that has always been so typical of the "enduring time" of tradition and ancestrality. It is to this timeframe that the logic of kinship has always referred and through which it has realized and externalized itself. The transformations in this field, however, perhaps explain "the sometimes violent rejection of ancestral and parental figures in response to what is understood as their absence, their impotence, or their withdrawal of protection."[125]

On the micro level of the household, the family and the lineage, the pressures caused by the changing demands on the social environment in the urban context are most tangibly present in newly emerging relations of authority and respect between the sexes as well as between generations. These new shapes and attitudes are most clearly illustrated in the current transformation of divisions of labor. Whereas some youngsters have gained financial power and social status by means of revenues from the diamond trade, most family heads are socially and economically reduced to the status of unemployed and inactive men in Kinshasa today. In Kinshasa only a tiny fraction of the active adult male population is employed in the formal sector and has a salaried job, while they do not easily find a niche in the informal economy either, for this space seems to offer an advantage to youngsters who are often more streetwise and therefore better equipped in terms of social skills to adapt to the flexibility that characterizes such an economic environment. Just as children rule in the second world of witchcraft, and just as this shadow world has taken over the first world, youngsters control the country's second economy which has become, in fact, the real economy. Also, many men are often absent from home. As elsewhere throughout Africa, Kinois men are caught up in processes of migratory labor and travel, such as in the diamond traffic or because of the war, or they have set up other households in various areas of the vast city that is Kinshasa. It is a well-known fact that the *tontines* and *mozikis*—the neighborhood units of cooperation, the church support groups, the small-scale production of goods for sale on the market, all of those social networks and daily strategies of survival—are basically the work of women and mothers. To say that this goes hand in hand with an erosion of male authority is stating the obvious, but it is a factor that may help to explain why witch-children seem to accuse women and maternal figures rather more frequently than men and elders. Where the socioeconomic shifts are mediated by gender, the discourse of witchcraft seems to graft itself upon new, female, figures of authority in which old notions of power now concentrate themselves, rather than upon the male elder, who had always embodied the ultimate personification of the witch. And when this occurs in a sociocultural landscape of kin based relations under strain, such shifts form an ideal ground for all kinds of further tensions and witchcraft accusations amongst adults or between the adults and the children under their care. For example, the realities of urban polygamy have called into existence a category of co-wives known as "rivals" (*mbanda*). Unlike rural polygamous households, these co-wives usually do not live together in the same house or even in the same *quartier*, and frequently they do not even know of each other's existence. The term *mbanda* also applies to the relationship between the wives of two brothers. When one brother dies, the other brother will often be under the obligation to offer shelter and material support to the deceased's children and wife, who then becomes a rival of his own wife. In many cases, the relationships between these rivaling women are very tense. The frequency by which the *mbanda* theme, with all of its tensions and conflicts, is used as a source of inspiration in popular Congolese song attests to the central place it occupies in the minds and lives of the Kinois:

Mama, oo mboka etumba oo.	Mother, nothing but problems in this town.
Libala nayaki mpasi oo.	So much suffering in this marriage of mine.
Nakutaki bana ya mbanda oo.	I found the children of his first wife there.
Lokola ngai nabotaka te,	Since I don't have children
Tika ko babondela ngai, lokola	they try to be nice to me because
mama na bango, atinda bango.	their mother told them so.
Mama, tia nalela.	Mother, understand me when I complain.
Mobali nayaki, apesaka ngai attention,	The husband I live with has warned me:
Mpo na bana na ye nakuta.	I should behave well towards the children I found
Abengalaka ngai mbanda na ndako,	upon entering his household. He brings his first wife
Akosa ngai, aye kotala bana.	to the house; he presents her to me and tells me
Soki nalobi, alobi na ngai,	she comes to visit the children. And when I protest,
oyo mama na bana oo.	he just tells me that she is the mother of his children.
Mama, tala likambo	Mother, there is still another problem:
Mwana nyonso bakobetaka.	Every child needs punishment from time to time.
Lokola ngai nabotaka te...	And I, I never had any children...
Jeudi, nabetaki mwana ya mbanda,	Thursday, I spanked the child of my rival,
Anyataki poto-poto ya mbula,	he dirtied himself in the mud
Aye konyata na yango bafoteye.	And then climbed onto the sofa.
Ntango mobali na ngai ayaki,	And when my husband came home,
au lieu atuna likambo,	instead of asking what had happened,
Asiliki wo wo.	he just became angry.
Alobi: nabota ya ngai mwana,	He said: Give birth to your own child,
Nabetaka wo.	and then you can spank it as much as you want.
Mama, bana ya mbanda, kobokolo te.	Mother, how can I raise the children of my rival?
Nzoto na ngai ekomi kokondo na	I lose weight because of these children
likolo ya bana naboti te oo.	I didn't even bring into the world.
Mobali mpe andima ngai te;	My husband no longer respects me;
Ngai ko libumu eboya zemi.	I can't have children.
Nakoma na ngai amela milangi.	I have become like someone who has swallowed
	a bottle [who is blocked, cannot get pregnant].
Mama, naboyi na ngai libala.	Mother, I abandon this marriage.
Nakozonga, soki nazwi zemi.	I will only return to it when I have given birth
	to a child myself.

[Orchestra OK Jazz, in. *Oyo mobali tapale*]

When a "rival" dies or when she is absent for a long period because she left in search of a better life in the diaspora or in the Angolan diamond trade, like Esther's mother, her children regularly end up in the recalcitrant care of one of her husband's co-wives. It is stated that "to take care of the child of one's rival, is to take care of a dangerous monster" (*kobokola mwana ya mbanda obokoli elima*). Especially when these children's father dies as well, they often find themselves in a very vulnerable and unprotected position. Such children end up very much marginalized in a family context in which they are merely viewed as a burden and an extra mouth to feed at a time when food is already too scarce to feed everyone. In many households in Kinshasa today, people eat only once every two days: one day a meal is prepared for the children and the next day for the adults. In such a context, children who occupy a structurally weak position in their kin group, or sometimes even end up with no family at all, are more likely to be singled out as witches. This applies even more strongly to children who already stand out in one way or another because of a mental or physical disability, for example, or because of their erratic or idiosyncratic behavior. In this way, I observed a witch-child in one church who obviously suffered from Tourette's syndrome.

The same socioeconomic changes have also contributed to a growing intergenerational rift. Certainly in a rural context, children and youngsters are often no longer willing to lead the same life as their parents, to build a small house with a grass roof, and to till the fields. Despite its miserable conditions, the city often continues to be viewed by rural youngsters as a space of independence and freedom offering an escape from the social control (also in terms of witchcraft) exerted by the village elders. In Kinshasa and other urban settings in Congo, youngsters frequently create spaces of independence for themselves. They join, for example, a prayer group or a small collaborative economic unit (equally named stable) of (often male) age mates who frequently, although not necessarily, share the same regional or ethnic background and usually live in the same neighborhood. Whereas the organization of a stable is often, in a gang-like fashion, characterized by a strict hierarchy between older and younger (*grands* and *petits*), or "fathers" and "sons" amongst its members, the prayer groups, who typically include both boys and girls, are much more structured around invented horizontal kinship ties within one generation rather than around vertical (intergenerational) relations. In these rapidly proliferating urban prayer groups, often splitoffs from or subgroups of more established adult churches, all members thus call each other "Brothers and Sisters in Christ." Often such groups consist exclusively of children and youngsters. They usually meet several times a week, often during nocturnal prayer events that start at sunset and end early the next morning. They provide the ideal site for children and youngsters to remove themselves from parental control and other relations of seniority.

In spite of the crisis which structures of seniority are currently undergoing, age obviously remains an important marker to place and position individuals in the societal context, but with this difference: there seems to be an important shift from *absolute* age (via a periodization from child to adolescent, adult and elder, ritualized in different rituals of passage that mark the transitions within the life cycle) to *relative* age (in a social logic of *grand* and *petit*) in which normal hierarchies between absolute age and gender categories become much vaguer. In this respect forty year-old men can still be students, and thus belong to an "adolescent" category, while twenty year-old *bana Lunda* are *patrons* and act like elders.

It is important to underscore that the new, more relative, social hierarchies which emerge in the changing social world are still modeled on age, and that it continues to be the "old" vocabulary of masculine gerontocracy that informs the transformed contexts and relations between the sexes and the generations. The principles of seniority and gerontocracy as such are not being dismantled, but have instead become the ground for a generational conflict, mediated by gender, in which the (urban) young claim for themselves the right to singularize and realize themselves as "authoritative elders," and to use the syntax of gerontocracy before one's time, as it were. The actual modes of adolescent self realization in the contemporary urban context (the right to monopolize the public space, the power to become the maker of a social network, the aspiration to become the pivotal point of mechanisms of redistribution within one's kin or peer group, that is, the power to position oneself, like an elder, as a good "giver," with all the rights and duties this entails) thus do not really differ much from the old modalities of the established gerontocratic model. Girls and young women, too, will try to become more independent vis-à-vis the old hierarchical relations of authority that prevail in the context of lineage and household. Just like their young male counterparts, they too will, in a certain way, replicate these structures while reversing the gendered power relations between the generations. Young women such as Esther's mother, for example, or Mado (in the next chapter) who leave husband, family and children behind to search for material wealth in the context of the Angolan diamond trade are called "dogs who break the leash" (*bambwa bakata singa*). If successful they gain independence thanks to their newly acquired financial power, but also because they have managed to become like successful "hunters" and elder men. This, for example, becomes clear in the way in which, in the Angolan context, many of these women manage to monopolize and manipulate to their own advantage strategies of marriage and alliance, normally a prerogative of male elders.

The temporalities used in sociological analyses are often too dependent on the instant. They lack time depth. In the configuration presented here, what may be perceived in the moment of the immediate as a "crisis" of longstanding models of gerontocracy and seniority is in reality, when put in a longer time frame, a gender and generation conflict in which existing patterns of authority remain, in a sense, indelible but are now being appropriated and accessed in new and flexible ways by different categories of social actors who were formerly excluded from these social sources and positions of power. The fact that this generational conflict does not unfold without difficulty is highlighted by the new discursive fields and practices of witchcraft which strongly focus on children, youngsters and women. The diabolization of children by adults may thus be understood as a dark allegory which tells us something about a deeply rooted anxiety which accompanies a broader societal transformation (which is itself linked to a generalized crisis of modernity, at least in the Central African postcolony). In this respect Africa does not differ from other places around the globe where the link between children and witchcraft (whether it is in terms of child abuse, child prostitution, Satanism and child sacrifice, pedophilia, organ trade, or death squads hunting down street kids) expresses in similar ways a feeling of deep crisis.[126] In the rural Luunda world of southwestern Congo, where I conducted my initial field research in the late 1980s and early 1990s, the maternal uncle who "eats" his sister's children is referred to as "the dog eating its own placenta" (Luunda: *kabw waadi zamu dieend*). In urban Kinshasa, however, it is now the placenta which devours the dog. While the satanization of children in the urban context is thus illustrative of a perverse inversion of more traditional witchcraft models, the examples from the West, from child abuse to organ traffic, document how children fall victim to the witchcraft of adults. Both types of society, however, deal with an intergenerational crisis in which the relation with one's "placenta," one's descendants, has become problematic, and in which the life stream has been inverted and the prospect of a future cannibalized. In Congo this is also expressed in the widespread feeling that society has, in apocalyptic terms, arrived at the end of times.

THE TRANSFORMATION OF THE GIFT

The destructurations and transformations of existing patterns of kinship which I touched upon above are accompanied by profound shifts in the structuring fields of gift, reciprocity and exchange. These have always underpinned social transactions, especially with regard to marriage and alliance. However, in Congo today, many young men and their families find it impossible to observe and respect the gift obligations and transactions that make a marriage possible. One vendor on Kinshasa's central market succinctly put it like this: *Tosalaka te, tobalaka te*, "we don't work, and [therefore] we don't marry." Therefore Kinshasa's youth have switched to an alternative marriage system, the *marriage raccourci*, the "shortcut" version in which youngsters de facto start living together, have a child and place both their families before a *fait accompli*, thereby shortcircuiting the gift cycle of marriage and bride wealth transactions. Needless to say, this in turn adds to the possible causes for conflict and witchcraft accusations occurring in the urban family context.

The transformed nature of the circulation of women not only changes the whole pattern of gift and reciprocity which underpins the total social field, and especially the relationships between agnates, uterines and allies, but it also touches on the cultural status of the maternal figure. This may explain why women and mothers, more often than men, are implicated in the accusations which witch-children in turn direct against adults. Witch-children's stories exemplify a recurring pattern in which children become witches through a poisoned gift offered by a man, as in Mamuya's or Omba's accounts, but more often still by a woman, a mother, grandmother, aunt, neighbor or market woman as in Esther's case. In all of these stories something is being communicated about the status of the gift and, more specifically, about the monetarization and commodification of gift patterns in both kin and non-kin based relationships.

The idioms of sorcery and witchcraft (*kindoki*), until recently indissolubly connected to kinship, reveal to what extent capitalism and kinship interpenetrate. As illustrated, for example, in Omba's account, in the Congolese imaginary the capitalist logic of buying and selling easily adapts to and even exemplifies the nocturnal logic of witchcraft. As Mauss has shown, within the logic of reciprocity and gift, closedness or blockage of flow is seen as socially negative.[127] This blockage, with the conflicts and violence it entails, is often expressed in terms of sorcery and witchcraft. In the autochthonous popular understanding of the capitalist logic, blockage is viewed to be necessary to make profits and maximize capital. In this interpretation, capitalism becomes an "economy of constipation," in which local notions of "*kula*-like" circularity and personalized reciprocity of the gift seem to be transformed into a linear and exclusive, negative model of transaction to which access is much more restricted. Here, the figure of the accumulating, non-sharing individual, the successful PDG, entrepreneur or diamond trader coincides with the figure of the witch. For a certain urban elite, for example, the "dinosaurs" of the Mobutu regime for a long time exemplified and provided a role model of this ideal entrepreneurship. However, when one tunes in to *Radio Trottoir*, the window on the popular imagination, it becomes clear to what extent this collective imagination views the successful entrepreneur and politician, or the rich person, in powerful images of witchcraft and cannibalism, for example in connection with the figure of the Satan, the *ndoki*, or the *mami wata* who provides money in return for the lives of one's own offspring, thus embodying the ultimate blockage and reversal of the lifeflow.[128]

As it is, there is nothing surprising in the linkage between witchcraft and (absence of) gift, for both are ambivalent and dangerous "total social facts."[129] Bewitchment has always been defined in a context of inverted and perverted social relations, and witchcraft has always been transmitted by means of the gift (whether through food, sex or other interactions). Similarly, gifts have always had the capacity to be poisoned, especially if they engage one in a relationship of exchange that is forced upon one. The witch itself has always been a fundamental figure of exchange. Setting in motion a destructive internal mechanism of redistribution and "eating," the witch, as a figure of crisis, has always defined negatively what extended social reciprocity and "eating together" or sharing means positively. Therefore, the witch, as nocturnal shadow or double, had a non-alienated relationship with the diurnal subject, not as its reflection but as an integral part of this dual relationship in which the gift operated as a fulcrum. The gift positions itself at the heart of the oscillation which allows the nocturnal double to contribute to the institutionalization of its other half.

At the same time, the more traditional, though far from static, dynamics of witchcraft enabled the constant creation and redefinition of kinship solidarity. Popular Luunda etiology and diagnosis, for example, distinguish between three possible "causes" (Luunda: *yisaku*, sing. *chisaku*) of illness, death and misfortune: death (*lufw*), witchcraft (*ulaj*) and non ancestral spiritual agencies (*mahaamb*). Each of these three "causes" may involve either one's agnatic and/or one's uterine descent group. The sorcerer or witch who causes evil may be located either on one's father's side (*ku utaatukw*) or on one's mother's side (*ku umaakw*). As the Luunda observe: "It is the one with whom you eat who will also kill you," meaning that ritual hindrance or witchcraft occurs only between relatives with whom one is most closely related in terms of consanguinity, commensality and other forms of sharing and reciprocity, corporeal intimacy or conjugality. In fact, a large interdependence exists between close relatives both on the level of the residential unit and on the level of the lineage. Luunda representations have it that a witch, ancestor or spirit never acts without reason. The cause has to be provoked (*kukokil yiteel*) to act against one. As such, the *mwiin chiteel*, "the one who provoked" the cause, bears as big a responsibility for the harm done as the actual agent (*chisuung*), that is, the actual witch, ancestor or *haamb* spirit that was the origin of the cause and carried it out. One's behavior may put the lives of one's relatives at risk through provoking a witch or another agent into action. Hence the Luunda say that "the bigger witch is the one who provoked." Therefore, deviant behavior (lack of respect, neglect of one's familial duties, refusal of hospitality, physical threats, insults and so on) from a member of one's household or lineage, is very much dreaded since it may provoke a witch, ancestor or spirit to act against one through ritual means. Moreover, it is believed that a witch never directly attacks the provoker him or herself. Luunda say that "the provoker will not die." Instead, the agent who effects the "cause" will try to strike the provoker by "eating" and eventually eliminating one or more of his/her close relatives. In short, the *chisaku* constitutes a vengeful attack upon the whole kin group, and no relatives of the provoker's are safe from this vengeful action. At the same time, this attack, provoked by a *mwiin chiteel* and carried out by an agency (witch or ancestor) from within the kin group (and mostly within the matriline), may also reinforce the solidarity between those relatives: "If a wild boar feeds on the field of a younger sibling, you must chase it off; otherwise it will start to feed on the fields of the older sibling tomorrow." Ranks are closed for a vengeful counterattack or therapeutic action, in order to prevent the *chisaku* from eliminating the whole kin group. It is at the level of the lineage, and on the responsibility of the lineage head, that action is undertaken by relatives of the victim. Very often, however, the problem is presented at an interlineage level as well, and the elders of the village's other lineages, as well as the head of the major and longest established lineage of the village, will be consulted. The council of elders may even advise a particular choice of action, including witchcraft. Such witchcraft is termed "the witchcraft of the elders" (*ulaj wa amakuluump*), i.e. accepted as a solution after a wide consensus.

Whereas older, rural discourses and practices related to witchcraft thus ultimately strengthened kinship solidarity and acted as local forms of conflict prevention and resolution, the newly emerging discursive formations surrounding witchcraft in the urban context contribute, on the contrary, to the weakening of kinship ties in rather dramatic ways. In many of the new charismatic churches and prayer movements, such as Mama Olangi's and many others, the members of the extended family are almost invariably labeled as *bandoki*, witches. Although this still seems to tie in with the older notion of witchcraft as something coming from within one's own kin group, in reality it constitutes a major change in the ways in which the demarcating lines between kin and non-kin are drawn. In a previous chapter I have commented upon the individualizing and singularizing drive that underlies much of these churches' actions and discourses. Significantly, the churches' attacks on extended family relations focus on the gift obligations which underpin these larger kin based solidarity networks. To underline their argument, the church leaders refer themselves to the Bible passage in which it is stated that one should earn a living and work "by the sweat of your brow," that is, through one's own effort. Those family members who come to ask a relative for food, shelter, money and other forms of support, have always been fully entitled to do so in the open gift logic of kin based solidarity and reciprocity that is so characteristic of the social architecture throughout Central Africa. Indeed, as I have explained, refusing such request constituted a provocation. In these Central African worlds, also, the vocabulary of kinship has always been used in much more encompassing ways as a metaphor for opening up kin based networks. By redefining strangers and outsiders as kin, for example, gift cycles were widened and new levels of trust summoned. In this way a political economy of gift exchange in the form of tributes between real, putative or fictive kin has always formed one of the most important organizational modes to create, enable, maintain and broaden the network of political relations. Tributary relations institutionalized the personal sphere and personalized the institutional level.

The new regimes of knowledge that are being installed in the urban context and have started to penetrate the rural hinterland through the churches' expansion introduce a radical break with these longstanding moralities of transmission and exchange. In these new religious arenas, the open social field of relations, which is constantly generated and renewed through the circulation and the flow of gifts and transactions between its members, is increasingly becoming more closed. Basically, all those who fall outside of the scope of the nuclear family are now being denied the right to insert themselves in such gift relations. What this means in practice is that they are not only being labeled as evil witches when they attempt to do so, but also that, as witches, they are redefined as non-kin.

Moreover, the new churches are contributing to a drastic redefinition of the gift itself. Referring themselves to Matthew 7:7, they have launched the phenomenon of *semence*, "seed," under the motto: "Give to God and he will give you back" (*pesa Nzambe, akopesa yo*). As such, all "gifts" made to the church become short or long term investments: One sows in order to harvest (more than the English "seed," the French word *semence* carries the double meaning of seed and semen and thus strongly suggests fertility and plenty, connecting the fields of sexuality, agriculture and material wealth). As such, the gift has become a life insurance:

Kikwit, December 15, 1996. As I was walking past the court building of Kikwit, a city 500 kms northeast of Kinshasa, my attention was drawn by a large gathering of people in and around one of the neighboring compounds. Walking towards the crowd I could make out the voice of a preacher. Bystanders informed me that he had come from Kinshasa on an evangelization campaign and represented a church called "The Church of Faith:" "God gave you life for free, He gave you everything that you possess, life, breath, money, everything. The God of Moses made you rich. And He never asked you for something in return. But today, this same God is asking you to give everything you owe to Him. God is testing you to make you understand the hidden dimension of his divine message. He is telling you: 'Test me; give me what you have and I will return it to you multiplied by two.' You have to give to your God through his intermediary, your *pasteur*. The *pasteur* has no salaried job. He has to eat; he has to feed himself; he has to feed and clothe his family with whatever he receives from the church members. You have to feed the servant of God. He has to eat a heavy breakfast with large tins of milk powder. It is only when he is in good health and strong that he will be able to accomplish the mission that God bestowed upon him. If you give the *pasteur* twenty dollars, God will give you back ten times more. It is stated in the Bible; God has taken this into account. If you give a shirt to the *pasteur,* God will give you ten shirts in return. Test God and you will see the miracles he will work in your life. In front of the altar, you can see two large baskets. Step forward and give whatever you have brought. God will give it back to you multiplied by ten. Don't leave the church with your money in your pocket. You will lose it upon your return home, for Satan is watching you closely too. He doesn't like people who come together to glorify God. You have two spirits in you. One will tell you: 'Give everything, don't hold anything back.' This is the spirit of God who works for you. The second spirit will tell you: 'Don't give everything. How are you going to pay all your bills?' This is a diabolical spirit. In order to recognize it as such, you have to be filled by the spirit of God. So I ask you to consider this matter carefully. God, who sees and knows everything, looks into the heart of each and every one of you. If you go home with something in your pocket, he will take away from you everything you owe. Brothers and Sisters in Christ, you have to know that our God is not poor. He is richer than we can imagine. All the wealth in the world belongs to him. He is the One who gives, and He is the One who takes away."

Thereupon people precipitated themselves to deposit money in the baskets: 100,000 Nouveau Zaires, 250,000 NZ, a hundred dollars. A man gave five hundred dollars. Before depositing the dollar bills in the basket, he addressed the churchgoers in the following terms: "I give five hundred dollars to my God. I am convinced that God will give me 1,000,000 dollars back." Everybody applauded him. The preacher then addressed him: "My Brother, God of Israel, our God, is a God of miracles. Don't be afraid. It shouldn't surprise you if God gives you back 5,000,000 dollars. And the others who didn't give everything they possessed will regret their greediness, but it will be too late. Brothers and Sisters in Christ! Do you see this notebook? Write your name and address in it, and whatever it was that you have given to God today, whether money, a mattress, a basket, a plot of land, a television, trousers, a shirt, 1,000 dollars... In this way we will verify if God will have given back ten times more. Brothers and Sisters! I am very happy to see that there are people here today who know the true dimension of the Holy Word and who give to God foreign valuta rather than local money. Our local money is unstable, it depreciates,

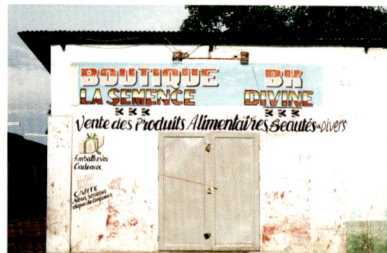

it loses its value day after day. Today, even if you give 10,000,000 NZ to God and God returns 20,000,000 NZ to you, what will you be able to buy with this money? Not very much! We can as well tempt God by giving him strong currencies, so that he can reimburse you with money that is strong. Nevertheless, even dollars, what are they worth, these dollars? We all know that, when our children come back from Angola with their dollars, this money doesn't last very long either. This is to tell you that even dollars are worthless in the face of God. But God's word always remains strong! If you doubt when you give to Him, your gift will be worthless."

Kinshasa, May 2001. In the "Free Church of Africa" (*Eglise Libre d'Afrique*, ELDA, a church movement that broke away from the Kimbanguist Church) Mama Kalonji gives her testimony:
My Brothers and Sisters, I died but I was resuscitated. When I died I went up to heaven. In Paradise [Lingala: *Lola*] I met the angels, but I did not see God. I can tell you this, however: All the gifts that we give in the church, I saw how these gifts are put to good use by God. God uses these gifts to build houses for us in Paradise. Those who do not contribute to God's work, and who refuse to give in the church, will find themselves in an unfinished house when they arrive in Heaven. Therefore, I beg you, give freely. To give is to prepare your house in Lola. In reality, the money, the Mercedes cars, the television sets that we give to the *pasteur* are stored for us by God. I, Kalonji, who are speaking to you, I am still a young woman. When I will be old, God will listen to my prayers, and he will render manifold what I gave to him because I "sowed" on time. To give is like sowing the seed. By giving to the *pasteur* I will be able to harvest later. Giving is keeping.

The gifts made to God and his intermediaries are called *nsinani* or, more frequently, *mabonza* or, with a French word, *dîme* (referring to the original biblical idea of giving a tenth of your possessions up to God). The phenomenon of *semence* (in many respects, a religious counterpart of the money pyramids and the chance games, the "Bindomanie," that became popular for a short while in Kinshasa in the early 1990s)[130] has taken over the daily reality in Kinshasa. References to *semence* on advertisements for churches and shops abound in every street: "the good sower" (*le bon semeur*), "seed in the soul" (*la semence dans l'âme*), "the good seed in the world" (*la bonne semence dans le monde*), "the sower" (*le semeur*), "the good seed" (*la bonne semence*), "the divine seed" (*la semence divine*), "the seed of God" (*la semence de Dieu*), "the good seed of life" (*bonne semence de vie*), and so on. Some counter-voices inside and outside of these churches (such as the popular Kin based actors Lokuli and Ngaluphar) have begun to criticize what they call "the commercial Gospel," "the prostitution of the Holy Spirit" (*kindumba ya molimo*), the "communities of lies" (*mangomba ya lokuta*) or "the communities of hunger" (*magomba ya nzala*), thereby indicating that these churches were, above all, created as a source of income for the preachers. Similarly, some criticism has been aimed at the *binzambi-nzambi*, the endless creation of new small churches that are perceived as an insult to God's greatness. Notwithstanding these criticisms, most "miracle churches" draw ever larger crowds, while the gifts, the "seeds" that are sown by the "believers" (*bandimi*), only continue to grow in importance. People "sow" watches, jewelry, diamonds, money, cars and houses to obtain a miracle, a job, a marriage (*mpo bazwa mabala*), healing (*mpo babika*), children (*mpo babota*), prosperity (*mpo commerce e prosperer*). In the midst of all of this, the "free" and spontaneous character of the gift (even though a gift is always embedded in a structure of obligation) is being redefined as a calculated act. Giving, to quote Mama Kalonji's words, has become keeping.

In summary, Kinshasa thus witnesses a total breach with older concepts regarding both the morality of gift exchange and the delineation of the relationships between kin and non-kin, inside and outside, or endogamous and exogamous. First, witchcraft is no longer something from within. Not only has the circle of kinship become much smaller through the restricting redefinition of lineage and clan relations imposed by the churches, but the outside world is also increasingly, and often in very brutal ways, penetrating the intimate circle of the nuclear family. Contrary to older forms of witchcraft, the witchcraft "new style" is wild, random and unpredictable, without clear direction or intention. This has also greatly affected local concepts of pathogenesis and has opened up the older etiological and diagnostic grid. Because the possible sources of witchcraft are oftentimes disconnected from kinship relations, the danger may now come from anywhere. One becomes bewitched in public places like markets and shops, and through relations with unrelated or anonymous people.

Secondly, what poses as gift in the social interaction is no longer what it appears to be. Underneath the visible gift lurks another invisible pattern which corrupts regular patterns of exchange. Crucial with regard to the new patterns of witchcraft is the emergence of the notion that one can be tied by a gift which poses as such, but which in reality creates a debt obligation. More important, the receiver of the gift does not even realize that he is actually contracting a debt and engaging in a relationship of a totally different nature: that of a nocturnal capitalism, with all that this entails: debts, unstable prices, interest rates, and laws of supply and demand. The gift of the witch who gives bread, biscuits, fish or fruit to children pretends to be a free gift in the initial establishment of the relation. But rather than being free, it turns into something else. In Omba's account, the witches' nocturnal village is described as a world of "give-give" (*donnant-donnant*), of "give and they will give you, receive and give back" (*pesa bapesa yo, bapesi yo, yo mpe pesa*). As such, not only are the rules changed because the logic of gift and counter gift is applied a posteriori, and hence turns what was a free gift into an obligation to return, but moreover there no longer exists a balance between gift and counter gift: a human life is expected in return for a biscuit. Furthermore, there is no longer a reason, a *chisaku* or cause, not even a provocation, to justify such a bewitching demand. Above all, this logic of unequal reciprocity is applied erroneously. For one, not only are the exchanged gifts and counter gifts of unequal status, but so are the exchange partners themselves. In normal circumstances, the receivers would not even be expected or supposed to give back if only because they are children and have not yet attained the required social status to position themselves as givers and engage in relationships of reciprocity.

The stories of the children, who are being pulled into the second world by unknowingly accepting a gift that does not reveal its true nature at first, mirror the mechanisms of debt creation that they experience in the first world reality. These often force them to stay in the street. A common practice among street children is *confisquer*. This practice creates what is called "fictive debts" through which a child is "forced into a debt" (*kokotisa na nyongo*) and cannot leave the street until the debt is repaid towards the street group of which he or she is a member. The gang will, for example, send one of its members to the market to sell some goods. Even if after a day the child was unable to sell the commodities, the group will nevertheless consider these goods as sold and will consequently claim from the child a sum of money that is equivalent to the goods' estimated selling price. Thus, both the market and the second world mirror each other. They force one into situations of social and economic debt and dependency through which one is tied or knotted into an intimate but unequal relationship with the claimant.

As noted before, the children's stories about how they were pulled in the second world often implicate women. The growing commodification of gift and kin based relations in the urban (and increasingly also the rural) world, combined with the fact that women have started to gain more economic, political and religious power than ever before and increasingly appear as the social actors who manipulate the gift, especially in relation to (their own) children, illustrates that even the most basic building block of kin relations, namely the relationship between mother and child, is touched by the profound transformations the urban context is currently undergoing.

On a different level, I contend that the changing perception of women and mothers is indicative of a growing alienation with, a liquidation of, the double, indicative also of the changing nature of junction and disjunction between first and second world, diurnal and nocturnal, or life and death that is operated by the gift. The image of the mother as witch goes radically against the deeply ingrained cultural model which views women (in their role of genitrix, mother, cultivator and cook) as the ultimate figures of physical and social reproduction, and thus as the generative forces behind the sociocultural weave. In the rural Luunda world, for example, as in most Central African cultures, the female body is conceptualized as relational body. Most obviously women "are with two bodies" (Luunda: *aadi ni mijiimb yaadi*) during pregnancy, but more generally, the female body is a social body that gives and receives and thus creates strong physical and social ties between the members of the household and beyond. In this way, Luunda women refer to themselves as "the little needle" (*kukeep kwa ndoong*) which sews together or repairs the social skin (*aam kapwakal kaanguy kateendaang*). The verb *kuteend* means "repair" as well as "feed" or "cause to grow."[131] Women are those who generate social ties and "knot" (*kunuung*) the links between the generations. In the contemporary urban context, however, it is precisely this "knotting ahead" (*kunuung kulutw*) of the life flow which has become problematic. Rumors and stories that have started to circulate in Kinshasa on a frequent basis comment upon this by making mention of mothers who give birth to witch-children or, even more dehumanizing, electric eels. Stories as illustrated in Pfumueto's comic strips include: "the monster-fetus which exits its mother's womb at night" (*Bebe oyo abimaka na zemi ya mama na ye na butu*), or "the woman who gives birth to an electric eel in Kinshasa" (*mwasi aboti nzombo na Kinshasa*).

The changing status of women and mothers is indicative of the cracks and flaws that have started to appear in the urban gift logic, and so is the conceptualization and the collective experience of children in terms of witchcraft. In alliance transactions children represent, even more so than wives, the supreme gift or the ultimate binding agents in the endless cycles of reciprocity and redistribution that underpin the societal field. As Lallemand has pointed out in a recent echo of Marcel Mauss, it is especially the circulation and the un-

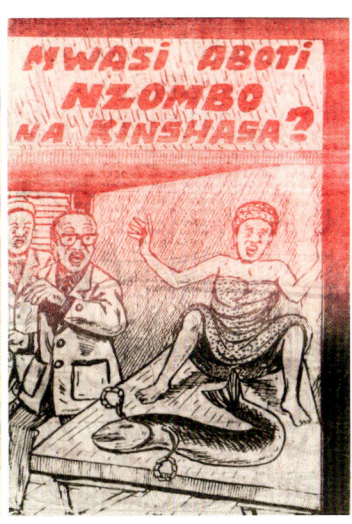

remitting movement of children between various kinship units which allow the formation of the social architecture of kinship, alliance and residence in what she calls traditional societies.[132] Lévi-Strauss' reinterpretation of Mauss' classic *Essai sur le don*, however, is in great part responsible for the fact that the role of children has disappeared from the analysis of the gift cycle and that the role of women as ultimate gift has been stressed so strongly instead.[133] And yet when rereading Mauss' essay, one is reminded not only of the fact that the processes of exchange of *oloa* and *tonga* in Polynesia are set in motion by the birth of a child, but that the child itself also becomes a gift, a *tonga*, and as such becomes an integrative part of the gift cycle itself.[134] Children thus appear both as medium and as actors in the creation and extension of kin relations and alliance: Without children, no gifts; and without gifts, no kin and allies. Therefore childless marriages in Congo usually end in the wife's return to and reintegration in her own family, together with the restitution of all the goods that were transferred during the marriage transactions from the side of the wife takers to that of the wife givers.

THE BREACH BETWEEN THE IMAGINARY AND THE SYMBOLIC

Much of the previous analysis embeds itself in what might be seen as a classic approach to witchcraft as an expression of social relations and processes. In such an approach to the witchcraft idiom, the social and structural tensions produced by intergenerational and crossgender relations are usually interpreted to be amongst the most important determinants of witchcraft accusations. Approaches of this nature have been criticized for their reductionism and instrumentalism, as well as their incapacity to reveal the autochthonous understandings and internal structures of symbolization.[135] Whereas such an approach does indeed not focus in depth on the inner meanings and ontological status of witchcraft and divination in the experiential reality of the Congolese subject, I believe it does shed light on the shifts that currently occur in the idiom of witchcraft itself. Furthermore, it also links these shifts to more profound societal alterations which touch more precisely on issues of ontology, local structures of symbolization, and the subjective experience of these realities.

While the emergence of witch-children is symptomatic of an underlying "crisis" of the gift, this crisis is itself emblematic of what Barry designates as the "weakening of the cultural tools of symbolization" (*défaillance des outils culturels de symbolization*) and what I have called a more generalized breach between the levels of the imaginary and the symbolic.[136] The gift is the ultimate mediator between these two levels. I would like to turn to the Lacanian gift doctrine in order to make this more explicit.[137]

In *Fonction et champs de la parole et du langage*, Lacan offers an interpretation of

Freud's observation of a toddler throwing away a bobbin and then pulling it back by means of the unreeled thread. The two movements are accompanied by the child's calling out "o" and "a", *fort*, there, and *da*, here. Through the play with the bobbin, the toddler symbolically masters the real absence of the mother. The bobbin represents the lost object and, not unlike the gift object in the cycle of gift and counter gift, it becomes a symbol of both presence and absence. The child thus learns that he can control in the symbolic domain what he loses in reality. The bobbin (the gift) is what Lacan calls an object "a": "the signified of all loss meeting the subject of its ascension towards social order and exchange."[138] Accessing the dimension of the ludic and the symbolic allows the subject to overcome the attraction of the reflection, of the image that other subjects return, or of the register of the imaginary. On the level of the unconscious, on the other hand, is situated everything that cannot be exchanged, symbolized, represented, given and returned. What psychoanalysis (or in another context ritual and hence the logic of gift and counter gift) envisages is the turning of the register of the imaginary into the dimension of the symbolic, of language and of exchange.

The classic interpretations of the gift by Lévi-Strauss and Lacan postulate the supremacy of the symbolic in relation to the imaginary. In this respect, the signified is to some extent subordinated to the signifier: symbols are imbued with a larger reality value than that which they symbolize, that is, the levels of the imaginary and of what Lacan calls "the real" (that which is neither imaginary nor symbolic). Godelier has recently offered a critique on these classic interpretations in which he turns around their primacy.[139] For Godelier, the levels of the symbolic and the real are materializations of the imaginary, which (re)creates and institutionalizes society. Here the symbolic is not a mental structure but encompasses an internalized social structure constructed by a social logic that is unconscious but that constantly externalizes itself as social essence in the domains of sexuality, power and politics. It is the concentration of the three orders of the imaginary, the symbolic and the *réel* which makes social reality, the social life of people, but it is the register of the imaginary that offers the fixed points from which a society invents itself.

To return to the Congolese context: the first world of social reality is only formed in relation to a second world, a mirror image which is rooted in a collective imaginary. That is what the conceptualization of the witch as the moment of inversion, shadow, or double means. The traditional figure of the witch works as an imaginary yet simultaneously real double, as imago and mirror. As a figure of crisis, the witch thereby enables the realization of its opposite.

In September 1999, while cruising in the streets of Kinshasa, I noticed an inscription, taken from a song by the popular musician Koffi Olomide, on one of the city's many taxi buses (*fula-fula* or *nzungu ya bana*).[140] The inscription read: *Réalité eza trucquage te*, "reality is no imitation, counterfeit or forgery". And yet the qualities of reality in Congo are no longer those of Lacan's *réel* (hence the importance of "appearance" and of the *faire semblant* in the Congolese context). Instead, the second world has become the first, just as the informal second economy has become the first economic reality. No matter which reading one prefers (the one offered by Lacan or by Godelier), it is clear that the processes of dedoubling and mirroring no longer find a comfortable place in the current Congolese context. Symbolization, in other words, no longer takes place or, more precisely, the qualities of the structuring of symbolization have changed. Thus, the linkages among the orders of imaginary, symbolic and real, have lost their simultaneity, they have disappeared or weakened, and can no longer be trusted or taken for granted. Today, the two sides of the mirror have not only become entangled, but they have radically collapsed into each other. It is at this very point that the mirror has lost its power of reflection. Rather, it opens up into the abyss of terror, a terror that is rooted in the fact that the grounds on which reality is constructed (the possibilities of representation and the capturing of relations in language) have themselves disappeared into the abyss of the two collapsing halves. The drastic transformation of the gift, as the most central binding agent between the levels of the imaginary, the real and the symbolic, is indicative of this more fundamental crisis.

Across cultures, children are one of the most powerful points of reference on which sociocultural imaginaries at the crossroads of sexuality and power graft themselves (and images of Bluebeard, Gilles de Rais or Tournier's *Le Roi des Aulnes* readily come to mind). In relation to the context of Congolese post-colonialism, the local collective imaginary is no longer symbolized, and (re)presented in the social reality of everyday life. Neither does it seem to underpin, institutionalize nor legitimate other levels. Through a severing of the ties that operate the mechanisms of junction and disjunction, and the generation of the simultaneous multiplicity that underpins processes of doubling and dedoubling, it has become ontological instead. The imaginary as such has swallowed and replaced social reality. This also has enormous consequences for the meaning and the production of violence in the Congolese *societas*. The dynamics of witchcraft have always opened spaces of violence, but this violence contributed to and enabled the turning of the drama of social disorder into its opposite. It established (social and symbolic) consensus or institutionalized the breach. In the current context, however, an imaginary of violence does seem to represent social violence, or offer a solution to it, to a lesser extent than it used to before. Instead it has itself become the unmediated reality. It is this fundamental change in the interplay between imaginary and symbolic, which is externalized and has crystallized in the figure of the child as witch. The witch-child is the terminus of a long process of disconnection in which the non alienated character of the relation with the double has gradually evolved to an alienated one. Here the relation with the double has ceased to be one of exchange and negotiation, and has turned from familiar to *mystique*. The shadow has become satanic and deadly as an image also of all the dead that have been rejected and forgotten but do not agree to become meaningless for the living.

Having said this, however, one should be wary of analytical models which suggest the dawning of new eras that require new means of understanding basic social processes or models that imply total loss or evacuation of meaning. The difference between experience and structure is important here. Despite the experiential frame of urban Congolese life, it is difficult to understand how one can have a world (or an imaginative process) without symbolization. No doubt the question also centers on the changing, and thus historical, character of such symbolization (its stability, collective power, its relation to "realism," its imagic form, its capacity to fixing ontology). Viewed in a more diachronic perspective, today's terminus might really turn out to be tomorrow's starting point for a further round of flexible transformations within continuing long term historical trajectories.

INVISIBLE CITIES III
MADO:
THE STORY OF A FEMALE DIAMOND SMUGGLER

Mado's narrative is set against the background of the diamond trade between Congo and Angola. Judging from multiple other conversations I had with both men and women from the Lunda Norte scene over the past ten years, her story is representative of the lives led by many Congolese women in the diamond territories UNITA occupied till 1998 (although some areas remained under UNITA control till Savimbi's death in 2002). Mado is a young woman in her early thirties, and a mother of five children. In September 1997, while returning from downtown Kikwit where I had been visiting a healing church, I walked along a well known busy parking lot where owners of four wheel drive cars were recruiting clients hoping to travel to Kinshasa, Kahemba and other towns. In the crowd I caught sight of Mado. She was negotiating the price of a place on board a Land Cruiser which was supposed to leave for Kinshasa that day. The French she was using was perfect and revealed a good school training, but the way in which she was dressed, the make-up, the gold necklaces she was wearing, her whole attitude betrayed her involvement in the diamond traffic which was then flourishing between Kinshasa and the Angolan province of Lunda Norte. After the driver made it clear that all the seats were already taken, she and a girlfriend slowly started to walk in the direction of the nearby Kimpwanza avenue, where they entered "The Forest" bar. Together with a friend, a school teacher who lived in the neighborhood, I followed them and after a couple of beers we struck up a conversation. The account which is rendered below was imparted to me on the following day, in the house of one of Mado's relatives.

1984 — MARRYING JOHNNY

I live in Kinshasa in the zone of Lemba and I am the mother of five children. I have just returned from Angola where I spent the last two years. I have been going to Angola ever since February 1984. I started going there because I was married to a student by the name of Johnny. He was studying medicine at the University of Kinshasa. We had to support ourselves financially. Our marriage didn't start like other regular marriages. Johnny and I were friends, and then I became pregnant. My parents chased me from the house. I had no choice but to go and live with Johnny. We tried to get by with the little money that we had. Then I gave birth to a boy, little Theo.

In 1984 Theo was four years old. There were a lot of rumors about diamonds in Angola. My husband decided to interrupt his studies to go to Angola. I tried to convince him to continue his studies and to give me the permission to go in his place. He finally accepted. But we didn't have any money to pay for the journey. We sold all the furniture that we had and with that money I traveled from Kinshasa to Tembo, a diamond town on the border with Angola. It took me five days to get there.

THE FIRST ENTRY INTO ANGOLA

In those days there was no problem with *guia*'s[141] to enter into Angola. People entered Angola illegally through a stretch of forest which has since been given the name of *corta mata*. After three weeks in Tembo, I entered Angola accompanied by some carriers. The bags with commodities that we carried with us for barter were dirtied so that they couldn't be perceived from afar. Otherwise one risked being arrested. We arrived at a village called Kiambamba where we hid in the bush. The carriers who knew the local language entered the village and made arrangements with the people there. What I mean by this is that they contacted villagers in possession of diamonds. They then returned with a list of goods which these people wanted in return for their diamonds. As soon as an agreement was reached, we left the forest to spend the night in the village. When the whole operation was over, we had no reason to stay there. As quickly as possible we returned to Congo. It happened frequently that the villagers themselves betrayed us and informed armed men of our presence. They would come and confiscate all of our goods. In spite of all these setbacks we weren't discouraged easily. On another trip we were ambushed. The soldiers [either UNITA fighters or MPLA troops] took everything, gave us a beating and left us more dead than alive.

THE FIRST "MARRIAGE" IN ANGOLA: THE UNITA SOLDIER

Personally, I suffered a great deal during another ambush. Four soldiers raped me and left with all the goods I had brought along. That is why, during those days, many women tried to marry soldiers in order to get protection. Me too. As soon as I had established a relationship with one of them, the "natives" [the Angolan soldiers] would give me diamonds to sell in Congo. They would also give me a list of goods which I had to purchase for them. When selling the diamonds you had to make sure that you respected the list at all costs. If some money was left after I had bought their things it became mine. When I returned with the goods to Angola the soldiers would be extremely pleased. They started to

trust me. Many people did business like that in Angola. As for me, I managed
to buy a house in Lemba and two more houses in Matete [two neighborhoods
in Kinshasa]. I paid for Johnny's studies. We [the Congolese] continued to
work like this for nearly six years before the Angolans woke up. Then many
people died.[142] Afterwards they started with the system of checkpoints at the
border. The *guia* system was put in place. The dollar entered the scene,
first at the Congolese side of the border in places like Tembo and Kahungula.
Before that, even in Congo, we used to prefer local money whenever we sold
our diamonds to the local *comptoirs* in Tembo. But the dollar started to rule
from 1987–1989 onwards. It was in that period also that traders started
to sell their diamonds directly in Kinshasa. Nevertheless the number of
comptoirs at the border continued to increase.

THE SECOND "MARRIAGE" IN ANGOLA: MITTERAND

Bit by bit I put an end to my relationship with my friend, the Angolan UNITA soldier.
Finally, he was transferred to another place. At some point in time UNITA
started to deny entrance into Angola to women. Only men were deemed
strong enough to work in the UNITA controlled diamond mining sites. UNITA
wanted diamonds badly in order to buy arms. The only way for a woman to
be allowed to enter Angola was in the company of her husband. You had to
be able to show a passport that stated that you were indeed married to so-
and-so. All of the Congolese women, open-minded as always, started to marry
at the border in order to gain access to Angola. I was taken by a man called
Mitterand. We entered Angola together and stayed there for a long time.
We were really married, Mitterand and I. I met him in 1989. He had traveled
to Angola repeatedly and was well-known there. Civilians and soldiers alike,
everybody respected him. He had a house and a car, and he was one of
the first Congolese to own a shop and a bar with electric light. We lived very
peacefully in Angola. Mitterand was a big chief. People even started asking
him to act as a judge in disputes between Congolese, between Angolans,
or between Congolese and Angolans. In short, he was an important man.
Too bad, though, that he did not have any formal schooling. He couldn't
even speak French and only a little Portuguese. He had left his native village
near Idiofa [in the Kwilu district of the province of Bandundu] in search of
adventure and he had ended up in Angola. There he worked in diamonds
and became a respected man. He was even allowed to carry his personal gun
around, so that he could defend himself in case someone attacked him.
He was an alcoholic and smoked marijuana all day long. I started smoking
that stuff because of him.

DANGEROUS LIAISONS AND THEIR CONSEQUENCES

From time to time I returned to Congo in order to buy more goods. In Kinshasa I told my husband [Johnny] what the situation was and what a woman had to do in order to enter Angola. He understood. I told myself that my husband, having seen how quickly we had become rich, could not really object to the situation. It took some persuasion but in the end he understood. I assured him that I was only acting with his and the children's best interests in mind. I returned to Angola. There I had the misfortune to become pregnant. I gave birth to a girl. She grew up with Mitterand and me during the next two years. Then, a UNITA officer fell in love with me. In the beginning I said no. Then he started to threaten that he would kill Mitterand if I didn't give in. I finally gave him what he wanted but on one condition: that we would be secret lovers. He accepted. After a while, however, Mitterand grew suspicious and became more and more jealous. Then there was an open conflict. I had to explain everything to Mitterand. One evening Mitterand was so angry that he fired a shot at the officer. The latter died on the spot. The situation really got out of hand. We had no choice but to flee. We managed to escape with our diamonds and dollars. After we left, UNITA killed eleven Congolese and wounded several more. We arrived at Tembo and from there took a flight to Kinshasa.

In Kinshasa I found myself in a difficult position. Mitterand ignored the fact that I was married to Johnny. We took a room in a hotel. On the third day I went home to visit Johnny. It was on a Sunday, I well remember. My husband was there. We embraced. I told him the whole story and asked to remain calm. I told him that we had brought a lot of dollars and diamonds worth a small fortune. In order to win this game we had to be flexible and think well before playing this last card which we call the card of good fortune. Johnny understood the whole situation. I returned to the hotel. The next day, Mitterand and I went to a *comptoir* downtown. The value of our diamonds was estimated at US$170,000. We decided to buy two houses: one for him and the other for me. We also wanted to buy a Land Cruiser as well as to open a shop selling luxury goods in Kinshasa. We also wanted to buy some real estate in Kikwit, with a view to constructing a big bar there. On top of that there would be some money left to give to relatives. I urged him to leave for Kikwit as soon as possible to start with the realization of our plans. For me it was a way to get rid of him. Finally we sold our diamonds for US$135,000. We bought the houses and the car as planned.

GETTING RID OF MITTERAND

We planned to travel to Kikwit two weeks later. In the meantime I went home every day and gave my husband US$42,000. For me it was a way to calm him down. I told him everything that Mitterand and I had done. I gave him the documents of all the new houses that I had bought. In all, we now had four houses in Kinshasa. My husband was very pleased. He proposed buying a car as well. I approved of his idea. He bought a Peugeot for US$3,000. A couple of days after that I left with Mitterand for Kikwit. He wanted to go to his village first.

After a week I pretended to be ill. He let me precede him to Kikwit. From there I took a plane to Kinshasa. He stayed in his village for nearly two months. The girl that I had with Mitterand stayed with me in Kinshasa. Johnny didn't object and treated her as one of his own.

When Mitterand arrived in Kikwit he sent me a message asking me to join him. I promised to come, but two months later I was still in Kinshasa. Mitterand was a real drunkard. He took other girls in Kikwit, and for me this presented an occasion to get rid of him. I convinced my husband to let me go to Kikwit in order to rid ourselves of Mitterand and reclaim our belongings there. Some other people had to intervene and persuade Johnny before he finally allowed me to go. I traveled to Kikwit and hid myself near Mitterand's house, together with some boys. Around midnight I asked one of the boys to knock at the door. Mitterand opened the door, half dressed. I jumped up, rushed into the house and saw another woman lying on the bed, totally naked. I yelled and cried till dawn. Then I went straight to the OR [*Office de Renseignement Militaire*, Military Intelligence Office]. My case was taken to court and Mitterand lost. I was given the house in Kikwit. I told Mitterand that as far as I was concerned we were divorced. Totally drunk, he signed the divorce papers. Two days later I returned to Kinshasa. My husband was very pleased with me. I told Mitterand that I would take him to court for the second time if he tried to follow me to Kinshasa. And for the rest of his life he will not be able to return to Angola either, because they are waiting for him there too. After a while, however, Mitterand did show up in Kinshasa. Fortunately we reached an agreement as to the other belongings that we had bought together. Our elders mediated between the two of us and we didn't have to go to court for the second time. Mitterand left me the Land Cruiser and we were now totally divorced.

LEAVING AGAIN FOR ANGOLA

In agreement with my husband I decided to return to Angola one more time. This time I didn't go to the border of Tembo, since they would remember that I had been involved in the death of a UNITA soldier. I went to Shakufwa instead [a village more to the east, near the town of Kahemba]. This was for my own security because the soldiers at Tembo would remember that an officer had been killed because of me, even though some years had passed. I entered Angola in the company of the son of my older sister, Mandola. This was in November 1996 and only now, in September 1997, have we come back to Congo. In 1996 the border was closed. During that period UNITA didn't give a *guia* to Congolese. Nobody could get in. We spent four months at the Congolese side of the border. After four months we noticed that the

number of *pincheurs* (as we call the courageous people who go to Angola to make a living), the number of *pincheurs* who were waiting in Shakufwa like ourselves, had diminished considerably. At first there had been at least three thousand people there. We understood that many of them had associated themselves to local villagers who helped them to enter Angola through the forest. We decided to do the same. We paid the amount of money that the guides asked from us. One night, the villagers came knocking on our door and we left that very same night, together with sixty-four other persons. We traveled during the night. During the day we were obliged to remain at the same spot, hidden under the trees of the savannah, or in the forest. We walked during the night. After seven days we arrived at a village.

We thought it would be better to stay in the bush and send someone to the village to check it out first and to see whether there were *mbila* [in Lingala: "palm tree," a name used to designate soldiers]. The guide left in the morning and returned late that same day. There were indeed some *magivel* [UNITA soldiers] present in the village. The guide had also seen how another group had entered the village and how the soldiers had given them *guia*'s allowing them to work in the diamond mines. Upon hearing this we decided to enter the village. The first soldier who caught sight of us was still a child. Amongst the soldiers in that village many were only fourteen or fifteen years old.

The little soldier stopped us and ordered us not to move. It wasn't my first time in Angola so I knew that it is always like this. The soldier whistled and a group of other soldiers appeared. We had a Luba boy [Luba: an ethnic group in Congo] in our midst who had never been in Angola before. When the soldiers started to fire in the air, he fainted and fell down. In the meantime the soldiers proceeded with the *rivista* [control]. They took most of the goods that we were carrying with us.

One of their officers started to divide us in two groups. He put all the women to one side. There were twelve of us in all. We were shown into a house where another group of five officers was drinking. When they saw us they started to yell *amigo, amigo*. One of them grabbed a Luba girl with a very light-brown skin. He cried out: *pora*! and left with her. We never found out what happened with her. In the meantime the group of men was severely beaten. We heard gunfire and cries for help. Afterwards we were informed that these men were really tortured. They were considered MPLA spies trespassing on UNITA territory.

In the house where they had taken us we were held by four drunken soldiers. One of them, the one with a revolver, started to undress. All he was wearing was a piece of dirty underwear. He then grabbed one of the women.

The woman in question fiercely resisted. He slapped her in the face, yelling "bitch." We advised the girl not to resist or else she risked being killed by that man, especially since he was totally drunk. They finally went to an adjacent room where he raped her. We, the other women, sat in silence for a long time. The two other officers left without a word. After a couple of hours they returned, accompanied by others who had just returned from a looting trip. We spent two nights in that village. On the third day each of us was given a *guia* which indicated which mine we had to report to. By chance, my nephew and I were sent to the same mine, Zombi, situated along the Kwango river. There were four women in my group.

THE THIRD "MARRIAGE" IN ANGOLA: OLD WILLY

At the Zombi mine there were lots of divers and diggers. When the *bana Lunda* ["the Children of Lunda," i.e. the Congolese youngsters who are diving and digging for money in Lunda Norte] and the soldiers noticed the arrival of four new women they started to invite us to their homes, giving us plenty of food and beer. Without much ado, four marriages were concluded. That is the law in Angola. The men there remain single for so long that they grab the first woman they meet. As for me, I married a certain Willy, and I made sure that my young nephew could live with us. Ya Willy [Old Willy] was a famous diver. I had to stay home while he went to work. My nephew found a job in the *laverie*, the "wash place" [sifting the gravel]. The *laverie* belonged to the "State" [UNITA]. In the evening they came home where their food and their bed awaited them. Each time Willy found a diamond, he gave it to me, and I kept it safely at home for him. My nephew did the same. Ya Willy regularly controlled the diamonds so that there couldn't be any discussion as to what belonged to whom.

We lived for four months like that in the Zombi mine, without finding many stones, however. At other mines we were hardly more successful. We did the tour of all the major mines, but we didn't come across the big stone that would allow us to return to Congo. In the Kwango mine we heard the rumor that there was an *ewawa* [a waterfall of diamonds] in the mine of Kayisese. We decided to go there. Many others did the same, and we all traveled together. After two days we arrived at Kayisese. When we arrived we saw two dead divers being hauled up from the river. There were more dead bodies under the water. There had been the kind of accident that we refer to as *ngele* [The canoes on the river have equipment on board to provide the divers with oxygen. Many canoes are tied together to allow them to stay on the same spot. When the cords break and the canoes start floating away or capsize, the divers are very vulnerable for they risk being cut off from their source of oxygen]. Many divers died that day; few were saved. This accident made the *ewawa* stronger. These people died because they were sacrificed to produce the diamonds. Their lives were at the base of the *ewawa*.

The next day the divers were buried. In Angola, and especially on the side of UNITA, all that matters is work. They always want to speed up the work tempo. They don't like to lose time over useless rituals. When someone dies at night, he is buried first thing in the morning, so that people can return to the river to continue with their work as quickly as possible. They need the diamonds to pay for their guns. If someone dies in the morning around eleven, those who are scheduled to work the next night are called upon to replace those who are burying the dead person.

After the burial, the "chiefs of the motors" [*dona moteur*, the owner of the diving equipment and usually the head of the ring or group (*écurie*) that collaborates in the hunt for diamonds] hired new divers.[143] Ya Willy was one of them. Two days later he started to work. There was an *ewawa* indeed! On his first day of work Ya Willy found an eight carat stone, closed and without spots, which would make a lot of money. That evening we organized a party. We drank a lot. Kayisese is a great mine. There are fantastic bars, there is electric light till dawn. There are always a lot of people in the bars. For the rest of the month we lived really well.

GETTING RID OF YA WILLY

After a month, our "bundle" of diamonds had grown considerably. Ya Willy wanted to return to Congo once and for all and he started to make plans to marry me upon our return. Since I was already married in Congo, I knew that I could not possibly go along with his plans. I decided that it was time to play a trick on Willy. I myself produced a letter which was addressed to me and seemingly came from Congo. In the letter, my family announced the imminent death of my mother. They begged me to come home as soon as I received their message so that I could take my mother to the hospital and pay for her bills. That day I cooked dinner. Then I went inside the house and stayed there for the rest of the day, adopting a sad air. When Willy came home, I made sure that big tears were rolling down my cheeks. He found me like that, sitting in my room. He was surprised to see that I was crying and asked me what was going on. I gave him the letter and while he was reading it I pretended to break down in tears. He was moved and tried to calm me down. He promised that he would find a solution. Then he left.

While he was gone, I called my nephew and informed him of my plans. He was very happy to hear what I had in mind. Together we decided upon our strategy. I told him: "If Ya Willy gives me the permission to return to Congo, I will ask you to accompany me. You, however, will pretend to resist the idea. You will only give in after several other people have tried to convince you of the necessity of your return." I asked him to act as if he were very sad. After that, Willy came home again in the company of one of his friends, who had also brought his wife. They did their best to comfort me. Willy promised to let me return to Congo so that I could look after my mother. I then told him that I didn't want to go alone. I asked Willy to accompany me. He said that he had too much work and besides, he had to take advantage of the *ewawa*. Then he proposed that my nephew would accompany me. The latter refused, according to plan. While the others tried to convince him, Willy and I made love, all night long till the morning. In the morning I told him that the money to hospitalize my mother constituted a major problem. Willy said he was willing to split the diamonds we had. I told him: "Before doing that, I want to make love to you again." And so we did. Afterwards he took the bundle containing the diamonds and we divided them in two equal parts.

Around six in the morning my nephew finally agreed to accompany me to Congo. Willy arranged the *guia* passes for us. At ten o'clock we boarded a Land Cruiser belonging to UNITA and they drove us to the border. The soldiers were sent on a reconnaissance tour. They dropped us off and we crossed the border without anyone controlling us. This is how we arrived in the New Congo. At the border everything was empty, not a soldier in sight. I arrived in Kikwit a couple of days ago. Now I have escaped from Willy.

GENDER RELATIONS IN LUNDA NORTE FROM A WOMAN'S PERSPECTIVE

You see, marriage in Angola differs substantially from marriage in Congo. I know that, after my departure, Willy, with his diamonds, will marry someone else and forget about me. There is no danger. For women in Angola men have a certain value in that they know how to work hard. Women refer to men as *bana misala* [Lingala: "the work children"], which means: workers, money machines, or servants. And they call us *ebunga*, "the stool on which one is seated." Men are easy to manipulate, they are vulnerable, especially if they have a bit of money. All you have to do is flatter them a little, that is it, that is all it takes for them to give in. It suffices that a man finds a woman to love and that is it, he is troubled and can only think about how to spend his money to prove to his woman that he loves her. A woman will always be a woman, no matter where she is. But in Angola, to tell you the truth, single women are treated as if they don't have any value. For a woman in Angola, therefore, it is necessary to have a husband. Once she is married, she gains in importance. But without someone to take care of her, she becomes a "mattress," everybody will sleep with her and she will be treated in the worst possible way. But if she is taken care of by a man, she becomes more "heavy" [important]. It is rare, though, to find a woman who is faithful to her husband in Angola. There are no faithful marriages. I think I do not have to explain this to you. Women go to Angola in search of money. That is their main goal. If they marry they do so for a good reason: because, after all, they are only human too, but, more importantly, to exploit men. Do you really think that we marry these guys to fulfill our sexual desires? If you do, you are wrong. What we are after is money. And for a woman in Angola it is easy to find money because she herself is a commodity. Because he is strong, a man can make money easily. A woman, on the contrary, has to manipulate a man in order to benefit from his money. Because men are naturally weak in front of a woman, they can easily be persuaded. It is from such marriages that the association between men and women springs. The Congolese woman is a "trade mark." It is easy to seduce the Angolans, because we, Congolese women, are prettier than our Angolan sisters. And the Angolan man is an easy catch. A woman who uses her brains and understands what her primary objectives in Angola are cannot return empty handed.

I, Mado, as for me, I cannot allow my younger sisters to start leading the same life as I have led. I sacrificed myself for the whole family and I hope that I am the only one in my family who has to suffer such a fate. Once your sister goes to Angola, know that you have lost her for the rest of your life. She will bring back money, but she will be worthless for everything else. I do not want to go into that in more detail.

EPILOGUE — KINSHASA, SEPTEMBER 1999

Upon her return to Kinshasa after our meeting in Kikwit, Mado took up her life with Johnny again. In 1998, however, she started an affair with another man. During the same period her former "husband" Mitterand went to court to reclaim part of the goods he had lost in the dispute with Mado some years before, and won his case. As a result, Mado ended up in Makala, Kinshasa's main prison. She was released two months later, after having won her own court case against Mitterand. She continues to live with Johnny and her lover, and makes plans for yet another trip to Angola.

THE POSSIBILITIES
OF THE (IM)POSSIBLE

Approached from the river, Kinshasa reveals itself in a different guise. On the river, amidst the sounds of silence, one is engulfed in the immensity of the water's surface, stretching out in endless shades of silver and gray, hardly distinguishable from the watery sky above, a large canvas on which the black silhouettes of fishermen, standing upright in their canoes, paint a hesitant ripple when throwing out their nets.

Turning to the other side, in the direction of the city, all one sees at first is a wide marshy strip of long green grass. Behind it, barely visible, a skyline of palm trees, lining the neighborhoods of Masina and Kingabwa. As one floats downstream, small makeshift pile dwellings appear, sheltering fishermen and others who make a living out of the river. And then, one by one, the ports of Kinshasa glide by.

At first they emerge only in audible form, as an approaching soundscape that gradually breaks up the river's silence. Voices shouting and yelling, the noise of machines, fragments of music carried across the water, the sound of metal upon metal, and the more subdued plops of wooden peddles entering the water.

Then one catches sight of a port now occupied by the United Nations. The unnatural white of their boats stands out against the background. On their white surfaces are painted, in large black letters, the acronym UN (*les Uns*, as the United Nations people are called in Kinshasa, in opposition to the "others," *les autres*, the Kinois themselves). And then follow the other ports: Port Baramoto, the Yacht Club, Beach Ngobila. Here, the river banks are packed with people. Behind them, old warehouses with barely readable names painted on the dirty cement of their façades, names like NOGUEIRA, reminders of a time when Greek and Portuguese traders provided the shops of Kinshasa with goods.

The riverbank itself is hidden from view by boats, lots of boats, but boats that no longer float, dead bodies, cadavers of boats, old steamers and ONATRA (*Office national des transports*) ferries, in every possible shade of rust eaten brown. The port is a cemetery. Sunk, immobilized, stuck in the mud and entangled with floating carpets of hyacinth, these boats were dismantled and turned into squatters' camps a long time ago. Still afloat, patiently waiting between these corpses, are hundreds of *baleinières*, large wooden boats with outboard motors, smelling of tar, dried fish and the penetrating odor of cassava. These are the boats that transport people and goods back and forth between the

Congo river and a vast network of waterways in the interior of the country. Like an octopus' sticky tentacles, the hinterland's riverarms thus firmly wrap around Kinshasa, connecting both in an endless ebbing and flowing of people and commodities.

Painted on each of the boats, in large, colorful letters, a name: "Satellite," "The City of Jericho," "L'Avenir" (The Future), "Tantine Henriette – Proverbs 13.11" ("Wealth hastily gotten will dwindle, but he who gathers little by little will increase it"). On one boat is written: "One day, the future will prove us right."

In *Of Other Spaces*, a text I will return to later on, Foucault writes about boats as the greatest reserves of the imagination.[144] But what if the imagination has been unmoored, and the ship itself has sunk? Even if, one day, the future proves the inhabitants of Kinshasa right, what will the shape of that future be? What elements, in an urban politics of the possible, could give form to the making and remaking of associational life in such an urban configuration? The riverbanks of Kinshasa reveal the stunning material geography of failing infrastructure, a spectacular architecture of decay which constitutes the physical life of crisis. At the same time, the boats' names reveal the local production of zones of desire, expectations and hope. Similarly, the myriad activities and the whole web of informal economies that have spun themselves around the river and the city as a whole, have given birth to multiple technologies of fixing and repairing. They form a constant reminder of the productivity of degradation and its capacity to invent new material structures and generate and moor social ties,[145] even if these social ties are often marked by their harshness. Kinshasa is a pitiless city with no place for the weak. Infrastructures of lack and incompleteness rarely generate a great capacity for compassion.

KINSHASA AND ITS (IM)MATERIAL INFRASTRUCTURE

SIMULACRA OF INFRASTRUCTURE | In ongoing discussions concerning the nature of the African city architects, urban planners, sociologists, anthropologists, demographers and others devote a lot of attention to the built form, and more generally to the city's material infrastructure. Architecture has become a central issue in western discourses and reflections on how to plan, engineer, sanitize and transform the urban site and its public spaces. Mirroring that discourse, architecture has also started to occupy an increasingly important place in attempts to come to terms with the specificities of the African urbanscape and to imagine new urban paradigms for the African city of the future. Indeed, one can hardly underestimate the importance of the built form

and of the material, physical infrastructure if one wants to understand the ways the urban space unfolds and designs itself. For example, studying the process of the "bunkerization" of the city, as it is called by its inhabitants, that is the fact that one of Kinshasa's crucial spaces, the compound, has evolved from an open space lined by flowers and shrubs in the 1940s and 50s to today's closed *parcelles,* surrounded by high walls that make the inside invisible to the street, would certainly contribute to a better understanding of the city's history of unraveling social relationships, its altered sense of security and its changing attitude towards the qualities of public and private.

However, as Kinshasa's ports reveal, the city's infrastructure is of a very specific kind. Its functioning is punctuated by constant breakdown. The qualities of failing often give the urban infrastructure the character of a simulacrum. For example, the television set, a status symbol, occupies a central place in the living room, but often it just sits there without functioning at all because there is nothing to plug it into, or because it broke down a long time ago, or because electricity has stopped to come. Often, while in Kinshasa, I am reminded of Mary Douglas' "*The Hotel Kwilu: A Model of Models.*" In this text she describes how she visits the Hotel Kwilu, located in the town of Kikwit, overlooking the Kwilu river:

"The Hotel Kwilu looks like a modest version of the Sheraton or the Marriott or any of a number of well-standardized airport hotels: modest by comparison, but grandiose in its setting. As I remember, it is a handsome building made of solid stone, with broad steps up to the front entry, a reception desk on the right, a big glass-roofed atrium in front, potted palm trees around, a bar to the left, and a restaurant beyond that, all calm, cool, and inviting. Before looking in I asked to see the bedroom. It was still in the accepted Sheraton style: clean, big, huge mirror, air-conditioning, twin beds, twin pictures on the wall, the telephone, the reading lamp, well carpeted, the bathroom en suite. Inside the bathroom, again: perfectly in style, the bath, the gleaming fittings on the hand basin, shower, hairwashing spray, the lavatory. Everything was there, not forgetting the bottle of drinking water. The only thing I thought was odd was that the bath was full of cold water. I wondered if the last guest had not left them time to clean it, but no, I was told this was to economize water. The candle and matches by the bed I took for an extra courtesy in case of emergency. [...]

The receptionist asked me to pay in advance so that they could procure the diesel fuel needed for refrigeration and electricity. He also said that the electric lighting went out at 8 o'clock, to save diesel. [...] However, when I got upstairs I found, with the help of the candle, that the taps did not run, the lavatory did not flush, the phone was not connected, nor the air-conditioning. But I rejoiced in the huge bath full of water, and a dipper for carrying water to the hand-basin and the lavatory."[146]

If Douglas had arrived at her hotel some hours before, she would have witnessed two women, with large plastic buckets on their heads, walking back and forth from a nearby public water tap all the way up to her room to fill the bathtub.

As with the Hotel Kwilu, Kinshasa is full of such disconnected figments, reminders, and echoes of a modernity that exists as form but no longer has the content that originally went with it. The fragments themselves are embedded in other rhythms and temporalities, in totally different layers of infrastructure and social networks. Failing infrastructure and an economy of scarcity therefore constantly delineate the limits of the possible, although they also generate often surprising possibilities, through a specific aesthetics of repair, by means of which breakdown is bypassed or overcome.

THE UNFINISHED CITY | Along the Bypass, the main road which coils around Kinshasa's southern and western parts, a dusty sand road leads to the commune of Mont Ngafula. This neighborhood emerged in the 1970s as a semi residential area for executives, functionaries and upcoming politicians. Many

compounds in this neighborhood are spacious, with lots of trees and green. But many houses were never finished. With the generalized breakdown that characterized the end of Mobutu's reign, the emerging middle class that bought building plots in this neighborhood was gradually cut off from its income. The (often spectacular) houses they had dreamt of building for themselves were left in various stages of unfinished abandon, impressing upon one the image of the city as a never ending, perpetual building site, a characteristic Kinshasa shares with many other African towns. Today, people live in the skeletons of their frozen dreams of progress and grandeur, in constructions of concrete and cement without doors, windows, roofs. Only the ground plan betrays the original aspirations.

Other, less fortunate inhabitants of this neighborhood witnessed how their houses disappeared overnight. During the rainy season, erosion is a constant threat in many parts of the city. Overnight, the erosion, which often finds its origin in deficient drainage, cuts through the sandy soil of Kinshasa's hills, leaving behind spectacular abysses in which houses, roads and other infrastructure disappear. Here Kinshasa becomes a cannibalistic city, literally devouring its own urban tissue. Today, in Kinshasa, erosion threatens whole neighborhoods in at least 400 different spots.

Together with the dust roads, the generally spacious and green compounds, though usually surrounded by high walls, give the commune of Mont Ngafula a rather rural character. As in most neighborhoods of Kinshasa, water and electricity reach this part of the city only sparingly. Water, for example, usually comes between 2 and 4 am, whereas electricity is made available according to a system of what Kinois refer to as *délestage*: in different sectors of the network, SNEL or REGIDESO, the national electricity and water companies, switch electricity and water off at certain times in order to feed other sectors. It is totally unclear which criteria determine the distribution over the various communes and neighborhoods. Some receive water and electricity during certain hours of the day (but unfortunately these hours often vary from one day to the next). Other parts of the city are supplied for weeks and then cut off for weeks. Some areas are not served for months while many neighborhoods are not even connected. Each of these cases sets in motion a carrousel of people. Girls and boys are sent out with buckets, tiles and cans to fetch water in nearby or more distant neighborhoods, fathers visit their friends to charge the batteries of their cell phones, and whole neighborhoods move elsewhere to watch soccer games in those compounds where there is a television set that works. When technologies remain silent or break down, and thereby give form to yet another level of invisibility that shapes the city, these lacks and absences generate new spheres of social interaction and different coping strategies and regimes of knowledge and power.

POSSIBILITIES OF INFRASTRUCTURE | Infrastructural fragments thus also enable the creation of new social spaces. A couple of years ago, on the corner between the main Bypass road and the entrance to the commune of Mont Ngafula, someone started building a FINA gas station. It took several years to complete, but the gas station finally opened in 2002. A couple of months later the owner placed a huge lamp post on the premise. Since the gas station used its own generator and therefore did not depend on the city for its electricity supply, the lamp kept burning. In no time at all, the lamp post gave birth to a large numbers of bars, a cyber café and a telephone shop around the station, while buses and taxis began to use this place as the terminus of their trajectory, thereby bringing even more people to the bars. Business at the nearby Fwakin Hotel started picking up again after many years. With fascination I observed how one lamp post transformed what was a quiet corner with little movement after nightfall into an important meeting point bristling with life till midnight. The process of random occupation of space also reveals the organic approach Kinois have to the production of the city. Space, in a way, belongs to whomever uses it, despite the halfhearted attempts of the city authorities to control the slow but unstoppable occupation and the progressive denser use of that space.

Simple material infrastructures and technologies, as well as their dysfunctioning and breakdown, thus create, define, and transform new sites of transportation, new configurations of entangled spatialities, new public spaces of work and relaxation, new itineraries and clusters of relations, new social interactions.

The *phonie* is a good example of how material infrastructure and technology create new forms of sociality and new topographies of propinquity,[147] how they can bring people into physical proximity with each other, how they generate new (trans)urban public spheres, or enable, maintain and carry forward existing social landscapes, networks and affiliations under changed circumstances. *Phonies* connect Kinshasa to the rural hinterland. Every *phonie* transmits messages to specific towns. As a result, people from the same ethnic or regional background meet at these *phonies*, where they often spend several days before getting in touch with the person they want to talk to at the other end. The *phonie*, therefore, provides a place, a social island within the city to maintain, strengthen and reactivate different, often pre-urban ties of locality and belonging.

However, such islands of communication, association, collaboration and proximity, with their possibilities of reimagining a different ethics for the current urban life, remain very dependent on the materiality of their infrastructure and are therefore very vulnerable. In the case of the *phonie* or the cyber café there is the constant dependence on hardware that is costly,[148] electricity that is interrupted all the time, radio transmitters that risk being damaged because of unstable voltage, solar panels that are hard to get by and easily break down, batteries of poor quality that have to be constantly recharged, computer viruses that infect all the city's PC's and are as difficult to get rid of as the viruses that attack the people of this city in real life. Beyond that, the existence of the *phonie,* for example, is strongly dependent on the absence of other, newer technologies. These may be more sophisticated and efficient but also more demanding, necessitating a larger investment or a higher degree of technical know how, which inevitably turns its users into mere consumers rather than producers or controllers of that technology. For example, as I write, the introduction of sophisticated cell phone technology by international communication multinationals in Congo is already turning the *phonie* meeting points and the social geographies they engender into archeological sites. In 2003, seven different telecommunication networks, each with its own international (American, South African, French, Belgian, Chinese) affiliations, were competing with each other to control the potentially vast Congolese telecommunications market (VODACOM, CELTEL, TELCEL, OASIS, AFRITEL, CCT [*Congo-Chine Téléphone*], COMCEL). In 2003, also, large parts of the interior were opened up through the implementation of cell phone technology in which these international companies invested a lot of money. For the first time ever, people in remote villages can call Kinshasa, Brussels, Paris or New York and reach beyond their own horizon within seconds. Wonderful as this is in itself, it also means that established forms of cooperation, communication and collective responsibility, with their specific social capital and the particular levels of trust they summon, will become obsolete and disappear in the very near future (no doubt to be replaced by something else).

INVISIBLE ARCHITECTURE | In spite of the fact that an analysis of the different physical sites through which the city exists and invents itself helps us to better understand the specific ways in which the materiality of the infrastructure generates particular sets of relations in the city, I would submit that in the end, in a city like Kinshasa, it is not, or not primarily, the material infrastructure or the built form that makes the city a city. The city, in a way, exists beyond its architecture. In Kinshasa, the built form is not, or is no longer, the product of a careful planning or engineering of the urban space. It is, rather, produced randomly in human sites as living space. Constantly banalized and reduced to its most basic function, that of a shelter, the built form is generated by this much more real, living city which exists as a heterogeneous conglomeration of truncated urban forms, fragments and reminders of material

and mental urban "elsewheres" (a lamp post, a radio antenna, a television screen, dreams of life in the diaspora). These are embedded into autochthonous dynamics and into an urban life that is itself produced through the entanglement of a wide variety of rhizomatic trajectories, relations and mirroring realities. They enjoin, merge, include, fracture, fragment and re-order the urban space through the practices and discourses of its inhabitants. Within these local dynamics, within these syncretic multiplicities, the cultural status of the built form seems to be of lesser importance, or rather, the material infrastructure that counts in the making of the city is of a very specific nature.

First of all, the infrastructure and architecture that function best in Kinshasa are almost totally invisible on a material level. Under the trees along most of the city's main roads and boulevards one finds all kinds of activities: garages, carpenter's workshops, showrooms for sofas, beds and other furniture, barber shops, cement factories, public scribes, florists, churches and a whole pleiad of other commercial activities and services. Yet, none of these take place in built structures. What one needs in order to operate a garage is not a building named "garage," but rather the idea of a garage. The only material element needed to turn an open space into a garage is a used automobile tire on which the garage owner has written the word *quado* (supposedly after the name of a well-known Belgian garage owner in the colonial period). One cord between two trees suffices to hang up the newspapers of the day, thereby creating a meeting place for the *parlementaires debout*, the people who gather under the trees to comment on the newspapers' content and erect their agora, their parliament, by means of a rhetorical architecture, the built form of the spoken word. These vibrant urban spaces teeming with all kinds of activities generate an infrastructure of paucity, defined by its material absence as much as by its presence. The built form that makes this possible is not made of cement and bricks but consists of the body of the tree under which people gather and meet, and the space between the trees that line the city's main roads. Short-cutting any dependence on unstable infrastructure and technologies, this is the level of infrastructural accommodation, the only level of accumulation also, that really seems to work.

BODY BUILDING | Secondly, in the African city, next to the body of the tree, the main infrastructural unit or building block is the human body.[149] Henri Lefebvre already noted that

"[...] there is an immediate relationship between the body and its space, between the body's deployment in space and its occupation of space. Before *producing* effects in the material realm (tools and objects), before *producing itself* by drawing nourishment from that realm, and before *reproducing itself* by generating other bodies, each living body *is* space and *has* its space: it produces itself in space and also produces that space. This is a truly remarkable relationship: the body with the energies at its disposal, the living body, creates or produces its own space [...]"[150]

To think of the body as having a space and being a space is important for a good understanding of the way in which a city like Kinshasa, itself a giant body, exists. It is in and through the body and its functions (producing and reproducing itself) that the multiple, interrelated practices and meanings of the various spaces in the urban context are mapped out. The mere fact that there are so many bodies moving, working, eating, drinking, making love, praying, dancing, suffering and starving together already gives the city its specific, often feverish, inner drive and rhythm. These bodies, as living entities, also create a certain order out of the chaos that is Kinshasa, or rather, they impose their own relational logic onto the city. "As a 'desiring machine' capable of creating order not only within itself but also in its environments, the

human body is active and transformative in relation to the processes that produce, sustain, and dissolve it," writes David Harvey. "Thus, bodily persons endowed with semiotic capacities and moral will make their bodies foundational elements in what we have long called 'the body politic.'"[151] The manner of production of space and time in the city is thus inextricably connected with the production of the body. Body and society reflect and are mirrored in each other. In the case of Kinshasa's street children, their bodies *are* the public space, or as they themselves state: "Our bodies belong to the public sphere, to soldiers and policemen, to the state, only our souls belong to God" (*nzoto ya Leta, molimo ya Nzambe*).

At the same time, the body is one of the few sites in the city through which the Kinois can transcend the raw functionalities of life as mere survival. The body is the site in which personal and collective geographies, experiences and imaginations meet and merge. It is a site in which desire and disgust, anxiety and dream materialize. Through all of these, it always produces a surplus and offers a road to something else, an extra, an elusive aesthetics that the harshness of the city and its infrastructures of decay do not offer otherwise.

In sharp contrast with the decrepit state of the city's material infrastructure, Kinois put a tremendous amount of energy not only in surviving, in feeding, clothing, healing and keeping their bodies alive, but also in building their bodies into a state of beauty and perfection. Throughout the city, young men obsessively train their bodies, exercise the machinery of each body part and build each muscle through boxing, wrestling, body building and other forms of physical training. Young men's coiffures have become increasingly com-

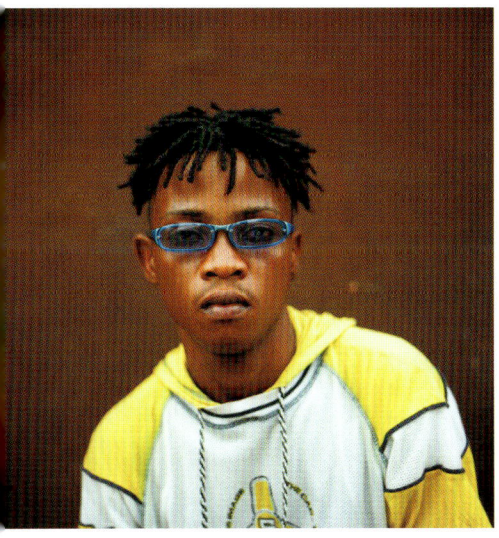 

plex, with intricate patterns and motifs that demand hours of work to accomplish. Women as well are constantly working at improving, decorating and transforming their bodies, by means of wigs, through their dress, or through the more dangerous but common practices of whitening the skin with the help of beauty products or fattening up the body by injecting hormonal preparations. For Kinois men and women, the body is the basic tool in the cultural realization of self, and in the creation of the city's private and public spheres. Certainly in Kinshasa's youth cultures (and youngsters make up the overwhelming majority of the city's inhabitants), identity is expressed corporeally as much as it is expressed discursively. The composite juvenile syntax of self realization materializes through the bodily dimensions of dress and dance. As I have noted before, the body often becomes the (sometimes subversive) site through which official political and cultural discourses and practices are questioned, reinvented or replaced by alternative forms of togetherness, conviviality, competition and success. And it is no coincidence that the loss of identity (as lived for example in the diasporic experience where one, often literally, becomes a non-identity, a *sans papiers*) is referred to in terms of a bodily loss (*kobwaka nzoto*, to shed or to throw one's body away).

THE SEX OF THE CITY | The physical body, with its specific rhythms, also determines the rhythms of the city's social body and ontologically grounds them. The comprehensive body work that is undertaken by the Kinois often generates specific forms of social life. For women, braiding hair is a collective enterprise, an occasion to meet, watch TV soaps together, or exchange news

and gossip. On another level, the women's associations and financial support groups, the more recreational *moziki* and the *likelemba* (a rotating saving and banking system amongst associated women) came into existence in Kinshasa in the 1930s and '40s and continue to play an important role in the attempts of Kinois women to overcome the economic crisis.[152] Historically, however, these forms of female associational life originated around specific sets of body-centered interests and in close relation with the ludic scene of fashion, music and dancing. Some of the earliest *mozikis,* such as *La Mode* and *La Beauté* consisted of women financing popular orchestras and launching new dress codes and fashions. The recent, more male oriented, cults of elegance known as Sape and *bilamba mabe* also testify to the importance of appearance in Kinshasa, where preachers, musicians, politicians and other figures of success embody to the full the biblical idea that one's body is a temple. In a very real sense, therefore, the most important building that goes on in Kinshasa is body building.

In summary, the (re)making of social coherence in the city is only partly generated through its material infrastructure. To a much greater extent, it is shaped through dynamic processes of a more immaterial, invisible, relational nature between the various actors that inhabit, use and produce the city through the collusion of both their bodies and their minds. Bodies, and the relational networks they generate in the urban space, form the locus of much of the "invisible modalities of urban action."[153] For example, local notions of power that define the nature of the urban space in general strongly draw from different sources of the imaginary including hunting, sexuality, initiation, and political leadership. These form the underlying fields of passion which the city

assembles in various ways to give form to local structures of power. Power, in all of these forms, is driven and spurred by a deeply rooted and oftentimes violently expressed politics of desire and longing. Hence, as Mbembe has pointed out so brilliantly, its fetishization in and through the body and its various parts (the mouth, the belly, the phallus).

The body is constantly encoding the local urban cosmologies that become visible throughout the whole range of activities within the city. The body moors the urban imagination of which it forms its most crucial site. And this urban imagination, which often expresses itself in strongly masculine terms, dreams the object of the city as a giant female body, legs spread apart, full of seduction and unfulfilled promises. And if, in the city's collective imagination, the sex of the city is female, the (male) subject of the city, therefore, is constantly aroused and excited. If the city is conceptualized as a woman (a temptress, a whore even, and occasionally also a mother), the urban mode of action, the taking possession of the city, is excessively male. The push and pull of the city forces the urban subjects into a constant erection, into constant excess, heterogeneity and dispersal, into an endless search for, and a realization of oneself through the fulfilment of all that throbbing desire, of all the promises the city makes but does never really deliver.

BODY AND ACCUMULATION | In Kinshasa, the major marker of success is lavish spending and excessive consumerism, a mode of action fully embodied by the *mwana Lunda* or diamond hunter. The successful *mwana Lunda* has "hands that spend easily" (*maboko pete pete*). He showers dollars as if they were peanuts. This spending behavior is referred to as *la boum, dijigunda, dijibunda*. The *boumeur* knows how to turn life into a party (*loyenge*). Many speak in this respect of "savoir vivre." The realization of this economy of desire and the sense of an urban "good life" is associated with the conspicuous consumption of bottled beer, western consumer goods and women (or men, as in the case of Mado). The city's socio-economic universe is, therefore, the exact opposite of Proverbs 13.11 ("wealth hastily gotten will dwindle, but he who gathers little by little will increase it"). To stick to the body metaphor, wealth is not defined within an economy of constipation, or through actions of closure and accumulation. Rather wealth functions in an economy of diarrhoea, of flux, of circulation, of injection into social networks, through which "eating," consumption, becomes socially productive and is converted into social wealth and social weight. The capacity to spend lavishly or, to put it differently, to spend in an excremental way, to ejaculate, to contract large debts even, creates a seductive and potent image of oneself, makes one visible, and is a sign of strength: "We are strong," *bana Lunda* say, "we can behave *au taux du jour*," that is, we have the financial means, the possibilities, we are, quite literally, "on top of things." Of such a person it is said that he is "planted like a pole," assuming a central, erect position in the public space, seen and heard by all.[154]

The underlying mode of action which is revealed in this excessive expenditure and spectacular consumerism (and which is adopted by both men and women, as the story of Mado illustrates) is one of hunting and capturing. It also means that, just as the level of infrastructure which functions best in the city is a zero degree infrastructure (the idea of a garage rather than an actual building named garage), the level of accumulation that is manageable and functional in the city within this mode of action is restricted to what many in the West would consider as the bare minimum. One could say that, in this city, accumulation (that is, accumulation which is not compository but which brings together more of the same) never really gets, or at least not in a lasting way, beyond the stage of the small heaps for sale along the road or at the market: a heap of gravel, or cassava flour or *makala* charcoal, a pile of soap bars, a stack of roots, a *sakombi* (measuring unit) of maize or beans, all of them quantities that are manageable, that are not meant to last and are immediately consumable. All that surpasses this level is surplus and is immediately dispersed, injected into a broader social network. In Kinshasa, accumulation mostly takes place on this human scale, that is, on the scale of the human body, which is the measuring unit, the yardstick, the *sakombi* of the city.

As the example of the *bana Lunda* shows, in this context, the body itself is the ultimate accumulation strategy. In a seminal essay on modes of self realization in Central Africa, Jane Guyer focuses on nineteenth-century African notions of accumulation. As she rightly points out

> "[...] the development of currency in Equatorial Africa may be associated with the relatively great importance of capture as a source, and destruction or immobilizations as destinations; that is [...] 'alienation'. In accordance with the principle of self-realization, the assets were not things at all but the singular persons who harnessed sources and controlled fates."[155]

Viewed as such, the process of capturing and subsequently spending (in other words, destroying) becomes a process of self realization. Through appropriation and consumption (rather than production or accumulation) a successful person singularizes himself in the urban context, and according to autochtonous modes of action that are rooted in much older, rural, models and moralities. These turn him into a strong, autonomous "true man" and "patron." The image of the hunter, with its explicit sexual connotations and with its specifically random, nondirectional temporality, in which good luck and uncertainty as much as rational planning play a major role, therefore continues to have a strongly epistemic power in the urban context. It offers the possibility of making and claiming identity and place in the urban context, and generates the specific ways in which the public good, in terms of resources and resource control, is imagined and managed.

THE CITY AND ITS SPACES OF HOPE

THE (IM)POSSIBILITIES OF THE POSSIBLE | The construction of urban identity in masculine terms remains, nevertheless, ambivalent insofar as it evolves around only one of two opposing aspects of male personhood. It favors the vision of singularized, autonomous manhood, a model which seems to be idealized by many youngsters, to the detriment of another aspect that is an inherent part of more "traditional" notions of male identity, namely that of social responsibility. This second, complementary aspect highlights, for example, the elder's capacity to weave the social network (often by means of the authority of his word) and give a tangible form to ties of reciprocity and solidarity. If, however, the city's mode of action has become that of the single, autonomous hunter, how, then, can this urban self realization be inserted in a wider social network? How to achieve this insertion when gerontocratic structures of authority and control no longer apply as before, and when former strategies for inclusion, such as the creation of a tributary network, or the circulation of gifts between family members and allies, have lost much of their cohesive force in the urban constellation? Today where could one locate the possibility for the (re)making of the group, the family, kinship structures, or other, alternative cooperative units? What counters the disintegration of larger overarching structures and mechanisms of inclusion, containment and closure? Where are entities of social cooperation and control embedded?

As Foucault already pointed out, the accumulation of capital or goods and the accumulation of people are two processes that cannot be viewed

separately.[156] This seems to apply all the more in an autochthonous universe where wealth in things and wealth in people often reinforce each other or are even interchangeable. Given the specific nature of the accumulation of capital and goods in Kinshasa (and Congo in general), on which level, then, does the accumulation of people, the making of groups, remain possible in the city? As with the accumulation of goods, the only scale on which the making of the group in the city seems feasible is, again, the scale of the human body, of

the individual who can insert himself into a relational network in which every participant can situate the other in relation to his own place within the larger social body.

The entities available to do so remain in the first place family and kinship structures. Even though they have lost much of their capacity to generate cohesion in the urban context, this does not mean that they no longer form a counterforce which attempts to criticize or channel the energy of masculine excess and heterogeneity in alternative ways in the urban locale.

The fact is that there are few existing alternatives for the renewal of associational life. The encroachment of the churches on public space is an illustration of the force of their vision of the city at the center of a new order that will start on Judgment Day. Nevertheless, the most powerful social critique of uncontrolled prodigality and other forms of excess in the realization of the urban self does not, in my view, come from the reinvented kin groups that are the churches, for these have themselves a very particular, and in the context of the city often problematic, attitude towards wealth, consumption and accumulation. Rather than strengthening group ties, many churches propagate a strongly singularizing and individualizing drive, and thereby divide existing social entities such as the family, which is itself redefined in nuclear terms in the churches. And yet, it is precisely the broader network of the extended family which used to offer a certain social security and produce the strongest moral criticisms against divisional drives and against an egoistic rather than a socializing singularization. It has always been there that the shift from the socio-logics of the warrior, the hunter and the phallus to that of the elder, the

lineage and, by extension, the mother, the household, the womb and the stomach takes place. Although this unit has often become a rather problematic one, as the wave of witchcraft accusations involving children illustrates most painfully, it remains perhaps the only one, within the urban realm of the possible, that is capable of channeling the energy of capture and dispersal, and of refocusing it, bringing it, quite literally, home again; the only one, also, capable of recapturing and rescuing the masculine figure of the hunter (and hunting praxis as such) from the field of a disappropriative imaginary of sorcery and witchcraft.[157] Even while in crisis, it is still the most important remaining unit to explore and redefine anew the rhythms of reciprocity, commensality, conjugality and gender relations in the urban context. Contrary to the public urban spaces and their modes of action, the forces in these fields spring from other, more basal sources, from much more feminine domains which mediate more than they are intermediate: the female domains of the household and, most importantly, the kitchen, the fireplace and the cauldron. The reappropriation of a male defined sexuality and its ensuing modes of action takes place in and through this intimate domain of the household. It is the household that forms the necessary complement of, and precondition for, any successful and lasting (social, political, economic) redefinition or the urban space as a gestational space.

Again, this is not to deny the ruptures and fragmentations that are currently reshaping the landscapes of kinship in Kinshasa. In the daily praxis that determines life in the city, the relational fields that make it possible for urban dwellers to redefine their lives in different terms are under a lot of strain and

have often become sites of struggle and conflict themselves. As illustrated throughout this book, the family unit, which materializes in space as a point of closure and containment while opening onto the possible insertion into wider social networks, has lost much of its capacity to do either. Its possibilities are becoming increasingly impossible. The city, therefore, is also the space where desire and longing remain unfulfilled, where dream and disillusion, or erection and impotence go hand in hand. Kinois, though spurred on by virile and potent dreams of self realization through capture, ejaculation and annihilation, are constantly annihilated themselves, reduced to the state of broken, hungry and diseased bodies, both by the conditions of pauperization that mark life in the city, and also by the nature of the urban imagination itself. "The male member is constantly erect and yet we are all impotent eunuchs," as Kinois writer Vincent Lombume Kalimasi expressed it in an interview I conducted with him. This also means that these mutually exclusive but simultaneously experienced states ultimately define Kinshasa as a space of schizophrenia. The immaterial, corporeal infrastructure, the architecture of the urban imagination, which makes the city, and makes it work, is at the same time also, inevitably, the infrastructure of its madness in the confrontation with the material lack and absence that punctuate the urbanites' daily life and discipline their bodies into misery.

THE POSSIBILITIES OF THE IMPOSSIBLE I: KINSHASA AND ITS UTOPIAS
Like every other city around the globe, Kinshasa too has produced its dreamers, visionaries and utopians. The internationally renowned, Kin based artist

Bodys Isek Kingelez builds futuristic, hypermodern alternative Kinshasas out of cardboard and colored paper. Mirroring Le Corbusier's Radiant City, his largest model is named *Ville fantôme*, a modernist utopia within the paradigms of the industrial metropolis. Here Kingelez' urban vision reveals itself as a utopia in overdrive, a Kinshasa for the third millennium, a future paradise full of architectural deliria in the form of luxurious towers and miraculously eccentric hotels. Between the airport and the city, the Bridge of Death separates the good from the bad souls. The latter are denied access to the city and disappear in an abyss that marks a division between the city and the rest of the world.[158] It illustrates well the fact that Kinois utopia almost always embraces the dimensions of eutopia and dystopia simultaneously.

The same visionary, modernist but also religious and moralist overtones may be found, in an even more outspoken way, in the objects made by Kinshasa's other utopian artist, Pume Bylex. Previously I referred to one of his works, *Humanity taken Hostage*, with its overt references to the Apocalypse. Bylex's quest is one for perfection, for God himself is perfect and He will only choose the perfect on Judgment Day. To achieve perfection, Bylex uses mathematics (symbolized by the recurrent little black and white squares in all of his work, and by the number three which returns in all of his objects, as well as in his name).[159] He also uses the modernist processes of industrial manufacturing (or a simulacrum thereof). For Bylex all of his objects and models should be reproducible, like industrial products, that is, made by what the artist refers to as "indirect emotion," by Abstraction and by Reason, independent from the person of the inventor, and therefore more perfect than objects produced through "direct emotion." Of course, his striving for perfection and his longing for a controllable universe put him in constant opposition to the city in which he lives and works, for Kinshasa is the epitome of imperfection, of the immediate and the concrete, of the irrational and the unexpected. All of Bylex's works of art, therefore, whether large models and plans such as The Tourist City (*la cité touristique*) or small objects such as his visionary armchairs, clocks or shoes, are enclosed in little glass boxes, poetic utopias with little hope of breaking out of their form, and constantly in danger of being contaminated by the urban chaos and madness in which they emerge.

What Kingelez and Bylex have in common with Kinshasa's architects and urban theorists (a rare species in this city without architecture or urban planning) is the utopian dream of abandoning the existing city, leaving it behind to construct a new capital alongside it. In interviews I conducted with Kinshasa's leading urban planners and architects, this belief in the modernist city constantly returns, unaware of the fact that this construction of an imagined future for a new Kinshasa, this total break with the city's past and its specific social practices, this denial of time, of history or, in the absence of an historical

awareness, of the urban collective memory, is bound to be a failure in the way similar projects, such as Brasilia, proved to be failures in the past.[160] As with the alternatives proposed by the charismatic churches, the model for a better society is located in a spatial or temporal elsewhere, with no real location in the here and now of the city as it exists. Utopias remain locked within the realm of pure possibility. They represent possibilities that are materially impossible and therefore they are not, it seems to me, a great force for changing the (urban) reality.

THE POSSIBILITIES OF THE IMPOSSIBLE II : KINSHASA AND ITS
HETEROTOPIAS | In the preface to *The Order of Things* Foucault notes :
"Utopias afford consolation : although they have no real locality there is nevertheless a fantastic, untroubled region in which they are able to unfold; they open up cities with vast avenues, superbly planted gardens, countries where life is easy, even though the road to them is chimerical." [161]

In the same preface he contrasts utopias, that is sites with no real place, unreal spaces which have a relation of inverted analogy with the real space of society, with the notion of heterotopia. For Foucault, heterotopias are effectively enacted utopias, places where it is possible to think or to enact all the contradictory categories of a society simultaneously, spaces in which it becomes possible to live heterogeneity, difference, alterity and alternate ordering. In *The Order of Things*, this place is language : heterotopias "dessicate speech, stop words in their tracks, contest the very possibility of grammar at its source." [162] In *Of Other Spaces*, a lecture Foucault first delivered for a group of architects a year after the publication of *The Order of Things*, he endeavored to give the concept of heterotopia a material referent. In every culture and every civilization, Foucault says in this short but beautiful text, there are

"real places – places that do exist and that are formed in the very founding of society – which are something like counter-sites, a kind of effectively enacted utopia in which the real sites, all the other real sites that can be found within the culture, are simultaneously represented, contested, and inverted. Places of this kind are outside of all places, even though it may be possible to indicate their location in reality."

Leaning heavily on Bachelard and his poetics of space, [163] he then goes on to identify some possible heterotopias : crisis heterotopias which spatialize states of crisis or the painful passage from one identity to the next (the boarding school, military service, the honeymoon trip), heterotopias of deviation (psychiatric hospitals, prisons, rest homes), the cemetery (as a space connected with all the individuals and all the sites of the city), the theater, the cinema, the garden, museums and libraries, fairgrounds and vacation villages, saunas and hammams, brothels and motel rooms, colonies and ships. All of these heterotopias are marked by their specific relationship to the poetics of space and time in a given society. They are spaces that place one in an elsewhere or a nowhere, that are capable of juxtaposing several otherwise incompatible spaces and sites in a single real space, that have the capacity to be heterochronic, to accumulate time or ground it to a halt; spaces also that are marked by specific systems of opening and closing, or that create room for illusion or compensation. They are, in short, the spaces that escape from the order of things, its standard forms of classification and accumulation, if only because they constantly conjure up the aesthetic through their appeal to the imagination and the oneiric.

What would a heterotopology of Kinshasa look like ? Where do the Kinois simultaneously contest the spaces in which they live, overcome the contradictions that shape their daily lives, and dream of another, mythic space ? What spaces should we focus our attention on to better understand the multiple forms of deviance, transgression and excess that the urbanscape of Kinshasa is constantly generating ? If, on the level of the general organization of the urban space, colonial Léopoldville was a heterotopia, it was certainly more of one for the Belgians than for their Congolese colonial subjects, for it allowed the colonizers to create a city that was "other," that was as perfect and as meticulous as the reality of the Belgian metropole was messy and unfinished. Hence the fact that the colonial capital became such a huge playground for Belgian architects. But where, for the Congolese inhabitants of this city, are located the places of "im-possibility," that is, the places where it is possible to live and imagine all the contradictory categories at the same time, and thereby to overcome these contradictions, even if just for a moment ?

In various guises, these questions have been at the heart of this book. In one more attempt to answer them, I would like to return to an image with which I opened the introduction, and which has been meandering like a thin red thread throughout the chapters of this book : the image of the mirror. If heterotopias exist through their capacity for simultaneity, the process of mirroring might help us to understand the nature of heterotopia, for mirrors of-

fer a particular point of entrance to reflect on the possibilities of simultaneity. I described Kinshasa as a vast mirror hall, reflecting different visions of the city, fracturing the urban universe into a series of multiple but simultaneously existing worlds, originating at different points in history yet speaking to each other. I have also endeavored to ground the analysis of the mirroring process, of the possibility of simultaneity, in the autochthonous understanding and experience of that simultaneity, with its processes of doubling and undoubling between obverse and reverse, visible and invisible, day and night, or heaven and hell. As I have pointed out, it is precisely the quality of this local capacity for simultaneous multiplicity that is undergoing a major change in the urban sphere today.

Foucault opens the first chapter of *The Order of Things* with a long description of *Las Meninas*, the famous Velasquez painting which can be admired in the Prado. It is a complex painting, picturing the painter painting a number of young girls in his studio. While we do not see the painting in the painting, but only the back of it, as the painter is viewing us, the spectators, we see the painter's back reflected in a mirror behind him. *Las Meninas* thus offers the peg on which Foucault hangs his reflection on the nature of representation, of the double, of visibility and invisibility, and of the process of mirroring itself. In *Of Other Spaces*, Foucault returns to the image of the mirror :

"I believe that between utopias and these quite other sites, these heterotopias, there might be a sort of mixed, joint experience, which would be the mirror. The mirror is, after all, a utopia, since it is a placeless place. In the mirror, I see myself there where I am not, in an unreal, virtual space that opens up behind the surface; I am over there, there where I am not, a sort of shadow that gives my own visibility to myself, that enables me to see myself there where I am absent : such is the utopia of the mirror. But it is also a heterotopia in so far as the mirror does exist in reality, where it exerts a sort of counteraction on the position that I occupy. From the standpoint of the mirror, I discover my absence from the place where I am since I see myself over there. Starting from this gaze that is, as it were, directed toward me, from the ground of this virtual space that is on the other side of the glass, I come back toward myself; I begin again to direct my eyes toward myself and to reconstitute myself there where I am. The mirror functions as a heterotopia in this respect : it makes this place that I occupy at the moment when I look at myself in the glass at once absolutely real, connected with all the space that surrounds it, and absolutely unreal, since in order to be perceived it has to pass through this virtual point which is over there."

In Kinshasa, the specular often becomes very spectacular. I would suggest that Kinshasa's basic heterotopia is not so much the object itself of the mirror, but rather the very process of mirroring, realized in all those spaces where the interplay between real and unreal, or visible and invisible is realized. This also means that the materiality of the heterotopia is of lesser importance. Kinshasa's heterotopias (such as the stage, the bar, the body, the street, the funeral), as realized non places with fictional qualities, are simultaneously real and placeless, everywhere and nowhere, unfolding themselves in the here and now, and yet very transient and volatile. Not that these heterotopias exist as mere figments of the imagination. There is a very real relation with existing social processes: they are available and materially present, but at the same time without any real and lasting connection to place or location.

In Kinshasa, this exhibitionist and theatrical city where the art of performance is of vital importance if one wants to exist socially, theaters and stages are effective heterotopias during the time of such performances. Today, the city's most important stage is undoubtedly the church. But once the prayers have died out, or the musicians have unplugged their guitars, these heterotopias revert back to the banality of the material fabric of the city. Bars, nightclubs and other crucial places in the context of Kinshasa are all such heterotopias. They can materialize anywhere. They move in and out of existence. They come into being in the oneiric time space of the night, itself the main mirror of the city, and then become mere houses again, in all their ordinary imperfection. And that imperfection is always there, as the shadow of the heterotopia, the nightmarish other half of the dream which is always only realized half way.

Unlike utopias, heterotopias do not, therefore, generate hope. What they do is something else. They offer a glimpse of the possibility of overcoming fragmentedness, the contradictions and ruptures that have scarred the face of the city's existence. But they never do so for long. If the cemetery is a heterotopia because it connects all the individuals and all the spaces of the city, it is also a constant reminder of the changed and problematic nature of death itself. If the body becomes the main urban stage through which one can realize oneself, it also remains, simultaneously, an extremely vulnerable, contaminated and violated entity, a body in danger. If the mirror is heterotopic, it is also very often, in the context of the city, a broken one (which makes for the impossibility of one overarching vision of the city). As I have argued throughout this book, the processes of mirroring have become problematic in the context of Kinshasa because of the changes that have occured in the possibilities of generating simultaneity. If heterotopias are the sociospatial anchors of an urban society that exists through the image, through appearance and through processes of mirroring and reflecting, they are also a constant reminder of the fact that the praxis and rhetoric of the image have been deeply affected, and that the mirroring profoundly distorts the relationship between image and reality. If language, the sheer force of the word, is perhaps the most powerful heterotopia through which the city imagines, invents and speaks itself, there remains the sneaking suspicion, the unspoken doubt that there no longer exists a one on one relationship between language and reality, that the paths of transfer between signifier and signified are undermined and that language itself has become a feeble instrument to explain and give meaning to the world in which one lives.

And yet, in the end, words seem to be the only weapons one has to defend oneself against the city. They are also the only tools, the most basic building blocks at the disposal of Kinshasa's inhabitants to erect the city over and over again. In the Central African cultural universe which brackets the urban world, words have always had a tremendous power. In these autochthonous realities, one has to be able to manipulate the word, to know "what speaking means," as Bourdieu would say, in order to exist socially.[164] The process of masculine singularization which I described above, finds its ultimate realization in a man's highly valued oratorical abilities. Speech, both in its political and aesthetic capacities, is what sets one man apart from the others. But male individuation and self appropriation is only fully achieved by the simultaneous development of his relational and intertwining social abilities. And these too are achieved through speech. In the cultural worlds of the Central African savannah, words "weave" the social network and make public space. In some of the many local languages spoken in Congo there is but one word to connote both "palaver" and the spool used to weave raffia threads into a tissue. Speech is therefore always colloquy. It is an essentially social act, always a speaking with others. And through their capacity to weave, words obtain a more maternal quality as well. In a very real way, speech is gestational. It makes "life ferment." For a man to speak is to "awaken" the world, and give birth to solutions to dissolve conflicts and strengthen ties of solidarity and support.[165] The legitimate public word shapes up especially as a demiurgical act of social reproduction and of world making, a culturally constructed (masculine) equivalent of female natural powers of physical reproduction and birth giving. And just as the spool picks up the raffia thread and "puts it in a line," that is, shoots it from left to right and vice versa in order to weave and produce texture, speech puts words in line, one behind the other, in order to produce a sentence. Speech therefore, like weaving, is about ordering the world.

As I noted before, in the preface to *The Order of Things* Foucault located the ultimate possibility of heterotopia emerging within language. His example is Jorge Luis Borges' famous Chinese Encyclopedia, with its incongruous classifying categories for animals (animals drawn with a very fine camelhair brush, animals having just broken the water pitcher, innumerable animals, animals belonging to the Emperor, and so on). The heterotopia of language is here the place, the non site, or the capacity, to create orders, to make the impossible possible or render it acceptable, to think the unthinkable, live the unliveable and speak the unspeakable. In a city where the ordering and accumulation of things rarely works beyond the simple architectures of the heaps of charcoal, loaves of bread or stacks of cassava roots for sale in the streets and markets, words provide the city dwellers with a potent tool to create other, alternative orders. In a city, also, in which the trans-substantiation of the Holy Spirit is constantly operating through the Word and investing the words of the believers with its force, it is not so difficult to believe in the sheer power of words to imagine the city anew. Words generate the quotidian poetry and prose of the city and form the foundation for urban culture, even if, as I have pointed out, they also form an intermediate zone where culture has often begun to drift away from its own codes, and where meaning has become destabilized. In this respect Kinshasa is a prayer, a mantric city. At every new beginning of the city is the word...

...AND THE WORD IS THE CITY

The city is a never ending construction. The city can never remain a passive victim. The city is, on the contrary, a place of possibility, the place that enables you to do and to act. We construct the city with our vices and virtues and therefore we have to accept the urban dwellers as they are, with their vices and virtues. The city is never or/or, it is and/and. The city is vice versa. Every city in the world is the depository of the nightmares and dreams of its inhabitants. It is an amalgam of the best and the worst. Never forget the worst. A city that is searching for its own identity inevitably generates incubi.

Human beings are fundamentally dynamic, in a movement towards the light, towards the sun. That is inherent in how they break their way : one's own dirt, one's own suffering becomes a starting point to break a way towards oneself, towards something different, towards the divine. And the more we move towards that verticality the more we construct our city and acquire the means of its construction. When I look at buildings and skyscrapers, I ask myself : what do they mean for me ? They illustrate mankind's aspiration towards the divine. The sky is the symbol of that dimension. That is what defines freedom. Whether or not you believe in God is not relevant here, whether or not you define freedom as God does not matter. What is of primary importance is that longing for something higher. All architecture translates that longing for the vertical, even if that architecture is only a hut. Through the act itself of tracing our path, even if it is a path which leads us through hunger and suffering, we somehow arrive.

And the city helps us to achieve that.

The city is a site of constant communion. It is not a place for anchorites and hermits. It is a place made of human beings, irrespective of who they are. It is a site of inclusion, made for serial killers as well as for drug addicts, for prostitutes, literate people, intellectuals, for all sorts of people. It is a site of dreams, where dreams encounter each other and become a single body.

However, on the level of our own experience of that urban environment, once one plunges into the life of the city and participates in it, it inevitably diversifies and becomes multiple. There is no urban crowd, there are multitudes. There are also many different cities in one. My city is not the city of a street kid, of an abandoned child who sleeps along a dirty river. And yet that child lives in Kinshasa as well. My city is not the city of a priest who does not frequent bars, who does not drink but goes home to read his Bible after mass. My city is not the city of a prostitute who throws her body away in order to survive. There are so many cities. There are the cities that one would like to murder, there are the cities that one loves, and there are the cities that one gives birth to every day. There is the city that exists in each of us, that each of us carries along. Everyone possesses his own imagined cities. And all these imagined cities wage war with each other in our imaginary. Some architecture is constructed, some exists only in our dreams. How many of us have not dreamt of living in an urban utopia ? The question is : what helps these dreams to become reality, to materialize into real cities which one can physically traverse from one end to the other ?

The fact is, we shouldn't spit upon the city. The city is a womb. I have often engendered this city through my writing and my words but it gave birth to me first. One therefore has to accept the city, anchored as it is in dust and dirt. One cannot spit upon the mother, the woman. One has to make do with her as she is. One loves her. One has to put up with her rotten spots, with the bodies of dead dogs rotting away in the street. One has to make do with what one gets. That doesn't mean that one has to accept or resign oneself to that dog rotting away. But first one has to ascertain that the dog is rotting away in view of the whole city. What other choice is there ? The city has to be constantly created. And wherever there is suffering, there will be people encountering each other. No city in the world just happened. No city emerged in a final form. All of them were constructed. Cities have to be made, and they make themselves. That is the unavoidable fate of the city. In this sense, Kinshasa is also self generating. It is its own creator. Therefore it is eternal. There will always be people to create and recreate the city, to regenerate or to destroy it, and then start all over again. It is a city that will accept its history yet to come. There is no finished city. All there is, is a historical quest. All it takes is confidence in oneself and in the other. This is a city that still has to learn a lot, but I believe it is learning fast. Maybe Kinshasa shouldn't try to follow the West. We could not catch up with it even if we tried. We would do better to follow the last one in the race, the hungry one, and follow the rhythm of his footsteps, the time of that hungry one. Of course, hunger signifies a lack of freedom. Somehow we have lost the equilibrium between the physical question and the beyond that creates freedom. Ready to accept and eat about anything, hunger reduces one to mere survival. But beyond that hunger lies something else. Kinshasa is not only stomach. We have the capacity to open up to that something else, but we haven't yet managed to surpass the problem of hunger, of death, of illness, of suffering. We haven't yet overcome the rupture.

And then, hunger and death do not only signify closure, they also enable the creation of an opening, if not physically then at least mentally. There are such streams of energy running through this city and we have not yet sufficiently explored them. Hunger might help us to learn how to do that, it offers a possibility. Hunger is a good starting point for this incessant search for a beyond, for it reveals the paradox in which we are living : a country so rich, with water, rivers, sun, forests, and yet with inhabitants so miserable. There is a hiatus somewhere, a void, and this void needs to be filled. It has to be filled by us, the inhabitants of this city, the initiated, the *shege*, the expatriates, the multitudes of people that make up this city. The city belongs to all of them. And they all have to constantly reinvent their own myths, their own stories of the street, to keep going and to offer themselves a semblance of direction for this world that keeps slipping through their fingers**.** The city is indeed a never ending construction.

[From an interview with Vincent Lombume Kalimasi, writer, Kinshasa, February 2004]

NOTES

1. Davies, 1998: 141. See also Spyer, 1998.
2. Mongo-Mboussa, 2002: 233.
3. *Africa on a Shoestring*, 199.
4. Foucault, 1975.
5. Bleys, 1996.
6. See Gilman, 1985; Pick, 1989.
7. Donzelot, 1979.
8. Comaroff, 1993: 305–306.
9. See Curtin, 1998.
10. See Lyons, 1992; Vaughan, 1991; Comaroff and Comaroff, 1997: chapter seven.
11. Boyd, 1936, quoted in De Boeck, 1994: 258.
12. Ranger, 1992: 256.
13. See Hunt, 1999; McCulloch, 1995. On the colonial attempts to create more productive and strong laborers, the *tshanga-tshanga* race, in the labor camps of the Katangese Union Minière, see De Meulder, 1996.
14. Lindenbaum and Lock, 1993: 303. See also Arnold, 1988; Butchart, 1998; Harrison, 1994; Headrick, 1981; MacLeod and Lewis, 1988.
15. For a detailed history of colonial architecture in Léopoldville and Congo see De Meulder, 2000. Personal reminiscences of a rapidly changing city are offered by Kolonga Molei, 1979. See also La Fontaine, 1970.
16. See De Meulder, 2000, chapter fourteen. See also de Saint-Moulin, 1970; de Saint-Moulin and Ducreux, 1969; de Maximy, 1984.
17. Mbuluku Nsaya, urban planner, personal communication, Kinshasa, February 2004.
18. On the notion of villagization see Devisch, 1996.
19. Even before, between 1920 and 1940, small gangs of youngsters appear on the streets of Léopoldville. These gangs recruited members primarily amongst the children of policemen and soldiers of the *Force Publique*.
20. Gondola (1997: 310) mentions in particular two films that introduced Buffalo Bill to the youthful Congolese audiences: the versions of Cecil B. DeMille (*The Plainsman*, 1936) and William Wellman (*Buffalo Bill*, 1944). Most popular, however, was *Pony Express* (translated as *Le triomphe de Buffalo Bill*), made by Jerry Hopper in 1953, in which Charlton Heston played the part of Buffalo Bill.
21. The fact that former rebel leader Kabila, imposing his "law" throughout the country in 1997, was referred to as "Sheriff" (and dressed accordingly, wearing a Stetson hat) is an immediate echo of 1950s Billism.
22. Today *bana Lunda*, young diamond diggers from Kinshasa and other towns in southwestern Congo who go to dig diamonds in the Angolan province of Lunda Norte, describe themselves as *kuntwalistes*, "those who go forward" (from kiKoongo *kuntwala*), echoing the Billies' slogan *tokende liboso*.
23. Jewsiewicki, 2003.
24. Lefebvre, 1991 [1974]: 123.
25. For an example of this tendency see Biaya, 1997.
26. Gasché, 1986.
27. Koolhaas, 1996: 724.
28. See Browder and Godfrey, 1997 on frontier urbanization and the creation of "rainforest cities" in the Brazilian Amazon.
29. The boomtowns of Tembo and Kahemba, in the administrative units of Kasongo-Lunda and Kahemba respectively, are a good example of these dynamics. In 1984, the *cité* of Kahemba officially counted 10,522 inhabitants (quartiers Kahemba, Mobutu and Sukisa). Ten years later the population of Kahemba had multiplied tenfold, with small aircraft flying in almost daily with goods and people from Kinshasa. Today the town of Kahemba is reducing in size again, due to the difficulties of accessing Angola since the end of 1998.
30. *Ngulu* means "pig" or "pork." The name refers to an older mythology that found its origins in colonial times, when it was believed that the rare Congolese who were invited to travel to Belgium by missionaries and others, were killed there and returned to Congo processed as corned beef, which was then distributed to the local population. Not without irony, the system of paying a musician or preacher for a fake real passport and visa in order to travel to Europe refers to these older beliefs. The *ngulu* system was exposed in 2003 when Papa Wemba, one of Congo's prominent musicians, was arrested on account of illegal human traffic.
31. *Fwa ku Mputu* is also the title of a novel written in Lingala by Bienvenue Sene Mongaba (2002) in which he tells the story of his own journey to Mputuville.
32. See Jewsiewicki, 1995: 56, plate 13; Jewsiewicki, 2003: 104, plate 28.
33. Harvey, 2003.
34. On urban rumors see also Obrist, 2000.
35. Yoka, 1999: 15.
36. Sontag, 1978: 180.
37. Ferme, 2001.
38. Mbembe, 2001: 144–145.

39 *Kindokinisme* is derived from the Lingala term *kindoki*, "witchcraft." The use of the neologism is significant in that it illustrates how the unpredictable transformations of reality constantly seem to require new conceptual frameworks.
40 Taussig, 1993.
41 Baudrillard, 1983.
42 Malinowski, 1985 [1922]: xv.
43 Appropriately, *Terra Morta* is the title of a novel by Castro Soromenho (1941), in which he gives an almost sociological description of the reality of diamond and rubber exploitation in the colonial society of the Angolan *sertão*, currently known as the province of Lunda Norte. For a nuanced view on the *chicotte* as symbol of Belgian colonialism, see Dembour, 1992. de Villers (1993) equally reminds us that the history of Belgian colonialism is much more complex and ambiguous than a one sided denunciatory interpretation allows for. On the Congolese section in the Tervuren Universal Exhibition of 1897 see Etambala, 1993; Jacques, 1897; Luwel, 1954. Apparently many more Congolese died during the exhibition. The organizers tried to conceal the fact of their death, but the news spread when inhabitants from Tervuren started a protest against the burial of "pagan" Africans in their churchyard. Following this protest, the bodies were buried in a collective grave. Only much later were the seven bodies of Ekia and his friends exhumed and reburied in their present graves.
44 See for example Mafikiri, 1996.
45 See Ngandu Kashama, 1992.
46 Bourdieu, 1990. See also S. Turner, 1994.
47 See Devisch, 1995; Mbembe and Roitman, 1995; Werbner, 2001.
48 Barthes, 1987: 101–102; de Certeau, 1988: 2.
49 de Certeau, 1988: 47, 101.
50 According to *Radio Trottoir* the "Golden Book" also contains the signatures of all the previous Belgian kings, starting with Leopold II. For an illustration of this see the painting by Tshibumba in Fabian, 1996: 91. See also Fabian, 1996: 88; Ndaywel, 1997: 539–49.
51 See Mudimbe, 1988: 4.
52 Bhabha, 1994.
53 The story was covered by *Le Monde* (May 23, 1995) and reprinted by the Kinshasa based newspaper *Le Soft*: "Dr Fontaine, Américain et missionaire, homme-hippopotame, s'est caché dans la rivière Kwilu pour venir épouvanter Kikwit. Son comportement est si néfaste qu'il est chassé de la mission Vanga quand il reprend la forme humaine; il pique alors une colère et décide de se venger de la ville ingrate." [Dr. Fontaine, American and missionary, man-hippopotamus, has been hiding in the river Kwilu to frighten Kikwit. His behavior is so destructive that he was chased from the mission of Vanga after he shifted back into his human shape. He then became so angry that he decided to take revenge on the ungrateful city.] One of the origins of the history of the oral transmission of the hippopotamus story may be traced to an actual event which took place in the mid 1980s, when an American party went for a swim in the Kwilu river and were attacked by a number of hippopotamuses. Several people, including some children, drowned in the tragedy, which was related to me in 1988 by one of the survivors, an American pilot working for the Protestant Mission Aviation Force. Around that same period, a Canadian Mennonite missionary, Mr. John Esau, had a boat accident on the Kwango river, in which two of his "boys" died. The missionary who, because of his strong build was nicknamed "the Elephant," was charged with their death and subsequently had to leave the country. In the late 1980s I heard several versions of the story of an American who returned from Congo to the United States, where he shifted into the shape of a hippopotamus to frighten people along the Potomac river. *Radio Trottoir* also circulated other versions of the poison story explaining the Ebola outbreak. In these, state agents from Kinshasa were held responsible for spreading poisoned fish in the city's markets.
54 Mamdani, 1996.
55 Terdiman, 1993. On the role of the Universal Exhibition within the modernist framework of the nation state see Harvey, 1996.
56 Lambek and Antze, 1996: xviii.
57 On nostalgia and globalization see Robertson, 1992.
58 Lowenthal, 1985: xxiv; see also Coombes, 1994; Phillips, 1995.
59 Bourdieu, 1990.
60 Augé, 1992; Mbembe, 2001; de Certeau, 1988: 47.
61 Kabamba, 1995: 53.
62 Zartman, 1995: 7.
63 See Callaghy, 1984; De Boeck, 1996; Schatzberg, 1988; Young and Turner, 1985.
64 Fabian, 1996: 269.
65 Kalulambi, 1997: 179.

66 This painting has been published in Jewsiewicki and Plankensteiner, 2001.
67 For a good introduction to Congolese music see Stewart, 2000.
68 Yoka, 1999: 164; see also Nlandu, 2002.
69 Bolya, 1980.
70 On millenarianist and apocalyptic movements throughout Africa see Corten and Marshall-Fratani, 2001; Laurent, 2003; Tonda, 2002; Weber, 2000. For a comparative perspective see Hall, Schuyler and Trinh, 2000; Robbins and Palmer, 1997; Stone, 2000.
71 For a brief introduction to Pume Bylex's oeuvre see Articlaut, 2003; Pivin, 1996.
72 Pume Bylex's original text on "Humanity taken hostage"

> **Perspectives et visions de l'œuvre**
> De gauche à droite la vision de l'envoyé spécial du diable: ici établit comme le commandant du dérèglement de la planète. Ce commandant au galon spécial est doté d'une puissance redoutable. A l'extrême droite; le diable, prince du ténèbre et amoureux du désordre, s'accroche sur la planète par son bec engrainé [sic]; pour exercer de toute son influence sur terre. Son bec engrainé lui évite également de se faire décroché du globe. Par sa langue rouge-vive, il lèche la planète pour la rendre lisse et légère; afin d'être très facile à transporter pour son commandant.
> Au centre du globe, l'homme est représenté comme "maître de l'environnement terrestre", pourvu des moustaches pour jouer son autorité. Mais ici, il est complètement aveuglé par le Diable: ne distinguant ni la vérité, ni la réalité. Par ailleurs, le commandant est premièrement galonné d'un grade spécial; soulignant qu'il est complètement agréé par son maître. Et deuxièmement, ses jambes sont en flèche pour traduire sa grande vitesse vers le désastre: c'est-à-dire, qu'il veut précipiter la planète vers la destruction radicale. Ses bras en aile (transportant le globe) au dessus duquel son maître se repose tout en s'y accrochant sévèrement. Les yeux du commandant sont grandement ouverts pour traduire ses cris ininterrompus en raison de stimulis musculaire. Ses dents en poignards d'attaque, témoignent qu'il cherche sans cesse à se débarrasser de son passage toute barrière gênante. Outre que ça, l'environnement qui cadre le diable et son envoyé spécial, est doté de part et d'autres; des champs de radars que le diable a imaginé pour entrer en communication avec tous les réseaux satellitaire que possède la terre.
>
> **Les perspectives notoires du commandant**
> Notes: Le commandant ou disciple du maître, présente en lui seul un aspect à triple formes:
> 1° La forme de "**la panthère**" pourvue de dents-poignards. Panthère dotée d'une antenne-corne (jaune dorée) lui permettant d'entrer en contact direct avec son maître (le Diable).
> 2° La forme de "**sauterelle-migrateur**" pour témoigner son insignation de pillard à vie (c'est-à-dire); qu'il terrorise la terre entière par son pillage qu'il se veut systématique.
> 3° La forme de "**la girafe-ailée**" ici, le grand et long cou de cette girafe lui permet de prendre son fourrage (ses victimes) à distance. Ses ailes sacrées et bleu-saphir nous révèlent sa promenade dans le néant. Et cette couleur choisie qu'est "le bleu" prouve à suffisance, sa fidélité aux interdits soumis du maître (le Diable).
>
> **Visions diverses**
> Les points métalliques incorporés dans le globe représentent les différents satellites de la terre. L'image des continents affaiblis, se détachants du globe.

73 Strathern, 1995.
74 See de Lannoy, Mabiala and Bongeli, 1986.
75 The religious movement which originated with Simon Kimbangu, a Kongo prophet, was considered an anti-colonialist resistance movement by the Belgian colonial administration. As a result, Kimbangu was imprisoned and died in detention. After his death, following independence, the movement flourished into a formal church under the guidance of Kimbangu's sons. Kimbanguism was recognized as official national religion by the Mobutu regime. Since May 2001, after the death of the last surviving son of Kimbangu, the church has been headed by one of Kimbangu's grandsons, a namesake of Simon Kimbangu's.
76 In effect, the members of this and other similar movements, including King Misele's, are constantly being harassed by the agents of the State. After some of the church's local branches in Kinshasa, the Lower Congo and Kikwit had been attacked by elements of the army in September 1996 (attacks in which at least three church members were killed and several others imprisoned), it became increasingly difficult for me to continue to visit this church

community, for I was suspected of gathering further information concerning the Dibundu dia Kongo on behalf of the State.
77 Douglas, 1978: 17.
78 See Meyer, 1998 for similar examples from Ghana on the religious production of modernity.
79 In the mid seventies Mobutu announced his economic masterplan called *Objectif 80* which would help Zaire to become an economic superpower by 1980: "*Première place: oui. Deuxième place: malamu. Troisième place: likambo te. Kasi quatrième place: non c'est non tokondima yango te.*" (The first place: yes. Second place: good. Third place: OK. But fourth place: no, we can never ever accept that.)
80 See Fabian, 1996, painting 68, *La mort historique de Lumumba*.
81 Jewsiewicki, 1996: 113. Since then, Lumumba-Christ reincarnated in Laurent Kabila. When Kisangani fell to Laurent Kabila's AFDL in March 1997, this was explained the next day by a Kisangani inhabitant as follows: "Jesus entered Jerusalem just like Kabila did in Kisangani. It's a coincidence. But Kabila is suffering a lot to liberate our people." (Associated Press Report of March 23, 1997 by Beth Duff-Brown). The fact that both Lumumba and Kabila were murdered and continue to be commemorated on the same day only strengthens the symbolic superimposition.
82 See Maffesoli, 1992.
83 See Ndaywel, 1993.
84 For other examples of the "transfiguration of politics" see also de Villers, 1995: 43; see also endnote 81.
85 Mbembe, 2001: 206. See also Augé, 1977: 153; de Certeau, 1988: 90.
86 See Devisch, 1996; Schatzberg, 1988; Stewart and Shaw, 1994.
87 Taussig, 1993.
88 Battaglia, 1993: 430. See also Casey, 1987; Connerton, 1989.
89 See T. Turner, 1994.
90 Lambek and Antze, 1996: xiii.
91 De Boeck and Devisch, 1994.
92 See also Nooter-Roberts and Roberts, 1995.
93 Mbembe, 2002: 640.
94 In the Angolan context, the technology of dismemberment also includes a practice known as *kuchaant* in the local Luunda vernacular, signifying the progressive slicing up of the living body.
95 See also French, 1994; Nordstrom, 1992; Scarry, 1985.
96 Douglas, 1995.
97 On connivance and zombification see also Stoller, 1995.
98 Labou Tansi, 1979: 17.
99 Mbembe, 2001: 197. See also Biaya, 1998; Grootaers, 1998; Vangu, 1997; Yamb, 1997.
100 Djungu-Simba, 1994.
101 This text is also quoted in de Villers, 1992: 192–194. See also Kamandji, 1998.
102 "Nos morts des zones périphériques sont de vrais morts. Quand on les enterre, on les oublie. Et lorsqu'on se souvient, on oublie quand même l'emplacement de la tombe. Nos morts sont périphériques, nos cimetières sont périphériques, et nos salaires sont périphériques!"
103 Bataille, 1971: 28.
104 Mbembe, 2001: 145.
105 Devisch, 2001: 116.
106 See Appadurai, 1996; Bayart, 1996: 143.
107 See for example Gupta and Ferguson, 1997a/b; Olwig and Hastrup, 1997.
108 Deleuze, 1990.
109 The material presented here is based on several periods of field research in Kinshasa (1999–2004), and more particularly in the context of prayer movements and healing churches, most of which had links with Pentecostalism and other "fundamentalist" branches such as Watchtower and Jehovah's Witness, as well as Seventh Day Adventists. I frequented churches in the neighborhoods of Masina, Bandalungwa, Lemba, Selembao, Ndjili and Kintambo, and conducted interviews with children, church leaders, parents and other relatives of the children involved.
110 See for example Douglas, 1999.
111 The NGO *Save the Children* gives an estimate of 2000 children who are the subject of such accusations in Kinshasa. In my view the estimate is rather conservative in that it is based on an extrapolation of the number of children brought to the churches to be exorcized. However, it does not take into account the high turnover of children in those churches and the constant production of new child-witches. For the rest, the joining of children and witches is of all times and all places. While in Europe, before 1600, witches were mostly elderly people, children were increasingly accused of witchcraft after that date. Not only were children victims of bewitchment, such as in the case of seventeenth century Salem, Massachusetts, but they were also accused of

bewitching others. In seventeenth century Europe, children were regularly burnt as witches, as attested by Midelfort's analysis of the Würzenberg witch trials of 1627–9, in which ten children between the ages of 6 and 20 were killed on account of witchcraft (see Midelfort, 1972: 179ff). The phenomenon of child-witches is not new to Africa either. For comparative material in recent years see for example Geschiere's analysis of *mbati*, a reportedly new type of child-witchcraft which started to appear among the Maka of southeastern Cameroon in the beginning of the seventies (Geschiere, 1980). What therefore seems to be exceptional in the Congolese case that I am dealing with here is above all its expansive scale.

112 See Ferguson, 1999; Comaroff and Comaroff, 1999; Augé, 1999.

113 For an insightful treatment of these themes in relation to the gift see Baudrillard, 1976 and, more recently, Godelier, 1996.

114 See Barthélémy Bosongo, "Les 'enfants sorciers', boucs émissaires de la misère à Kinshasa" (*Agence France Presse*, October 13, 1999). During the same period BBC2 Newsnight devoted a whole program to the phenomenon of witch-children in Kinshasa. On March 28, 2000, APA (*Agence Presse Associée*) reported: "108 children abandoned by their families because of witchcraft issues have been presented to the press in the Center for Exorcism and Recuperation of Children (*Centre d'exorcisme et de récupération des enfants*), in Masina Pascal, during a celebration organized by the Evangelical Church of Jesus Christ in Congo (*l'Eglise évangélique de Jésus-Christ au Congo*). These children, aged between five and fifteen years (boys and girls), were exorcized and helped by the Reverend Kikutu Kamboma, in view of their functional reinsertion in society." See also the Dutch *NRC Handelsblad*, March 24, 2000: "Mothers in Congo give birth to 'witches,'" as well as Karine Ancellin Saleck's article "the sufferings of child-witches" (*le calvaire des enfants sorciers*) on the Amnesty International website (March 1, 2002), and BBC's Mark Dummett's report from January 17, 2003: "DR Congo's unhappy child 'witches'." Most recently (November 18, 2003), MONUC (*Mission de l'Organisation des Nations Unies en RD Congo*) published an article by Christophe Boulierac on its website: "The bad fate of so-called child-witches in RDC" (*le mauvais sort des enfants dits sorciers en RDC*).

115 For an interesting work on "emplotment" and the therapeutic use of narrative see Becker, 1997.

116 Van Zyl Slabbert et al., 1994. See also De Boeck and Honwana, 2000; Honwana and De Boeck, 2004.

117 De Boeck, 2004

118 *Lard* derives from do*llar*, which is commonly spelled as *dollard* in Congo, but it also makes reference to the French word for "fat," as in *faire du lard*, "to become fat."

119 Undoubtedly, the word *shege* has West African roots. In Hausa *shege* means "bastard," and it is a word parents use a lot to insult their children into behaving better, or working faster (Adeline Masquelier, personal communication).

120 On urban gossip in *Radio Trottoir* surrounding the sexual escapades of young girls (the so-called "séries 8," those born in the 1980s) see Nlandu-Tsasa, 1997: 97ff.

121 Other popular *pasteurs*, religious leaders and churches in Kinshasa today include Soni Kafuta (of the *Armée de l'Eternel*, the Eternal Army), Soni Mukwenze (of *La Restoration*, Restoration) the recently deceased Mutombo (of *Ministère Amen*), Mama Olangi (of the church CFMCI), Tata Ghonda (of *Le Dieu des Africains*, The God of the Africans), Pasteur Kiziamina, Dieu Mukuna, and the church Hidden Manna (*Manne Cachée*). On the appropriation of media technologies by charismatic and Pentecostal churches in Ghana and Nigeria see also Hackett, 1998. In 2003, confronted with the growing impact of these West African movies, the Congolese government temporarily banned them from the TV screens.

122 Although it falls outside of the scope of this chapter, this issue also raises all kinds of legal and judicial problems. Often the adult thus accused turns to a justice of the peace, who can only state his incompetence in witchcraft related matters. Contrary to some other African countries such as Cameroon (see Fisiy and Geschiere, 1990), witchcraft is not included in the Congolese penal law. Judges are therefore forced to step out of their legal role to adopt a more informal mediating position in the conflict in question. In doing so they adopt a role that comes much closer to that of the authoritative elder in the more familiar process of palaver and kinbased conflict negotiation.

123 Barry, 1998–99: 143.

124 See Geschiere, 1997.

125 See Lambek, 2000: 12.

126 See, for example, Comaroff, 1997; La Fontaine, 1997; Scheper-Hughes and Hoffman, 1998.
127 See also Taylor, 1992.
128 In many respects the contract with the *mami wata* is the local version of Faust's contract with his devil. As Berman (1988) has pointed out, the figure of Faust is itself central to the emergence and development of capitalism and modernity. See also Fisiy and Geschiere, 1991; Warnier, 1993.
129 See Latouche, 1998: 154ff.
130 See Jewsiewicki, 1992.
131 Compare with the Luunda practice of *kuteend wa kuteend*: when a girl, sometimes even before her birth, has been promised by her parents to an older man (often one of the girl's father's age mates), the future husband will care for her "like a mother" as long as she lives with her parents and until she has come of age to enter a new household. In such a case the man will regularly offer gifts to his future bride: meat from the hunt, cloth and other small presents. These gifts are called *kulil mwaan*, "the feeding of the child," or *kuteend wa kuteend*, "making grow."
132 Lallemand, 1993.
133 It should be noted, however, that, contrary to exchange based models of kinship and social organization which have ignored the role of children, descent based models, beloved of English Africanists, have far less. Thus while they have not always focused on children as such, they devoted much attention to issues of transmission between generations, as in the analysis of rites of passage and the like.
134 "In this society, where cross-cousin marriage is the rule, a man gives his child to his sister and brother-in-law to bring up; and the brother-in-law, who is the child's maternal uncle, calls the child a *tonga*, a piece of feminine property. [...] It is then a 'channel through which native property [...] or *tonga*, continues to flow to that family from the parents of the child. On the other hand, the child is to its parents a source of foreign property or *oloa*, coming from the parties who adopt it, as long as the child lives.'" (Mauss, 1967: 7). Compare with the French original: "Ainsi, l'enfant, que la soeur, et par conséquent le beau-frère, oncle utérin, reçoivent pour l'élever de leur frère et beau-frère, est lui-même appelé un *tonga*, un bien utérin [...]. Or, il est 'le canal par lequel les biens de nature indigène [...], les *tonga*, continuent à couler de la famille de l'enfant vers cette famille. D'autre part, l'enfant est le moyen pour ses parents d'obtenir des biens de nature étrangère (*oloa*) des parents qui l'ont adopté, et cela tout le temps que l'enfant vit.' [...] En somme, l'enfant, bien utérin, est le moyen par lequel les biens de la famille utérine s'échangent contre ceux de la famille masculine." (Mauss, 1985 [1950]: 155–156).
135 See Niehaus, 1997. See also De Boeck and Devisch, 1994.
136 See Barry, 1998–99: 156.
137 This reading of Lacan is largely based on Nicolas' presentation of Lacan's gift theory (Nicolas, 1986). See also Godbout, 1992: 178.
138 Lacan, 1966: 180: "[...] le signifiant de toute perte rencontrée par le sujet par son accession à l'ordre social et à l'échange."
139 Godelier, 1996.
140 *Fula-fula*: from English "full." *Nzungu ya bana*: "the children's cooking pot," for the bus allows its owner to bring home some money in the evening to feed his children.
141 *Guia*: a document sold by UNITA along the frontier between Congo and Angola. Only with such a passport, obtained at a UNITA checkpoint referred to as *poste avançado,* could one enter or exit the UNITA controlled areas.
142 She refers here to the progressive intrusion of the Lunda Norte area by UNITA troops in the late 1980s. This UNITA presence developed into a war over Lunda Norte (*epaka Lunda*) after the Angolan presidential elections in 1992. Intense fighting led to a de facto division of Lunda Norte in 1994, when MPLA had assured itself of the control over the diamond mining town of Cafunfo, while UNITA controlled the areas around the Kwango river. With the presence of UNITA the diamond trade also became increasingly dollarized. The dollarization of the diamond business led to a spectacular inflation of the living cost in Lunda Norte, where even wild tomatoes are sold for dollars. As Mado and others call it, the dollar has become "kitchen money" (*mbongo ya cuisine*), and US$ 1,000 is hardly sufficient to cover the cost of food for a week.
143 Most of the revenues of the diamond diving go to the *dona moteur*, although the divers earn good money as well. The least prestigious member of the group is the *mwetiste*, whose job it is to keep the pirogue or the small rubber boats on the same spot in the water with the help of long poles. The *mwetiste* also helps the divers to pull the sacks of sand and gravel out of the water. Divers who are not associated

with a *dona moteur* and dive without the necessary gear are called *kazabuleurs* or *zolo-zolo*.
144 Foucault, 1986.
145 Simone, 2001.
146 Douglas, 1992: 296–297.
147 On the city and the politics of propinquity see for example Copjec and Sorkin, 1999.
148 To operate a *phonie* necessitates a long and strenuous administrative trajectory and is a very expensive business for most Kinois. First one has to rent a place to set up one's office (in 2003, this meant a US$ 150 deposit and a rent averaging US$ 30 to US$ 50 a month), buy some office furniture (US$ 200) and, above all, the necessary hardware. A pair of radio transmitters easily costs US$ 2,500. To that one has to add equipment to stabilize the electric current (US$ 100), a battery (US$ 80), a generator and the equipment to set up the antenna. On top of that, the use and exploitation of a *phonie* is strictly controlled by the government and is therefore subject to a whole array of taxes. Before one can start to operate a *phonie* there is a long and often unpredictable ride among the various administrative units involved. From the Ministry of Communications (PTT) one needs to obtain an exploitation license (US$ 1,000) and a technical control card (US$ 500). These cannot be obtained without filling in certain application forms (US$ 50). Then the administration starts to "study the demand," a study which necessitates an "access tax" (US$ 200). Once this process is completed, one is assigned certain radio wave frequencies (between US$ 30 and US$ 100 per frequency) and a radio wave configuration map. From the Ministry of Communication, the whole file is transferred to the Ministry of the Economy. There one has to pay for a national identification card (US$ 150 if the *phonie* is used for commercial purposes). In order to obtain this card, one has to pay a "motivation fee" of US$ 100. Even then, it might easily take a year before one obtains this card. In order to obtain all the documents in each ministry one has to address a letter to the service involved. Of course, this entails further expenses. From the Ministry of the Economy it goes to the office of Counsel for the Prosecution where one buys the appropriate forms (US$ 20) to obtain a number in the commercial register (US$ 150). With this number one addresses the National Intelligence Service (ANR) who will deliver a Conformity attestation (US$ 350 for Congolese citizens, US$ 1,000 for expatriates), renewable each year. Finally, the commune where the *phonie* is to be installed will first inspect the place, draw up an environmental report (US$ 80), deliver an authorization to start operating the *phonie* (US$ 100), as well as another exploitation permit (price unknown) and levy a small yearly municipal tax. As one can imagine, each of the stages of this long process is accompanied by complex negotiations embedded in a whole range of formal, semiformal and informal relations.
149 This is a point well made by Abdoumaliq Simone. See Simone, 2003; in press.
150 Lefebvre, 1991: 170. See also Pile, 1996.
151 Harvey, 2000: 99.
152 See Comhaire-Sylvain, 1986 on some of Kinshasa's important women's associations in the '40s and '60s. On the subject of the *likelemba* see also Bouchard, 2002.
153 Simone, 2003.
154 See De Boeck, 1999 for a more elaborate analysis of patterns of expenditure.
155 Guyer, 1993.
156 Foucault, 1995 [1975]: 221.
157 Practices and discourses of sorcery easily blend in with the hunter's universe, and bring out fundamental ambivalences inherent in the hunting practice. In some respects, the hunter's solitary and autonomous character likens him to the sorcerer. Hunting, in all its aspects from the shooting of an animal to the cutting up and the distribution of its parts, is therefore also viewed as a model that refers to the anti-order of sorcery and witchcraft. Both sorcerer and hunter are engaged in actions of killing, trapping and shooting.
158 On Kingelez see Magnin, 2003.
159 Pume's utopian project code name is "Byl," a name composed of three letters of which the *b* is the second letter of the alphabet, the *y* the 25th and the *l* the 12th, together 39 (= 3+3×3). This formula includes Pume himself, for he is his father's third son, as well as Christ, who died at the age of 33. "Ex" stands for exposition.
160 Interviews with Professors Fernand Tala Ngai and Romain Buluku Nsaya, Kinshasa, February 2004. For an anthropological critique on Brasilia see Holston, 1989.
161 Foucault, 1994 (1966): xviii.
162 Foucault, idem.
163 Bachelard, 1957.
164 Bourdieu, 1982.
165 For a more detailed ethnography of speech in southwestern Congo see De Boeck, 1998b: 38ff.

REFERENCES

Africa on a Shoestring. 2001 Melbourne: Lonely Planet Publications.

APPADURAI, A.
1996 Disjuncture and Difference in the Global Cultural Economy. In *Modernity at Large. Cultural Dimensions of Globalization*. Minneapolis: University of Minnesota Press: 27–47.

ARNOLD, D. (ed.)
1988 *Imperial Medicine and Indigenous Societies*. Manchester: Manchester University Press.

ARTICLAUT, F.
2003 *Pume Bylex plasticien*. Montreuil: Les Editions de l'œil.

AUGÉ, M.
1977 *Pouvoirs de vie, pouvoirs de mort*. Paris: Flammarion.
1992 *Non-lieux: introduction à une anthropologie de la surmodernité*. Paris: Seuil.
1999 *The War of Dreams. Studies in Ethno-Fiction*. London: Pluto Press.

BACHELARD, G.
1957 *La poétique de l'espace*. Paris: Presses Universitaires de France.

BARRY, A.
1998–99 Marginalité et errance juvéniles en milieu urbain. La place de l'aide psychologique dans les dispositifs de prise en charge des enfants de la rue. *Psychopathologie africaine* XXIX, 2: 139–190.

BARTHES, R.
1981 *Camera Lucida: Reflections on Photography*. New York: Hill and Wang.
1982 *The Empire of Signs*. New York: Hill and Wang.
1987 *Michelet*. New York: Hill and Wang.

BATAILLE, G.
1971 La notion de dépense. In *La Part maudite*. Paris: Seuil.

BATTAGLIA, D.
1993 At Play in the Fields (and Borders) of the Imaginary: Melanesian Transformations of Forgetting. *Cultural Anthropology* 8 (4): 430–442.

BAUDRILLARD, J.
1976 *L'échange symbolique et la mort*. Paris: Gallimard.
1983 *Simulations*. New York: Semiotext(e).

BAYART, J.-F.
1996 *L'illusion identitaire*. Paris: Fayard.

BECKER, G.
1997 *Disrupted Lives. How People Create Meaning in a Chaotic World*. Berkeley: University of California Press.

BERMAN, M.
1988 *All that is Solid Melts into Air. The Experience of Modernity*. Harmondsworth, Middlesex: Penguin.

BHABHA, H.
1994 Signs Taken for Wonders: Questions of Ambivalence and Authority Under a Tree Outside Delhi, May 1817. In: *The Location of Culture*. London: Routledge.

BIAYA, T.K.
1997 Les paradoxes de la masculinite africaine. Une histoire de violences, d'immigration et de crises. *Canadian Folklore Canadien* 19 (1): 89–112.
1998 La mort et ses métaphores au Congo-Zaïre, 1990–1995. In: J.-L. Grootaers (ed.) *Mort et maladie au Zaïre*. Tervuren / Paris: Institut Africain-CEDAF / L'Harmattan (*Cahiers africains* 8 (31–32): 89–127).

BLEYS, R.
1996 *The Geography of Perversion: Male-to-Male Sexual Behaviour Outside the West and the Ethnographic Imagination, 1750–1918*. New York: New York University Press.

BOLYA, S.
1980 Lobi pe mokolo. Instantanés de la crise à Kinshasa. *Demain L'Afrique* 47: 70–71.

BOUCHARD, H.
2002 *Commerçantes de Kinshasa pour survivre*. Paris: L'Harmattan.

BOURDIEU, P.
1982 *Ce que parler veut dire. L'économie des échanges linguistiques*. Paris: Fayard.
1990 [1980] *The Logic of Practice*. Cambridge / Oxford: Polity Press / Blackwell.

BOYD, J.
1936 Problems of African Native Diet. *Africa* 9: 145–149.

BROWDER, J.O. and B.J. GODFREY
1997 *Rainforest Cities. Urbanization, Development and Globalization of the Brazilian Rainforest*. New York: Columbia University Press.

BUTCHART, A.
1998 *The Anatomy of Power: European Constructions of the African Body*. London: Zed Books.

CALLAGHY, T.M.
1984 *The State-Society Struggle: Zaire in Comparative Perspective*. New York: Columbia University Press.

CALVINO, I.
1974 *Invisible Cities*. New York: Harcourt Brace Jovanovich.

CASEY, E.
1987 *Remembering: A Phenomenological Study*. Bloomington: Indiana University Press.

COMAROFF, J.
1993 The Diseased Heart of Africa: Medicine, Colonialism, and the Black Body. In: Lindenbaum, S. and M.M. Lock (eds.) *Knowledge, Power, and Practice: The Anthropology of Medicine and Everyday Life*. Berkeley: University of California Press.

COMAROFF, J.
- 1997 Consuming Passions: Child Abuse, Fetishism, and "The New World Order". *Culture* 17: 7–19.

COMAROFF, J. and J. COMAROFF
- 1997 *Of Revelation and Revolution Volume 2. The Dialectics of Modernity on a South African Frontier.* Chicago: University of Chicago Press.
- 1999 Occult Economies and the Violence of Abstraction: Notes from the South African Postcolony. *American Ethnologist* 26 (2): 279–303.

CONNERTON, P.
- 1988 *How Societies Remember.* New York: Cambridge University Press.

CONRAD, J.
- 1983 [1902] *Heart of Darkness.* Harmondsworth: Penguin.

COPJEC, J. and M. SORKIN (eds.)
- 1999 *Giving Ground. The Politics of Propinquity.* London / New York: Verso.

COOMBES, A.E.
- 1994 *Reinventing Africa. Museums, Material Culture and Popular Imagination.* New Haven / London: Yale University Press.

CORTEN, A. and R. MARSHALL-FRATANI (eds.)
- 2001 *Between Babel and Pentecost. Transnational Pentecostalism in Africa and Latin America.* Bloomington / Indianapolis: Indiana University Press.

CURTIN, PH.
- 1998 *Disease and Empire. The Health of European Troops in the Conquest of Africa.* Cambridge: Cambridge University Press.

DAVIES, I.
- 1998 Negotiating African Culture: Toward a Decolonization of the Fetish. In: Jameson, F. and M. Miyoshi (eds.) *The Cultures of Globalization.* Durham / London: Duke University Press.

DE BOECK, F.
- 1994 When Hunger Goes Around the Land: Food and Hunger in Luunda Land. *Man (Journal of the Royal Anthropological Institute of Great Britain and Ireland)* 61 (1): 257–282.
- 1996 Postcolonialism, Power and Identity: Local and Global Perspectives from Zaire. In: R. Werbner and T. Ranger (eds.), *Postcolonial Identities in Africa.* London: Zed Books.
- 1998 a Beyond the Grave: History, Memory and Death in Postcolonial Congo/Zaire. In: R. Werbner (ed.) *Memory and the Postcolony: African Anthropology and the Critique of Power.* London: Zedbooks.
- 1998 b The Rootedness of Trees. Place as Cultural and Natural Texture in Rural Southwest Congo. In: N. Lovell (ed.) *Locality and Belonging.* London: Routledge.
- 1999 Domesticating Diamonds and Dollars: Identity, Expenditure and Sharing in Southwestern Zaire (1984–1997). In: B. Meyer and P. Geschiere (eds.) *Globalization and Identity. Dialectics of Flow and Closure.* Oxford: Blackwell.
- 2001 a Dancing the Apocalypse in Congo: Time, Death and Double in the Realm of the Apocalyptic Interlude. In: J.-L. Grootaers (ed.) *Millenarian Movements in Africa and the Diaspora.* [Special issue of the *Bulletin des Séances de l'Académie Royale des Sciences d'Outre-Mer* 47].
- 2001 b 'Des chiens qui brisent leur laisse': Mondialisation et inversion des catégories de genre dans le contexte du traffic de diamant entre l'Angola et la République Démocratique du Congo (1984–1997). In: L. Monnier, B. Jewsiewicki and G. de Villers (eds.) *Chasse au diamant au Congo/Zaïre.* Paris: L'Harmattan.
- 2002 Kinshasa: Tales of the "Invisible City" and the Second World. In: Okwui Enwezor et al. (eds.) *Under Siege: Four African Cities Freetown, Johannesburg, Kinshasa, Lagos.* Kassel: Hatje Cantz Verlag.
- 2004 La frontière diamantifère angolaise et son héros mutant. In: J.-F. Bayart and J.-P. Warnier (eds.), *Matière à politique. Le pouvoir, les corps et les choses.* Paris: Karthala.

DE BOECK, F. and R. DEVISCH
- 1994 Ndembu, Luunda and Yaka Divination Compared: From Representation and Social Engineering to Embodiment and Worldmaking. *Journal of Religion in Africa* 24 (2): 98–133.

DE BOECK, F. and A. HONWANA (eds.)
- 2000 *Enfants, jeunes et politique.* Special Issue of *Politique Africaine* 80.

DE BOECK, F. and M.F. PLISSART
- 2003 Geographies of Exclusion: Churches and Childwitches in Kinshasa. *Beople: A Magazine about a Certain Belgium* 6: 46–58.

DE CERTEAU, M.
- 1988 *The Writing of History.* New York: Columbia University Press.

DE LANNOY, D., SEDA DIANGWALA MABIALA and YEIKELO YA ATO BONGELI (eds.)
- 1986 *Tango ya ba noko, Le temps des oncles, recueil de témoignages zaïrois.* Brussels: Les Cahiers du CEDAF.

DE MAXIMY, R.
- 1984 *Kinshasa, ville en suspens. Dynamique de la croissance et problèmes d'urbanisme: étude socio-politique.* Paris: Editions de l'Office de la Recherche Scientifique et Technique Outre-Mer.

DELEUZE, G.
1990 *Pourparlers. 1972–1990*. Paris: Minuit.
DEMBOUR, M.-B.
1992 La chicotte comme symbole du colonialisme belge? *Canadian Journal of African Studies* 26 (2): 205–225.
DE MEULDER, B.
1996 *De kampen van Kongo: Arbeid, kapitaal en rasveredeling in de koloniale planning*. Amsterdam / Antwerpen: Meulenhoff / Kritak.
2000 *Kuvuande Mbote. Een eeuw koloniale architectuur en stedenbouw in Kongo*. Antwerpen: Uitgeverij Houtekiet / De Singel.
DE SAINT-MOULIN, L.
1970 Ndjili, première cité satellite de Kinshasa. *Cahiers Economiques et Sociaux*, VIII (2): 295-316.
DE SAINT-MOULIN, L. and M. DUCREUX
1969 Le phénomène urbain à Kinshasa. Evolution et perspectives. *Etudes congolaises* XII (4).
DE VILLERS, G.
1992 *Zaïre 1990–1991: Faits et dits de la société d'après le regard de la presse*. Brussels: Les Cahiers du CEDAF, 1–2 [Zaire, Années 90, vol 2].
1993 Témoignages zaïrois sur la période coloniale. In: Jean Tshonda Omasombo (ed.) *Le Zaïre à l'épreuve de l'histoire immédiate*. Paris: Karthala.
1995 *De Mobutu à Mobutu. Trente Ans de Relations Belgique-Zaïre*. Brussels: De Boeck-Wesmael.
DE VILLIERS, G.
1978 *Panique au Zaïre*. Paris: Plon.
1997 *Zaïre adieu*. Paris: Editions G. de Villers.
DEVISCH, R.
1995 Frenzy, Violence, and Ethical Renewal in Kinshasa. *Public Culture* 7: 593–629.
1996 "Pillaging Jesus": Healing Churches and the Villagisation of Kinshasa. *Africa* 66 (4): 555–586.
2001 Sorcery Forces of Life and Death among the Yaka of Congo. In: G.C. Bond and D. Ciekawy (eds.) *Witchraft Dialogues. Anthropological and Philosophical Exchanges*. Athens, Ohio: Ohio University Center for International Studies.
DJUNGU-SIMBA, CH.
1994 *Sandruma: on demon-cratise!* Kinshasa: Les Editions du Trottoir / As-Editions.
DONZELOT, J.
1979 *The Policing of Families*. New York: Pantheon.
DOUGLAS, M.
1978 *Cultural Bias*. London: Royal Anthropological Institute of Great Britain and Ireland. (Occasional Paper n° 35).
1995 Forgotten Knowledge. In: M. Strathern (ed.) *Shifting Contexts: Transformations in Anthropological Knowledge*. London / New York: Routledge.
1992 The Hotel Kwilu: A Model of Models. In: M. Douglas, *Risk and Blame. Essays in Cultural Theory*. London: Routledge.
1999 Sorcery Accusations Unleashed: The Lele Revisited, 1987. *Africa* 69 (2): 177–193.
ETAMBALA, ZANA AZIZA
1993 *In het land van de Banoko: de geschiedenis van de Kongolese/Zaïrese aanwezigheid in België van 1885 tot heden*. Leuven: Steunpunt Migranten-Cahiers 7.
FABIAN, J.
1996 *Remembering the Present. Painting and Popular History in Zaire*. Berkeley: University of California Press.
FANON, F.
1986 [1952] *Black Skin, White Masks*. London: Pluto Press.
FERGUSON, J.
1999 *Expectations of Modernity. Myths and Meanings of Urban Life in the Zambian Copperbelt*. Berkeley: University of California Press.
FERME, M.C.
2001 *The Underneath of Things. Violence, History, and the Everyday in Sierra Leone*. Berkeley: The University of California Press.
FISIY, C. and P. GESCHIERE
1990 Judges and Witches, or How is the State to Deal with Witchcraft? Examples from Southeastern Cameroon. *Cahiers d'études africaines* 118: 135–156.
1991 Sorcery, Witchcraft and Accumulation: Regional Variations in South and West Cameroon. *Critique of Anthropology* 11 (3): 251–78.
FOUCAULT, M.
1994 [1966] *The Order of Things. An Archaeology of the Human Sciences*. New York: Vintage Books.
1977 *Discipline and Punish: The Birth of the Prison*. New York: Pantheon.
1986 Of Other Spaces. *Diacritics* 16 (1): 22–27.
FRENCH, L.
1994 The Political Economy of Injury and Compassion: Amputees on the Thai-Cambodia Border. In: T.J. Csordas (ed.) *Embodiment and Experience. The Existential Ground of Culture and Self*. Cambridge: Cambridge University Press.
GASCHÉ, R.
1986 *The Tain of the Mirror. Derrida and the Philosophy of Reflection*. Cambridge, Massachussets: Harvard University Press.
GESCHIERE, P.
1980 Child-Witches against the Authority of their

Elders. Anthropology and History in the Analysis of Witchcraft Beliefs of the Maka (Southeast Cameroon). In: R. Schefold, J.W. Schoorl and J. Tennekes (eds.) *Man, Meaning and Society. Essays in honour of H.G. Schulte Nordholt. Verhandelingen van het koninklijk Instituut voor Taal-, Land- en Volkenkunde* 89: 268–299.

1997 *The Modernity of Witchcraft. Politics and the Occult in Postcolonial Africa.* Charlottesville / London: University Press of Virginia.

GIDDENS, A.

1991 *Modernity and Self-Identity. Self and Society in the Late Modern Age.* Cambridge: Polity Press.

GILMAN, S.L.

1985 *Difference and Pathology: Stereotypes of Sexuality, Race and Madness.* Ithaca, New York: Cornell University Press.

GODBOUT J. T.

1992 *L'esprit du don.* Paris: Editions La Découverte.

GODELIER, M.

1996 *L'enigme du don.* Paris: Fayard.

GONDOLA, CH. D.

1997 *Villes miroirs. Migrations et identités urbaines à Kinshasa et Brazzaville 1930–1970.* Paris: L'Harmattan.

GROOTAERS, J.-L.

1998 'Reposer en désordre': enterrements et cimetières à Kinshasa à la lumière de la presse zaïroise (1993–1996). In: J.-L. Grootaers (ed.) *Mort et maladie au Zaïre.* Tervuren / Paris: Institut Africain-CEDAF / L'Harmattan. (*Cahiers Africains* 8 (31–32): 11–61).

GUPTA, A. and J. FERGUSON (eds.)

1997 a *Culture, Power, Place. Explorations in Critical Anthropology.* Durham: Duke University Press.

1997 b *Anthropological Locations. Boundaries and Grounds of a Field Science.* Berkeley: University of California Press.

GUYER, J.

1993 Wealth in People and Self-realization in Equatorial Africa. *Man* 28 (2): 243–265.

HACKETT, R.I.J.

1998 Charismatic/Pentecostal Appropriation of Media Technologies in Nigeria and Ghana. *Journal of Religion in Africa* XXVIII, 3: 258–277.

HALL, J.R., P.D. SCHUYLER and S. TRINH

2000 *Apocalypse Observed. Religious Movements and Violence in North America.* London: Routledge.

HARRISON, M.

1994 *Public Health in British India: Anglo-Indian Preventive Medicine, 1859–1914.* Cambridge: Cambridge University Press.

HARVEY, D.

2000 *Spaces of Hope.* Edinburgh: Edinburgh University Press.

2003 The City as a Body Politic. In: J. Schneider and I. Schusser (eds.) *Wounded Cities. Destruction and Reconstruction in a Global World.* Oxford / New York: Berg.

HARVEY, P.

1996 *Hybrids of Modernity. Anthropology, the Nation State and the Universal Exhibition.* London: Routledge.

HEADRICK, D.R.

1981 *The Tools of Empire: Technology and European Imperialism in the Nineteenth Century.* Oxford: Oxford University Press.

HOCHSCHILD, A.

1998 *King Leopold's Ghost. A Story of Greed, Terror and Heroism in Colonial Africa.* Boston / New York: Houghton Mifflin Company.

HOLSTON, J.

1989 *The Modernist City. An Anthropological Critique of Brasilia.* Chicago / London: The University of Chicago Press.

HONWANA, A. and F. DE BOECK (eds.),

2004 *Makers and Breakers, Made and Broken. Children and Youth as Emerging Categories in Postcolonial Africa.* Oxford: James Currey.

HUNT, N.R.

1999 *A Colonial Lexicon of Birth Ritual, Medicalization, and Mobility in the Congo.* Durham, N.C.: Duke University Press.

JACQUES, V.

1897 Les Congolais de l'Exposition Universelle Bruxelles-Tervueren. *Bulletin de la Société d'Anthropologie de Bruxelles* 16: 183–244.

JEWSIEWICKI, B.

1992 Jeux d'argent et de pouvoir au Zaïre: la "bindomanie" et le crépuscule de la Deuxième République. *Politique Africaine* 46: 55–70.

1995 *Chéri Samba: The Hybridity of Art.* Westmount, Québec: Galerie Amrad African Art Publications.

1996 Corps interdits. La représentation christique de Lumumba comme rédempteur du peuple zaïrois. *Cahiers d'Etudes africaines* 141–142, XXXVI–1–2: 113–142.

2003 *Mami Wata. La peinture urbaine au Congo.* Paris: Gallimard.

JEWSIEWICKI, B. and B. PLANKENSTEINER

2001 *An/Sichten. Malerei aus dem Kongo, 1990–2000.* Vienna / New York: Springer Verlag.

KABAMBA, M.

1995 *La dette coloniale.* Montreal: Humanitas.

KALULAMBI PONGO, M.

1997 *Etre Luba au XXe siècle.* Paris: Karthala.

KAMANDJI, G.-M.

1998 Rites mortuaires a Kinshasa: traditions et innovations. In: J.-L. Grootaers (ed.)

Mort et maladie au Zaïre. Tervuren / Paris: Institut Africain-CEDAF / L'Harmattan. [Zaïre, Années 90, volume 8].

KOLONGA MOLEI
1979 *Kinshasa, ce village d'hier*. Kinshasa: SODIMCA.

KONE, A.
1997 *Les coupeurs de tête*. Abidjan / Saint-Maur: CEDA / Editons Sépia.

KOOLHAAS, R.
2000 *La ville générique*. Architecture d'aujourd'hui 304: 70–77

LABOU TANSI, S.
1979 *La vie et demie*. Paris: Seuil.
1997 *Kinshasa ne sera jamais*. In: *L'autre monde: Ecrits inédits*. Paris: Editions Revue Noire.

LACAN, J.
1966 Fonction et champs de la parole et du langage. In: *Ecrits I*. Paris: Seuil.

LA FONTAINE, J.
1970 *City Politics. A Study of Léopoldville 1962–63*. Cambridge: Cambridge University Press.

LA FONTAINE, J.
1997 *Speak of the Devil: Allegations of Satanic Child Abuse in Contemporary England*. Cambridge: Cambridge University Press.

LALLEMAND, S.
1993 *La circulation des enfants en société traditionnelle. Prêt, don, échange*. Paris: L'Harmattan.

LAMBEK, M.
2000 Nuriaty, the Saint and the Sultan. Virtuous Subject and Subjective Virtuoso of the Post-Modern Colony. *Anthropology Today* 16 (2): 7–12.

LAMBEK, M. and P. ANTZE
1996 Introduction: Forecasting Memory. In: Antze, P. and M. Lambek (eds.) *Tense Past. Cultural Essays in Trauma and Memory*. London/New York: Routledge.

LATOUCHE, S.
1998 *L'autre Afrique. Entre don et marché*. Paris: Albin Michel.

LAURENT, P.-J.
2003 *Les pentecôtistes du Burkina Faso. Mariage, pouvoir, guérison*. Paris: Karthala.

LEFEBVRE, H.
1991 [1974] *The Production of Space*. Oxford: Blackwell.

LINDENBAUM, S. and M. LOCK
1993 Body Politics – Past and Present. In: Lindenbaum, S. and M. Lock (eds.) *Knowledge, Power, and Practice: The Anthropology of Medicine and Everyday Life*. Berkeley: University of California Press.

LOWENTHAL, D.
1985 *The Past is a Foreign Country*. Cambridge: Cambridge University Press.

LUWEL, M.
1954 De Congolezen op de Tentoonstelling van 1897. *Revue Congolaise illustré* 26 (4): 41–44.

LYONS, M.
1992 *The Colonial Disease: A Social History of Sleeping Sickness in Northern Zaïre, 1900–1940*. Cambridge: Cambridge University Press.

MCCULLOCH, J.
1995 *Colonial Psychiatry and "the African Mind"*. Cambridge: Cambridge University Press.

MACLEOD, R. and M. LEWIS (eds.)
1988 *Disease, Medicine, and Empire: Perspectives on Western Medicine and the Experience of European Expansion*. London: Routledge.

MAFFESOLI, M.
1992 *La transfiguration du politique: la tribalisation du monde*. Paris: Grasset & Fasquelle.

MAFIKIRI TSONGO
1996 Pratiques foncières, phénomènes informels et problèmes ethniques au Kivu (Zaïre). In: G. de Villers (ed.) *Phénomènes informels et dynamiques culturelles en Afrique*. Brussels/Paris: Institut Africain-CEDAF/L'Harmattan.

MAGNIN, A.
2003 Interview de Bodys Isek Kingelez. In: *Bodys Isek Kingelez*. Brussels: La Médiatine.

MALINOWSKI, B.
1985 [1922] *Argonauts of the Western Pacific*. London: Routledge and Kegan Paul.

MAMDANI, M.
1996 *Citizen and Subject. Contemporary Africa and the Legacy of Late Colonialism*. Princeton, New Jersey: Princeton University Press.

MAUSS, M.
1985 [1950] Essai sur le don. Forme et raison de l'échange dans les sociétés archaïques. In M. Mauss *Sociologie et anthropologie*. Paris: Quadrige / Presses Universitaires de France.
1967 *The Gift. Forms and Functions of Exchange in Archaic Societies*. New York / London: W.W. Norton & Company.

MBEMBE, A.
2001 *On the Postcolony*. Berkeley: University of California Press.
2002 On the Power of the False. *Public Culture* 38: 629–641.

MBEMBE, A. and J. ROITMAN
1995 Figures of the Subject in Times of Crisis. *Public Culture* 7 (2): 323–352.

MEYER, B.
1998 "Make a Complete Break with the Past." Memory and Postcolonial Modernity in

Ghanaian Pentecostalist Discourse. In: R. Werbner (ed.), *Memory and the Postcolony. African Anthropology and the Critique of Power.* London: Zed Books.

MIDELFORT, E.
1972 *Witch-Hunting in Southwestern Germany 1562–1684.* Stanford: Stanford University Press.

MONGO-MBOUSSA, B.
2002 *Désir d'Afrique.* Paris: Gallimard.

MUDIMBE, V.Y.
1988 *The Invention of Africa: Gnosis, Philosophy and the Order of Knowledge.* London / Bloomington: James Currey / Indiana University Press.

NAIPAUL, V.S.
1980 *A Bend in the River.* Harmondsworth: Penguin.

NDAYWEL È NZIEM, I.
1993 *La société zaïroise dans le miroir de son discours religieux (1990–1993).* Brussels/Paris: Centre d'Etudes Africaines/L'Harmattan.
1997 *Histoire du Zaïre. De l'héritage ancien à l'âge contemporain.* Louvain-la-Neuve: Duculot.

NGANDU KASHAMA, P.
1992 La chanson de la rupture dans la musique Zairoise moderne. In: M. Quaghebeur and E. Van Balberghe (eds.) *Paper blanc, Encre Noire. Cent Ans de Culture Francophone en Afrique Centrale (Zaire, Rwanda et Burundi).* Brussels: Labor.

NICOLAS, G.
1986 *Don, rituel et échange marchand.* Paris: Institut d'Ethnologie, Musée de l'Homme.

NIEHAUS, I.
1997 "A Witch Has No Hor." The Subjective Reality of Witchcraft in the South African Lowveld. In: P. McAllister (ed.) *Culture and the Commonplace. Anthropological Essays in Honour of David Hammond-Tooke.* Johannesburg: Witwatersrand University Press.

NLANDU, T.
2002 Kinshasa: Beyond Chaos. In: Okwui Enwezor et al. (eds.) *Under Siege: Four African Cities Freetown, Johannesburg, Kinshasa, Lagos.* Kassel: Hatje Cantz.

NLANDU-TSASA, C.
1997 *La rumeur au Zaïre de Mobutu. Radio-trottoir à Kinshasa.* Paris: L'Harmattan.

NOOTER-ROBERTS, M. and A.F. ROBERTS
1995 Memory in Motion. In: M. Nooter-Roberts and A.F. Roberts (eds.) *Memory. Luba Art and the Making of History.* New York/Munich: The Museum for African Art/Prestel.

NORDSTROM, C.
1992 The Backyard Front. In: C. Nordstrom and J. Martin (eds.) *The Paths to Domination, Resistance and Terror.* Berkeley: University of California Press.

NZEY VAN MUSALA
n.d. *Cité cimetière.* Kinshasa: unpublished theater play.

OBRIST, H.U.
2000 Urban Rumors. In: R. Koolhaas et al., *Mutations.* Barcelona / Bordeaux: ACTAR / Arc en reve centre d'architecture.

OLWIG, K.F. and K. HASTRUP (eds.)
1997 *Siting Culture. The Shifting Anthropological Object.* London: Routledge.

PHILLIPS, R.
1995 Why Not Tourist Art? Significant Silences in Native American Museum Representations. In: G. Prakash (ed.) *After Colonialism. Imperial histories and Postcolonial Displacements.* Princeton: Princeton University Press.

PICK, D.
1989 *Faces of Degeneration: A European Disorder c. 1848–c.1918.* Cambridge: Cambridge University Press.

PIVIN, J.-L.
1996 The Genius and the Forger. *Revue Noire* 21: 5–11.

RANGER, T.
1992 Godly Medicine: The Ambiguities of Medical Mission in Southeastern Tanzania, 1900–1945. In: Feierman, S. and J.M. Janzen (eds.) *The Social Basis of Health and Healing in Africa.* Berkeley: University of California Press.

ROBBINS, T. and S.J. PALMER (eds.)
1997 *Millenium, Messiahs, and Mayhem. Contemporary Apocalyptic Movements.* London: Routledge.

ROBERTSON, R.
1992 Globalization and the Nostalgic Paradigm. In: R. Robertson *Globalization. Social Theory and Global Culture.* London: Sage.

SCARRY, E.
1985 *The Body in Pain. The Making and Unmaking of the World.* Oxford: Oxford University Press.

SCHATZBERG, M.
1988 *The Dialectics of Oppression in Zaire.* Bloomington/Indianapolis. Indiana University Press.

SCHEPER-HUGHES, N. and D. HOFFMAN
1998 Brazilian Apartheid: Street Kids and the Struggle for Urban Space. In: Scheper-Hughes, N. and C. Sargent (eds.) *Small Wars. The Cultural Politics of Childhood.* Berkeley: University of California Press.

SENE MONGABA, B.
2002 *Fwa-ku-Mputu. To lisolo ya moto oyo akanaka Poto pene akufa.* Brussels: Editions Mabiki.

SIMONE, A.
2001 Straddling the Divides: Remaking Associational

Life in the Informal African City. *International Journal of Urban and Regional Research* 25 (1): 102–117.
2003 Reaching the Larger World: New Forms of Social Collaboration in Pikine, Senegal. *Africa* 73 (2): 226–250.
In press *For the City Yet To Come.* Durham: Duke University Press.

SONTAG, S.
1978 *On Photography.* London: Allen Lane.

SOROMENHO, C.
1956 [1941] *Camaxilo [Terra morta].* Paris: Présence Africaine.

SPYER, P. (ed.)
1998 *Border Fetishisms. Material Objects in Unstable Places.* New York / London: Routledge.

STEWART, G.
2000 *Rumba on the River. A History of the Popular Music of the Two Congos.* London: Verso.

STEWART, C. and R. SHAW (eds.)
1994 *Syncretism / Anti-Syncretism: The Politics of Religious Synthesis.* London: Routledge.

STOLLER, P.
1995 *Embodying Colonial Memories: Spirit Possession, Power and the Hauka in West Africa.* New York / London: Routledge.

STONE, J.R.
2000 *Expecting Armaggedon. Essential Readings in Failed Prophecy.* London: Routledge.

STRATHERN, M.
1995 Nostalgia and the New Genetics. In: Battaglia, D. (ed.) *Rhetorics of Self-Making.* Berkeley: University of California Press.

TAUSSIG, M.
1992 Culture of Terror-Space of Death: Roger Casement's Putumayo Report and the Explanation of Torture. In: N. B. Dirks (ed.), *Colonialism and Culture.* Ann Arbor: University of Michigan Press.
1993 *Mimesis and Alterity. A Particular History of the Senses.* London: Routledge.

TAYLOR, C.C.
1992 *Milk, Honey and Money. Changing Concepts in Rwandan Healing.* Philadelphia: University of Pennsylvania Press.

TERDIMAN, R.
1993 *Present Past. Modernity and the Memory Crisis.* Ithaca/London: Cornell University Press.

TONDA, J.
2002 *La guérison divine en Afrique centrale (Congo, Gabon).* Paris: Karthala.

TURNER, S.
1994 *The Social Theory of Practices. Tradition, Tacit Knowledge and Presuppositions.* Cambridge: Polity Press.

TURNER, T.
1994 Bodies and Anti-Bodies: Flesh and Fetish in Contemporary Social Theory. In: T.J. Csordas (ed.) *Embodiment and Experience. The Existential Ground of Culture and Self.* Cambridge: Cambridge University Press.

VANGU NGIMBI, I.
1997 *Jeunesse, funérailles et contestation socio-politique en Afrique.* Paris: L'Harmattan.

VAN ZYL SLABBERT, C. MALAN, H. MARAIS, J. OLIVIER and R. RIORDAN
1994 *Youth in the New South Africa.* Pretoria: Human Science Research Commission.

VAUGHAN, M.
1991 *Curing Their Ills: Colonial Power and African Illness.* Stanford: Stanford University Press.

WARNIER, J.-P.
1993 L'économie politique de la sorcellerie en Afrique Centrale. In: G. Gosselin (ed.) *Les nouveaux enjeux de l'anthropologie. Autour de Georges Balandier.* Paris: L'Harmattan.

WEBER, E.
2000 *Apocalypses. Prophecies, Cults and Millenial Beliefs through the Ages.* London: Pimlico.

WERBNER, R. (ed.)
2001 *Postcolonial Subjectivities in Africa.* London: Zed Books

YAMB, G.
1997 Thanatocratie, servitude ou démocratie?: essai sur le sens du jeu de la mort sur la scène politique africaine. *Zaïre-Afrique* 37 (311): 29–47.

YOKA, LYE M.
1995 Le Fossoyeur. In *Lettres d'un Kinois à l'oncle du village.* Brussels/Paris: Institut Africain-CEDAF/ L'Harmattan.
1999 *Kinshasa, signes de vie.* Tervuren / Paris: Institut Africain-CEDAF / L'Harmattan.

YOUNG, C. and T. TURNER
1985 *The Rise and Decline of the Zairean State.* Madison: University of Wisconsin Press.

ZARTMAN, I.W.
1995 Introduction: Posing the Problem of State Collapse. In: I.W. Zartman (ed.), *Collapsed States. The Disintegration and Restoration of Legitimate Authority.* Boulder, CO: Lynne Riener.

INDEX

accumulation *27, 43, 235, 242, 243, 244, 247, 248, 255, 259*
accumulation and body *242*
    capture *8, 18, 19, 42, 44, 156, 243, 249, 250*
    capturing *43, 91, 125, 208, 242, 243*
accumulation of people *244, 247*
Adoula *83*
aesthetics of repair *228*. See also productivity of degradation
agrarian urbanity *34*
    See also post urbanism
AIDS *22, 23, 85, 131, 132, 168, 169, 170, 173*
altered structures of solidarity *133*
    See also: gift, kinship, family
Antwerp *20, 21, 45*
Antze, Paul *86, 114*
Apocalypse *75, 81, 97, 98, 252*
apocalyptic interlude *93, 98, 131*
Appadurai, Arjun *156*
appearance *9, 36, 54, 59, 82, 95, 111, 208, 240, 257*
architecture of decay *226*.
    See also invisible architecture
Augé, Marc *87*
authenticity *108, 109*
autopsy of crisis *79*
Bachelard, Gaston *254*
bana Lunda *43, 125, 182, 242, 243*
banalization of death *135*
Bandalungwa *31, 37, 121, 151, 155, 157*
Bangala *31*
bar *37, 41, 49, 53, 56, 69, 72, 75, 95, 162, 180, 211, 213, 214, 228, 257*
Barry, Aboubacar *188, 206*
Barthes, Roland *8, 75, 81, 82, 156*
Barumbu *30, 36, 37, 162*
Bataille, Georges *135*
Bateke plateau *32*
Baudouin, King *83*
Baudrillard, Jean *59, 161*
Bayart, Jean-François *156, 157*
Beach Ngobila *14, 15, 225*
Beija, Dona *187*
Benjamin, Walter *91*
Bhabha, Homi *84*
Bible *15, 65, 81, 85, 93, 96, 97, 99, 100, 106, 128, 129, 199*

bilayi *38, 64, 172*
Billism *36, 37, 38, 39*
Bindomanie *202*
Binza *72, 84*
biomedicine *28, 114*
Birindwa *187*
Black Zionism *111*
Bodo *91, 92, 155*
body *8, 15, 26, 27, 28, 31, 46, 50, 54, 63, 64, 65, 67, 71, 73, 78, 82, 85, 86, 87, 99, 102, 113, 114, 115, 117, 118, 121, 124, 126, 127, 129, 130, 131, 133, 136, 142, 146, 148, 150, 155, 163, 164, 166, 172, 178, 180, 183, 188, 205, 235, 236, 237, 238, 239, 240, 241, 242, 243, 247, 248, 257, 260*
body and accumulation *242*
body building *236, 238, 240*
Book of Revelation *96, 97, 98, 102, 173*
Borges, Jorge Luis *258*
Bosch, Hieronymus *92, 100*
Boula, Matadi *84*
Bourdieu, Pierre *80, 87, 258*
Brazzaville *14, 16, 45, 83*
breccia *20*
bunkerization *227*
Bylex, Pume *100, 102, 252*
Cafunfo *122, 213*
Calvino, Italo *8, 13, 16, 17*
Camp Luka *33, 37, 103, 133*
Camp Mobutu *35*
Castoriadis, Cornelius *156*
cell phone technology *231*
Certeau, Michel de *82*
Chamber of Death *97*
Chokwe *115, 116*
Christian fundamentalism *54, 95, 96, 100, 158, 173*
Cité *28, 35, 72*
Cité Mama Mobutu *35*
Cité Verte *72*
cités indigènes *29, 30*
cités jardins *30*
Coastmen *46*
collective imaginary *47, 77, 91, 125, 173, 207, 208*
colonial administration *27, 31, 103*
colonial imperialism *24, 86*
colonial medicine *27*
colonialism *20, 26, 28, 33, 34, 77, 84, 87, 103, 107, 109*

colonialist modernity *27, 28, 34, 46, 84, 85, 87, 160, 184*
Comaroff, Jean *26*
comptoir *45, 214*
comptoir economy *45*
Congo river *14, 16, 110, 162, 164, 226*
Conrad, Joseph *22*
Cowboy *39*
crisis *18, 20, 34, 39, 58, 59, 60, 79, 80, 81, 82, 83, 86, 87, 95, 100, 103, 113, 114, 118, 127, 145, 156, 158, 160, 161, 170, 173, 175, 182, 189, 193, 194, 196, 206, 207, 208, 226, 240, 249, 254*
crisis of the gift *161* See also gift
crisis of meaning *58, 59*
dead *16, 17, 57, 58, 67, 71, 73, 75, 76, 81, 82, 116, 117, 122, 124, 127, 128, 129, 130, 131, 132, 133, 134, 135, 136, 137, 147, 159, 163, 183, 209, 212, 219, 225, 260*.
    See also living dead
death *9, 21, 27, 58, 60, 63, 75, 76, 77, 81, 82, 85, 87, 91, 94, 95, 96, 97, 99, 103, 104, 109, 110, 111, 113, 114, 117, 119, 121, 124, 128, 129, 131, 132, 133, 134, 135, 153, 155, 156, 157, 159, 163, 168, 170, 178, 185, 188, 194, 196, 205, 211, 216, 221, 257, 261*
    See also banalization of death
dedoubling *71, 153, 159, 208*
    See also double, doubling
dégénérescence *24*
Deleuze, Gilles *157*
De Meulder, Bruno *7, 27, 31, 34*
demonization *56, 98*. See also satanization, Verteufelung
desire *17, 125, 160, 226, 238, 241, 242, 250*
de Villiers, Gérard *22*
Devisch, René *34, 80, 112, 115, 156, 162, 206*
diabolical *73, 150, 169, 170, 199*
Diaka, Mungul *67*
diamond *39, 42, 43, 44, 45, 46, 48, 77, 88, 121, 122, 123, 124, 125, 126, 132, 164, 168, 178, 182, 190, 192, 193, 195, 211, 212, 213, 218, 219, 220, 242*
diamond economy *121*
diamond-hunter *42*
    See also bana Lunda

279

diaspora *45, 47, 49, 120, 163, 173, 192, 235*
Dibundu dia Kongo (DKK) *106*
difference *24, 28, 40, 41, 91, 193, 209, 254*
dismemberment *121, 125, 127*
divination *115, 116, 117, 206*
double *16, 57, 59, 60, 61, 75, 118, 156, 157, 159, 166, 196, 198, 204, 207, 209, 256*
doubling *159, 208, 256*
Douglas, Mary *108, 227*
dream *57, 102, 143, 148, 149, 178, 188, 238, 250, 252, 255, 257*. *See also* oneiric
dynamics of witchcraft *158, 196, 208 See also* witchcraft
Ebola *22, 82, 83, 85, 114, 135*
economy of constipation *195, 242*
economy of scarcity *228*
economy of the occult *160 See also* witchcraft
economy of violence *77, 119, 160*
Eglise des Noirs en Afrique *103*
Eglise du Christ en Afrique Noire des Apôtres du Congo (ECANAC) *103*
Eglise Libre d'Afrique *202*
Ekobo *134*
Emeneya, "King" Kester *78, 80, 82*
emplotment *175*
entangled spatialities *231*
Entzauberung *86, 158*
Equateur *31, 63, 150, 151*
ethnic affiliations *53, 56*
evacuation *45, 209*
Exhibition *21, 22, 24, 77, 86*
expenditure *43, 242*
family *26, 30, 53, 56, 63, 69, 71, 76, 81, 88, 126, 133, 134, 136, 137, 143, 144, 146, 150, 153, 168, 170, 172, 174, 177, 178, 181, 182, 183, 188, 189, 190, 192, 193, 195, 197, 198, 199, 203, 206, 221, 222, 244, 248, 250*
Fanon, Franz *46*
fetish *19*
fictive debts *204*
figure of succes *43*
Fonds d'Avance *30*
Force Publique *31, 36, 168*
forest *15, 22, 41, 42, 50, 75, 78, 164, 177, 212, 217, 218*
Foucault, Michel *24, 226, 244, 247, 254, 256, 258*

four eyes *9, 58, 145*. *See also* witchcraft
Franco, Luambo Makiadi *51, 91, 94, 120*
Freud, Sigmund *207*
funeral wake *78, 95, 134*
gangs *23, 36, 37, 38, 39, 171, 172, 192, 204*
geographies of perversion *24*
gerontocracy *133, 161, 193, 194*
Geschiere, Peter *127, 159, 188, 189, 195*
Giddens, Anthony *108*
gift *See also* reciprocity
    commodification of gift *204*
    crisis of the gift *161*
gift cycle of marriage and bride wealth *195*
gift exchange *198*
gift logic *56, 197, 205*. *See also* logic of reciprocity and gift
gift obligations *194, 197*
gift transformation *194, 208*
Gizenga, Antoine *83, 84, 109*
Glissant, Edouard *22*
glossolalia, *8*.
    See also speaking in tongues.
Godelier, Maurice *161, 207, 208*
Gombe *29, 30, 84, 164, 167, 168*
Gondola, Charles Didier *16, 17, 36*
Guyer, Jane *243*
habitus *80, 87, 125, 127*
Halbwachs, Maurice *113*
Harvey, David *238*
Heart of Darkness *15, 22*
heterotopia *254, 255, 256, 257, 258, 259*
Hindubill *39, 64*
Hochschild, Adam *77*
hunter *36, 41, 42, 43, 44, 242, 243, 244, 248, 249*
image *7, 8, 9, 13, 14, 15, 16, 20, 21, 22, 26, 36, 43, 45, 46, 47, 57, 59, 77, 83, 102, 105, 130, 155, 156, 177, 205, 207, 209, 229, 242, 243, 255, 256, 257, 258*
image and reality *59, 258*
imaginary *20, 21, 41, 46, 47, 59, 60, 61, 77, 89, 91, 92, 100, 119, 121, 125, 126, 155, 156, 157, 158, 160, 161, 173, 195, 206, 207, 208, 209, 240, 249, 260*
imagination *8, 17, 21, 22, 39, 44, 56, 82, 85, 96, 112, 156, 195, 226, 241, 250, 255, 257*
Independence *48, 83*
informal economies *45, 226*
interbellum *30*

intersubjectivity *56*
invisibility *23, 132, 170, 230, 256*. *See also* politics of invisibility
invisible *9, 13, 16, 22, 23, 24, 50, 52, 56, 57, 58, 63, 64, 69, 95, 127, 132, 139, 155, 156, 157, 159, 170, 203, 211, 227, 233, 235, 240, 256, 257*
invisible architecture *233*
invisible modalities of urban action *240*
Jewsiewicki, Bogumil *39, 50, 91, 109, 202*
juvenile syntaxis of self realization *239*
Kabamba, Maguy *88*
Kabila, Laurent *33, 37, 40, 80, 83, 94, 109, 110, 111, 119, 172, 178, 182, 184*
Kafuta, Soni *54, 119, 186*
Kahemba *7, 44, 45, 124, 211, 216*
Kahungula *124, 213*
Kalimasi, Vincent Lombume *250, 261*
Kalina *28, 29*
Kalle, Pepe *47*
Kalulambi Pongo, Martin *91*
Kandolo *16*
Karishika *186, 187, 188*
Khan, Kublai *16*
Kikwit *7, 22, 42, 82, 83, 85, 107, 126, 135, 198, 211, 214, 215, 216, 221, 223, 227*
Kimbanguism *103*
Kimbangu, Simon *103, 110, 111*
Kimbanseke *33, 136*
Kingabwa *225*
Kingasani *33, 164*
Kingelez, Bodys Isek *252*
Kinkole *31*
Kin-Malebo *16*
kinship *26, 26, 88, 112, 116, 133, 160, 161, 173, 189, 192, 194, 195, 196, 197, 198, 203, 206, 244, 248, 249*
Kintambo *16, 28, 29, 30, 36, 37, 71, 122, 151, 152*
Kisenso *33*
knotting *106, 118, 205*
Koné, Amadou *75*
Koolhaas, Rem *44*
Kungu Pemba *82, 83, 84, 87, 109*
Kutino, Fernando *54, 186*
Lacan, Jacques *156, 206, 207, 208*
Lallemand, Suzanne *205, 206*
Lambek, Michael *86, 114, 189*
Le Corbusier *20, 21, 252*

Lefebvre, Henri *40, 236*
Lemba *31, 37, 45, 69, 75, 97, 127, 157, 211, 213*
Leopold II, King *20, 21, 76, 77, 83, 104*
Léopoldville *16, 20, 28, 30, 31, 35, 36, 39, 255*
Lévi-Strauss, Claude *206, 207*
Limete *30, 36, 41, 46, 84, 109, 148*
Lingala *31, 36, 39, 41, 47, 57, 58, 66, 88, 117, 125, 126, 177, 185, 186, 202, 218, 222*
Lingwala *30, 36*
Lipopo *16, 30*
liquidation of the double *61* See also double, doubling
living dead *127, 132.* See also dead
logic of reciprocity and gift *161, 195* See also gift logic
Lokuli *202*
Lumbu *16*
Lumumba, Patrice *20, 41, 67, 83, 93, 94, 109, 110, 111*
Lunda Norte *39, 43, 45, 77, 121, 122, 124, 125, 182, 211, 213, 219, 222*
lupemba *171, 172*
Luunda *115, 118, 121, 194, 196, 197, 205*
Luunda aetiology *196*
Mabanga *16*
Makala *33, 103, 223*
Makoma *168*
Malange *124*
male identity *244*
Malebo Pool *16*
Malinowski, Bronislaw *76, 78*
Malweka *33*
Mama Olangi *186, 197*
Mama Yemo hospital *35*
Mamdani, Mahmood *86*
Mami Wata *39*
Mangwana, Sam *95*
Marley, Bob *111*
Masina *33, 45, 94, 96, 101, 119, 121, 136, 157, 160, 163, 164, 225*
Matadi *30, 84*
material infrastructure *226, 231, 233, 235, 238, 240.* See also possibilities of infrastructure
Matete *31, 37, 93, 213*
Matonge *31, 46, 136, 164, 180*
Mauss, Marcel *80, 195, 205, 206*
Mbamu *16*

Mbembe, Achille *57, 80, 87, 111, 121, 127, 133, 155, 156, 241*
Mbonge, Ebale *136*
memory *15, 17, 43, 44, 81, 85, 86, 87, 89, 91, 92, 94, 102, 103, 106, 111, 113, 114, 115, 116, 117, 125, 127, 137, 158, 166, 189, 253*
memory crisis *81, 86, 87, 103*
métissage *52*
Michelet, Jules *81, 82*
Midgi *85*
mimetic *34, 46, 59, 111*
Mimosa *16*
mirror *8, 13, 17, 18, 19, 20, 28, 40, 43, 44, 45, 46, 54, 57, 58, 76, 116, 117, 146, 204, 207, 208, 228, 255, 256, 257.* See also reflection.
mirroring realities *18, 235*
Misele, "King" *103, 107*
mission medicine *26*
Mobutist *34, 35, 88, 91, 103, 107, 108, 109, 110*
Mobutu *35, 44, 45, 48, 50, 79, 80, 83, 84, 85, 88, 103, 109, 110, 114, 119, 136, 137, 147, 160, 178, 195, 229*
modernism *20, 28*
modernist *21, 28, 33, 34, 41, 49, 77, 86, 87, 108, 252*
Modernization *46*
Moke *91*
Mont Ngafula *33, 139, 228, 230*
Monsengwo, Monseigneur *110*
movie theater *36, 39, 165*
moziki *240*
Mpadi, Simon *103*
Mpeve ya nlongo *116*
Mpiana, J.B. *121*
Mudimbe, Valentin *84*
mukanda circumcision ritual *38, 44*
Mulele, Pierre *109*
multiplication of the uncle *134* See also family, kinship
mutation *19, 20, 182*
mystique *58, 209*
Naipaul, V.S. *22, 46*
Ndaywel è Nziem, Isidore *83, 87, 91, 110*
Ndjili *31, 37, 45, 103, 119, 121, 150, 157, 164, 178*
ndoki *195*

necromancy *71*
necropolis *133*
necropolitical *121*
new patterns of witchcraft *203* See witchcraft
Ngaba *33, 46, 67, 75, 130*
Ngaliema *20, 30, 36, 133*
Ngaluphar *202*
nganda *37, 53*
Ngiri-Ngiri *36, 37*
Ninja *40*
nocturnal consumption *183* See occult
nocturnal market *147.* See occult
nostalgia *86, 87, 94, 102, 103, 111*
Nzey, Van Musala *133*
objectification, *8*
occult *56, 67, 110, 155, 160, 183*
Office de Cités Africaines *31*
Office de Cités Indigènes de Léopoldville *31*
Okri, Ben *186*
Olomide, Koffi *162, 208*
oneiric *17, 92, 95, 161, 188, 255, 257*
Orchestra OK Jazz *191*
palimpsestual *8, 106, 109, 113, 117*
Papa Wemba *46, 54, 184*
parcelle *53, 72*
parlementaires debout *50, 235*
Pasha, Emin *21*
phonie *53, 231*
physical life of crisis *226.* See crisis
political economy of gift exchange *198.* See also gift
politics of invisibility *170*
Polo, Marco *16*
possibilities of infrastructure *230*
possibilities of simultaneity, *256* See simultaneity
post urbanism *34.* See agrarian urbanity
private *28, 31, 52, 53, 54, 56, 77, 83, 127, 158, 159, 172, 174, 175, 186, 227, 239*
productivity of degradation *226*
public *28, 35, 39, 40, 50, 52, 53, 54, 55, 56, 63, 94, 95, 97, 113, 114, 119, 127, 158, 159, 160, 161, 164, 167, 173, 174, 175, 176, 177, 182, 184, 188, 189, 193, 203, 226, 227, 228, 231, 235, 238, 239, 242, 243, 248, 249, 258*

public confession *173, 175, 176, 177, 188*
public space *39, 40, 53, 55, 56, 95, 113, 158, 159, 164, 175, 182, 188, 193, 226, 231, 238, 242, 248, 258*
Radio Trottoir *50, 51, 52, 53, 63, 82, 83, 85, 110, 136, 185, 195*
reciprocity *56, 112, 161, 194, 195, 196, 197, 204, 205, 244, 249*
　See also gift
redistribution *43, 44, 126, 193, 196, 205*
reflection *7, 17, 18, 20, 21, 54, 57, 58, 112, 130, 155, 196, 207, 208, 256*
Renkin *31*
representation *9, 14, 17, 22, 50, 57, 59, 103, 108, 109, 161, 208, 256*
resistance *19, 49, 84, 103, 107, 112*
reterritorialization *36, 39*
Return to Authenticity *88*
Righini *45, 121*
rumba *78, 94, 95, 155*
rumor *50, 52, 63, 82, 185*
ruralization *40, 41*
Saint-Jean *37*
Sakombi Inongo, Dominique *110*
Salongo *45, 67, 121*
Samba, Chéri *50*
Sape *54, 240*
Sartre, Jean-Paul *156*
satanization of children *194*
Savimbi, Jonas *211*
second world *9, 56, 57, 58, 102, 128, 131, 136, 137, 148, 150, 151, 152, 153, 156, 161, 163, 170, 173, 178, 185, 190, 204, 205, 207, 208*
secrecy *52, 53*
seed *198, 202*
Selembao *33, 157, 163, 170, 172*
self realization *43, 44, 189, 193, 239, 243, 244, 250*
semence *198, 202*
sequestration *24*
shadow economy *35, 57*
　see informal economies
shege *158, 167, 184, 261*
Shengen *184*
simulacra of infrastructure *226*
simultaneity *189, 208, 256, 257*
simultaneous multiplicity *57, 156, 256*
Sontag, Susan *56*
space/time compression *86*

spaces of hope *244*
speaking in tongues *177, 179*
speculation *26, 28, 46*
　See image, mirror, reflection
speculum *20, 28*
　See image, mirror, reflection
Stade Kamanyola *35*
stage *14, 20, 53, 54, 56, 119, 184, 185, 186, 242, 257*
Stanley *20, 21, 28*
state
　beyond the state *89*
　integral state *88*
　nation state *24, 26, 48, 77, 86, 89, 91, 102, 113*
Strathern, Marilyn *102*
street children *14, 40, 55, 94, 159, 163, 164, 165, 166, 167, 168, 172, 174, 181, 184, 188, 189, 204, 238.*
　See also witch-children
symbolization *206, 208, 209.*
Tabu Ley, Seigneur Rochereau *52, 75, 120*
Tansi, Sony Labou *4, 133*
Tata Ghonda *108, 186*
Taussig, Michael *59, 77, 113*
Tembo *44, 45, 121, 212, 213, 214, 216*
témoignage *56, 63*
Terdiman, Richard *86*
Tervuren *21, 76, 77, 86*
thanatocracy *133*
theatralization *54*
Tip, Tippo *21*
topographies of propinquity *231*
Tournier, Michel *208*
truncated urban forms *233*
Tshibumba *83, 91, 109*
Tshisekedi, Etienne *110, 132*
Tungila *124*
undoubling *71, 256*
　See double, doubling, dedouble
unequal reciprocity *204*
　See gift
unfinished city *228*
urban polygamy *190*
Utex, *29*
utopia *17, 102, 111, 252, 254, 256, 260*
Velasquez, Diego *256*
Verckys *104*

Verteufelung *173*
　See satanization, demonization
Village Bercy *41*
Village Syllo *41*
Ville *28, 30, 164, 252*
Weber, Max *86, 96*
Wendo Kolosoy *120*
Wenge Musica *120*
Werrason *41, 48, 49, 120, 121*
witch-children *156, 157, 163, 169, 170, 171, 174, 175, 182, 190, 195, 205, 206*
　See also street children
witchcraft, *58, 61, 64, 85, 86, 112, 116, 126, 127, 131, 145, 148, 149, 150, 151, 152, 153, 157, 158, 159, 160, 163, 168, 172, 173, 174, 176, 179, 180, 182, 183, 186, 188, 189, 190, 192, 194, 195, 196, 197, 203, 205, 206, 208, 219*
　See also new patterns of witchcraft
World Exhibition *21, 22, 24*
Yoka, Lye Mudaba *134*
Yolo *31, 37*
youth crisis *182*
youth culture *39, 239*
Zaiko *38*
Zaireanization *35*
zombification *127, 129*

LIST OF ILLUSTRATIONS

Cover: Street child in the bar *Vis-à-Vis*, Quartier Matonge, Commune of Kalamu.
6   Portrait of a young girl accused of witchcraft, Commune of Selembao.
12   Sunken steamer on the Congo river.
17   View of downtown Kinshasa, Commune of Gombe.
18 – 19   The *Maisaf* bar, Avenue Kasa-Vubu, Commune of Bandalungwa. *Maisaf* is the abbreviation of *Maison africaine*, a shelter for Congolese students in Ixelles, Brussels.
22   Statue of king Leopold II and the feet of a statue which represented his envoy Stanley, Commune of Limete.
23   Statue of Stanley and his boat, Commune of Limete. Both statues were torn down and moved to two separate warehouses in Limete after Independence.
25   Mural painting: *Work: The Base of Progress*.
27   School blackboard: *Framework. The Punishments*.
29   *Place des travailleurs* (also known as *Place Forescom*), Commune of Gombe.
32 – 33   Rond Point Victoire, Quartier Matonge.
37   Young musicians rehearsing, Commune of Mont Ngafula.
38   *Chez Volcan*. Body building, Commune of Barumbu.
42   Neighborhood in the Commune of Kisenso.
43   School complex and garden, Quartier Matonge.
44   Playing in the street, Yolo Nord, Commune of Kalamu.
47   Dry cleaner *La modernisation*. Bus stop Abeti, Commune of Lemba 1999 and 2001. (Photo at left by Filip De Boeck).
48   Porte de Namur, Quartier Matonge, Kinshasa.
49   Porte de Namur, Matonge, Ixelles (Brussels).
51   Women selling food in street market, Binza IPN.
52   Old compound in the Commune of Barumbu.
55   Wedding, *Foire Internationale de Kinshasa*, Commune of Lemba.
60   *Le Bloc*, night life in Quartier Bisengo, Commune of Bandalungwa.
61   Bar *Kimpwanza*, Commune of Kasa-Vubu.
62   Portrait of painter Chéri Samba in his workshop, Commune of Ngiri-Ngiri, April 2000.
68   Interior of house, Yolo Sud, Commune of Kalamu.
70   Portrait of painter Moke in his workshop, Commune of Kinshasa, May 2001.
74   Blackboard in a church, Commune of Masina.
78   Bar in the Commune of Bandalungwa.
90   View of the *Boulevard du 30 juin*, the Belgian embassy and the SOZACOM tower, Commune of Gombe.
92   Portrait of painter-preacher Bodo in his compound, Commune of Kinshasa, May 2001.
93   Painting by Bodo.
96 – 99   Murals with religious themes.
104   Gathering of adepts of the Apostolic Church of John Maranke, in an abandoned UN refugee camp, Quartier Mpasa, Commune of Nsele.
106 – 107   Idem.
119   Musicians from the orchestra Wenge Musica BCBG (J.B. Mpiana), Commune of Gombe, 2001.
120   Bar *Saint-Tropez*, Rond Point Victoire, Quartier Matonge.
121   Barber shop with portrait of musician Ngiama Makanda (Werrason) in a priest's outfit and with a leopard's head.
123   Police office.
128   Blackboard *Les morts ne sont pas morts*, Commune of Lemba.
135   Funeral chapel in the street, Commune of Kintambo.
137   Undertaker's, Commune of Selembao.
138   Children accused of witchcraft in a church, Commune of Selembao.
140 – 141   Portraits of children who are being exorcized in a church, Commune of Selembao.
144   Witch-finder, along the Bypass Road, near Cité Verte.
148 – 153   Portraits of children accused of witchcraft.
154   Aquarium, Commune of Lingwala.
159   Girl sleeping on tombstone, Cemetery of Gombe.
165   Central Market, Commune of Gombe.
166 – 167   Street children, Central Market, Commune of Gombe.
169   Girls meeting in a compound, Commune of Kintambo.
174   Announcement of a prayer meeting, Commune of Bandalungwa.
175   Church ELIM, The Light of the World, Matonge.
177   Prayer meeting at Mama Olangi's, Commune of Limete.

181 Mural at the entrance of bar, Binza Gendarmerie.
184 Portrait of Papa Wemba before a concert in the Commune of Masina, May 2001.
184 – 185 During a Papa Wemba concert, Commune of Masina, May 2001.
186 – 187 Wrestling competition, Commune of Ndjili, Quartier 1.
200 – 201 *La semence*. Mural paintings.
205 Comic strips by Papa Mfumu'eto I.
210 Furniture for sale along the Bypass Road, Commune of Mont Ngafula, Quartier Masanga Mbila.
215 Selling furniture in the street, Commune of Masina.
217 Interior of colonial villa, Commune of Gombe.
220 Selling furniture, Binza Okapi.
224 View of the Congo river from Port Baramoto.
227 Tree in front of the Grand Hotel, Commune of Gombe.
229 Kimbanguist School, threatened by erosion, Binza Gendarmerie.
232 – 235 Public scribe, barber shop (with portrait of J.B. Mpiana) and *parlementaires debout* in the Eucalyptus woods along the Boulevard Lumumba, Commune of Ndjili.
236 – 241 Portraits of young musicians from the orchestras *QBG International* (Prince Shongo I, Pitchoi Bonpetit, Bijou Star Ami Simbal, Ousman Dirabolé, Delop Massapidi, Atueka Anaklé), *Nouveau monde international* (Jessy Ugue, Otchoudi, Jackson Mangumbi, JR) and *Weka Musica* (Gelor Dilou, Fiston Nzala, Linduku Munga, Gadens Ngeto, Tacle Mambo). See also photo on p. 37.
243 – 251 Accumulating heaps: shoes, lamp shades, second hand clothes, herbs for medical purposes, sunshades with religious inscription, wheel covers, bags of food (gifts from Italy and Belgium), charcoal, medicinal plants, cassava flour, white sand, gravel, money, bread and peanuts. (Photo of *cambistes* (money changers) on p. 250 by Filip De Boeck).
253 Portrait of artist Pume Bylex, Masina, Quartier Petro-Congo. April 2000.
255 *L'avenir*. Mural painting.
262 Children playing in the street, Yolo Sud.
270 Playing checkers, Mont Ngafula.
278 Making a photo portrait, Commune of Kimbanseke.

283 Photo Studio, Commune of Kimbanseke.
285 Mural decoration in barber shop.
286-287 Schoolchildren.

COLOPHON

FILIP DE BOECK is Professor of Anthropology at the Catholic University of Leuven, Belgium. He is Director of the Institute for Anthropological Research in Africa (IARA). His other publications include *Makers and Breakers. Children and Youth in Postcolonial Africa* as well as a documentary film, *Cemetery State*.

Amongst **MARIE-FRANÇOISE PLISSART**'s publications figure most prominently *Droits de Regards* (with Jacques Derrida, Editions de Minuit), *Right of Inspection* (The Monacelli Press) and *Bruxelles Horizon Vertical* (Editions Prisme). She is also the author of a short film, *L'occupation des sols*.

This book was first published as a sequel to the exhibition **KINSHASA, THE IMAGINARY CITY**. This project was commissioned by the Ministry of the Flemish Community for the Venice Architecture Biennial held from 9 September through 7 November 2004. The commissioner of the exhibition in the Belgian Pavilion was Katrien Vandermarliere, director of the Flemish Architecture Institute (Vlaams Architectuurinstituut – VAi). The curators of the exhibition were Filip De Boeck and Koen Van Synghel. The presentation comprised photographic and video material by Marie-Françoise Plissart.

Design : Dooreman
Typesetting : Wilfrieda Paessens

www.lup.be
ISBN 978-90-5867-967-3
D/2014/1869/16
NUR: 761

© 2004   Ludion Ghent-Amsterdam
© 2004   Filip De Boeck
© 2004   Marie-Françoise Plissart
© 2014   Authorized reprint by Leuven University Press / Presses Universitaires de Louvain / Universitaire Pers Leuven. Minderbroedersstraat 4, B-3000 Leuven (Belgium).

All rights reserved. Except in those cases expressly determined by law, no part of this publication may be multiplied, saved in an automated datafile or made public in any way whatsoever without the express prior written consent of the publishers.